ISLAMIC NATURAL LAW THEORIES

Islamic Natural Law Theories

ANVER M. EMON

OXFORD
UNIVERSITY PRESS

This book has been printed digitally and produced in a standard specification in order to ensure its continuing availability

OXFORD
UNIVERSITY PRESS

Great Clarendon Street, Oxford OX2 6DP
United Kingdom

Oxford University Press is a department of the University of Oxford.
It furthers the University's objective of excellence in research, scholarship,
and education by publishing worldwide. Oxford is a registered trade mark of
Oxford University Press in the UK and in certain other countries

Reprinted 2012

British Library Cataloguing in Publication Data
Data available

Library of Congress Cataloging in Publication Data
Data available

ISBN 978-0-19-957900-6

Printed and bound by CPI Group (UK) Ltd, Croydon, CR0 4YY

Jacket illustration: The 'Bismillah' in calligraphy on the cover
is recited by Muslims and found in the Qur'an. It can be translated
as: 'In the Name of God, Most Gracious, Most Beneficent'.
This translation conveys two characteristics of God that
feature centrally in the theological debates underlying
competing Islamic natural law theories.

Basmalah in Muhaqqaq. Ink on paper, Turkey, 18–19th
century. © V&A Images/ Victoria and Albert Museum, London.

To my parents,
Akhtar and Rashida,
for all they have made possible

Acknowledgments

This work has been a labor of love for approximately nine years, and has benefited substantially from a great many people. It is also my first book and so affords me a chance to acknowledge certain people who have been an important part of my life and work, although they may not have contributed directly to this particular book. All have contributed in direct and indirect ways to my thinking, although none bear any responsibility for errors in this book. Any errors remain my responsibility alone.

This study started as my PhD dissertation, and I want to thank the members of my committee for their unswerving support of my work and vision. The late Robert I Burns, SJ (1921–2008), one of America's most noted historians, took an early interest in my work, and taught me more than just about medieval legal history. He lived the virtues of intellectual commitment, professionalism, and integrity. His lessons to me—as mentor, scholar, and citizen—are the pillars on which I have attempted to build my own approach to scholarly research and teaching. Patrick Geary has been a role model to me in more ways than he knows. To him I owe a deep debt of gratitude for his academic guidance, advocacy and profound integrity. In pre-modern Islamic history and historical theory, I wish to thank Michael Morony and Gabriel Piterberg, both of whom always kept me historically grounded. Stephen Munzer's contribution to my training in legal philosophy provided the fundamental building block that led to my seeing something in the pre-modern Arabic sources that I would have otherwise missed. Lastly, I want to thank Michael Cooperson and Michael Fishbein for their guidance in all things Arabic, and Teofilo Ruiz for his commitment to graduate training and development.

Other scholars prepared me (and continue to advise me) for a life of academic research. I especially want to thank Harry Bader, Taimie Bryant, Marianne Constable, Marie Failinger, Noah Feldman, Alison Frazier, Paul Kahn, Anthony Kronman, Roger Louis, Ellen Lust, Janet Meisel, David Sklansky, and Suzanne Last Stone for their support and contribution to my intellectual pursuits over the years. In the field of Islamic law and legal history, I have had the good fortune to benefit from the generosity and insights of many leading scholars: Kecia Ali, Abdullahi Ahmed An-Na'im, Wael Hallaq, Bernard Haykel, Baber Johansen, Joseph Lowry, Chibli Mallat, Ziba Mir-Hosseini, David Powers, and Adel Omar Sherif. Khaled Abou El Fadl contributed to my early graduate training in Islamic law and legal history. I also want to thank my fellow-students, and now colleagues, who from 1999 to 2003 and 2003 to 2005, were my toughest interlocutors at UCLA and Yale Law School respectively, and who continue to inspire me: Michael Bednar, Benjamin Berger, Oonagh Breen, Conor Hanly, Raphaela Henze, Maciej Kisilowski, Sayeed Rahman, and Mairaj Syed.

At the University of Toronto, I have benefited from the enthusiasm and support of wonderful and generous colleagues: Lisa Austin, Joseph Carens, Bruce Chapman, Yasmin Dawood, David Dyzenhaus, Mohammad Fadel, Darlene Johnston, Audrey Macklin, Jennifer Nedelsky, Denise Réaume, Arthur Ripstein, Lorne Sossin, Ernest Weinrib, and Melissa Williams. Ahmed Saleh, a graduate student and budding scholar of Islamic law, has been of great help in reviewing the manuscript, as were Rahat Godil and Nafisah Chowdhury. I want to thank Sabrina Bandali, who expertly helped to prepare the index. My dean, Mayo Moran, has been an important and enthusiastic believer in my research, and I wish to thank her and the Faculty of Law for all they have done to support this project and others over the years that I have been a member of the Faculty.

Robert Gibbs, of the University of Toronto, has been a special friend and colleague. We have spent countless hours discussing the intersection of reason, religion and legal philosophy. He has challenged me on many levels, and in doing so has contributed to my thinking on the ideas at the core of this book. I owe him a debt of gratitude for his friendship and unflinching support. Together, we are recipients of a generous grant from Canada's Social Science and Humanities Research Council (SSHRC) on Islamic and Jewish Legal Reasoning. I wish to thank the SSHRC for its support of this and other related research, and all our fellow readers who have been part of that project.

I am profoundly indebted to three mentors who model the very best that university life has to offer. Denise Spellberg of the University of Texas has been a mentor and friend since I started graduate school in 1996. She has been nothing short of inspirational. Her friendship and devotion to her students have taught me how significant a teacher can be in the lives of her students. I can only hope to be the same kind of teacher to my future students. Owen Fiss of Yale Law School has been the model of the legal scholar that I hope to emulate. His scholarly breadth, his commitment to ideas, and his openness to the spectrum of intellectual possibilities have inspired me to challenge what are otherwise perceived as constraints, intellectual and otherwise. Richard Bulliet of Columbia University has been a mentor and friend in ways that I cannot begin to recount. His creative and imaginative approach to Islamic history reminds me to push constantly against what can sometimes be walls and boundaries of thought in the world of academia.

Many thanks go to Oxford University Press, and in particular to Alex Flach, for supporting this project from the very beginning. Natasha Knight, Emma Barber, and Emma Hawes were the epitome of professionalism and efficiency throughout the production process. OUP generously provided me a highly proficient and efficient copyeditor in the person of Nicola Freshwater, whose assistance in copyediting the entire text improved its clarity. The anonymous reviewers showed considerable generosity in their comments and suggestions. They saw in this project possibilities that I hope I have fulfilled with this book. Their reviews made this a much better study.

It is customary in acknowledgment sections to thank family and friends at the end. I always found that peculiar, until I had to write this section of the book. Now I understand why: words are simply not sufficient. Nonetheless, I shall try. I want to thank my parents, Akhtar and Rashida, whose support has been nothing short of unending and selfless. To them I dedicate this book. As it turns out, their support of my academic endeavors started well before I was ever a graduate student. When I was a teenager in high school, my father would often go to various conferences, and purchase Arabic books on Islamic law. Although he does not read Arabic fluently, he would purchase them in the hopes that some day either he would be able to delve into the sources, or he could give them to a student of the Islamic tradition. As it turned out, I was that student.

My friend Peter Pham has pushed me to go farther than I often thought possible, and has never been afraid to point out my errors. I will always treasure his friendship. My friend William Kwong has been a brother to me for nearly two decades. His friendship and advice have been virtual constants in my life, and I have cherished them deeply and immensely. His deep commitment to all he pursues is a testament to the integrity he lives everyday, and from which I have learned so much. And last (but definitely not least), I want to thank my wife, Allyssa J Case, for her love and friendship, her partnership in a life of the mind, her efforts to always keep me grounded, and most especially for inspiring me to be better than I am.

Contents—Summary

Contents

I

Introduction

A book on Islamic natural law theories might, at first blush, raise some eyebrows. Natural law is popularly understood as a legal theory associated with the Christian West, and principally concerned with the authority of reason as a source of law. Hence the title might be perplexing because of a popular view of religious argument generally, and Islamic legal rulings specifically, as characteristically deriving from an authority, rather than from claims based in reason. The title might also raise eyebrows if read as an attempt at intellectual hegemony. Various studies of the Islamic world have criticized previous scholarship that framed, couched, and translated Islamic concepts and ideas into a Western paradigm of knowledge and understanding, without due attention or regard to the particularities presented by the relevant Islamic paradigms.[1] Consequently, the title of this book may read as yet another example of this criticized strain of academic literature. Lastly, the title may be unsettling because of the use of the term 'natural law', as opposed to focusing directly on the place of reason in Islamic law. Islamic legal history is no stranger to debates on reason. However, this study shows that pre-modern Muslim jurists philosophized about the natural world in order to develop a theory of the authority of reason as a source of Sharīʿa.

The anxieties about the title are in part founded on certain premises about reason, authority, law, and Islam that this study

[1] Wael Hallaq makes this point forcefully in his critique of 'Islamic law' as insufficient to capture the full scope of meanings captured by Sharīʿa. Wael Hallaq, *Sharīʿa: Theory, Practice, Transformations* (Cambridge: Cambridge University Press, 2009) 1–6. For a critique of contemporary social theory and its impact on reflecting the particularity of Islamic history and tradition, see Bryan S Turner, *Orientalism, Postmodernism and Globalism* (London: Routledge, 1994).

seeks to challenge. To differentiate between reason and religion, as if the latter has limited, if any, rational foundations is not uncommon among some secular liberal theorists. As Jeremy Waldron entertainingly writes, '[s]ecular theorists often assume that they know what a religious argument is like: they present it as a crude prescription from God, backed up with threat of hellfire, derived from general or particular revelation. . . .'[2] The authority of religious argument is supposed to arise from source-texts and divine authority. Religious argument is presumed to require a type of obedience that for some, such as Max Weber, is based on 'complete personal devotion' as opposed to 'ethical, aesthetic, or other such point of view.'[3] To inquire into the authority of reason in a religious legal system would seem, from this point of view, inapposite at best. And yet numerous studies about natural law in the Western intellectual tradition show the above view to be more caricature than characteristic of the authority of reason in religious traditions. Whether we look to the medieval Aquinas[4] or later theorists along the lines of Suarez, Grotius and Puffendorf, we find efforts to understand the authority of reason within a religious frame. More recent natural law theorists proffer natural law inspired models of practical reasoning.[5] Some historians of natural law suggest that its historiography denotes a narrative of disintegration.[6] Legal philosophers take issue with the sometimes intuitive features of natural

[2] Jeremy Waldron, *God, Locke, and Equality: Christian Foundations in Locke's Political Thought* (Cambridge: Cambridge University Press, 2002) 20.

[3] Max Weber, *Economy and Society: An Outline of Interpretive Sociology*, Guenther Roth and Claus Wittich (eds), 2 vols (Berkeley: University of California Press, 1978) 1:242.

[4] Thomas Aquinas, *Treatise on Law (Summa Theologica, Questions 90–97)* (1956; reprint, Washington, DC: Regnery Publishing Inc, 1998); Anthony J Lisska, *Aquinas's Theory of Natural Law: An Analytic Reconstruction* (Oxford: Clarendon Press, 1996).

[5] John Finnis, *Natural Law and Natural Rights* (1980; reprint, Oxford: Clarendon Press, 1993); Germain Grisez, *Christian Moral Principles*, vol 1 of *The Way of the Lord Jesus* (1983; reprint, Quincy, Illinois: Franciscan Press, 1997); Germain Grisez and Russell Shaw, *Fulfillment in Christ: A Summary of Christian Moral Principles* (Notre Dame: University of Notre Dame Press, 1991); Robert P George (ed), *Natural Law: Contemporary Essays* (Oxford: Oxford University Press, 1992); Mark C Murphy, *Natural Law and Practical Rationality* (Cambridge: Cambridge University Press, 2001).

[6] Pauline C Westerman, *The Disintegration of Natural Law Theory: Aquinas to Finnis* (Leiden: Brill, 1998).

law reasoning.[7] Nonetheless, the extant and vast scholarly discourse on natural law should, at the very least, caution those who resort to caricature when considering the authority of reason in religious law.[8]

Natural law as an analytic concept, though, is not limited by the geographic or historical provenance from which it may have emanated and taken root in the popular imagination. The philosophical questions that underlie competing theories of natural law are arguably inherent in any legal system. Indeed one of the animating features of this study is to illustrate how legal philosophy generally, and natural law specifically, can provide an insightful frame of reference for understanding pre-modern Islamic legal theory. Of course, the fact that we are addressing a tradition as old as Sharīʿa requires us to ensure that its particularities are given a sufficiently robust voice, in order to avoid historical anachronisms or over-eagerness to find a common philosophical ground where none may exist.

To challenge the assumptions that underlie what may be initial anxieties about the title, this book examines what is herein called Islamic natural law. In particular, the book presents competing premodern theories about the ontological authority of reason in Sharīʿa. *Ontological authority* is used here to capture the idea of reason as an authoritative source of Sharīʿa norms, alongside revealed scripture and other authoritative source-texts. In this sense, this study addresses juristic debates about whether reason is a source of Sharīʿa norms. Muslim jurists have debated whether reason is an authoritative source of Sharīʿa norms that reflect the divine will on issues where revealed scripture or other authoritative source-texts are silent (*min qabla wurūd al-sharʿ*). This study will show that the debates on this issue were fundamentally linked to theological and philosophical considerations about nature as a site where fact and value are fused. To study the ontological authority of reason by reference to a natural law frame distinguishes this study from debates about reason as a tool of epistemic or methodological analysis. This is an important

[7] JW Harris, 'Can you believe in natural law? [Review of John Finnis, *Natural Law and Natural Rights*]' (1981) 44 MLR 729; Neil MacCormick, 'Natural Law Reconsidered [Review of John Finnis, *Natural Law and Natural Rights*]' (1981) 1 OJLS 99.

[8] Indeed, as Waldron suggests, liberal political theorists committed to Lockean conceptions of equality would do well to recognize the content Locke's religious values contributed to his philosophical exposition on equality. Waldron, *God, Locke and Equality*.

distinction, if only to ensure that this study is not confused with others that address the authority and scope of interpretation in Islamic law, known as *ijtihād*. Debates about *ijtihād* in Islamic law have been around for many decades, with special vehemence in the 20th century when Muslims sought to reform Islam and Muslim societies amidst the changes brought by modernity.[9] This study on Islamic natural law theories, while not irrelevant to the debates on *ijtihād*, is nonetheless philosophically different and distinct.

Between History and Legal Philosophy: A Note on Methodology

Before introducing the historical and theoretical background that informs this study, a preliminary note on methodology is in order. This study straddles the disciplines of Islamic law, legal philosophy, and history, each of which makes methodological demands that this study aims to satisfy, although with the knowledge that some readers may be disappointed. As a work of legal philosophy, this study traces the idea of natural law in Islamic legal history. The focus on law is not intended to suggest that no other field of Islamic literature addresses naturalistic reasoning. Indeed, Muslim philosophers have also offered accounts of naturalism, and a study of their contributions to naturalist philosophy would be of great interest.[10]

[9] Much of the debate about reason and interpretation is embedded in the controversy over whether Muslims can perform *ijtihād* or renewed interpretation on matters already addressed by precedent. Both in the scholarly and popular press, the doctrine of *ijtihād* offers theorists and reformists alike an important doctrinal concept for reflecting upon questions of moral agency, modernity and the law. For scholarly works on *ijtihād* and the debates about whether it was closed or not, see Shaista P Ali-Karamali and Fiona Dunne, 'The Ijtihad Controversy' (1994) 9 *Arab Law Quarterly* 238. The historical validity of this alleged closure has been substantially questioned and critiqued in the scholarly literature. Wael B Hallaq, 'Was the Gate of Ijtihad Closed?' (1984) 16 *International Journal of Middle East Studies* 3. However, modern self-proclaimed reformers nonetheless consider their calls for a new *ijtihād* to be novel and perhaps even edgy. See eg Irshad Manji, *The Trouble With Islam Today: A Muslim's Call for Reform in Her Faith* (New York: St Martin's Press, 2004).

[10] Thérèse-Anne Druart, 'Metaphysics' in Peter Adamson and Richard C Taylor (eds), *The Cambridge Companion to Arabic Philosophy* (Cambridge: Cambridge University Press, 2005) 327–49; Sami S. Hawi, *Islamic Naturalism and Mysticism: A Philosophical Study of Ibn Ṭufayl's Ḥayy b. Yaqẓān* (Leiden: Brill, 1974).

However, this study is instead focused on how pre-modern Muslim jurists theorized not simply about what nature is and the knowledge it can offer, but also (and most significantly) about the *authority* of naturalistic reasoning in the law.

This study presents a history and explanation of an idea in Sharīʿa, thereby situating it in the realm of intellectual history. Subsequent to the linguistic turn in the humanities and social sciences, which questions the objectivity historians can attribute to 'facts' of the past, such as ideas,[11] one might follow Quentin Skinner and suggest that such a history of ideas is untenable. According to Skinner, an idea does not exist independent of the expressive 'illocutionary force' of an author:[12]

> To be precise, Skinner argues that to understand an utterance we have to grasp both its meaning and its illocutionary force, where its meaning comes from its sense and reference, and its illocutionary force derives from the conventions that determine what the author was doing in making it.[13]

Likewise the historian Gabrielle Spiegel has argued that to determine the historical meaning of a text, the historian must investigate the 'social logic' of the text or, in other words, the context that may have informed the meaning of the language that the author used to convey a particular meaning.[14] Both Skinner and Spiegel are concerned about objectivity in the human sciences, and the inevitability of the subjective affecting the explicit and implicit meaning of a given text. This approach certainly preserves the role of the historian in light of the 'linguistic turn'. Consequently, a project about the 'idea' of natural law in Islamic legal theory might approach the topic by focusing on particular authors, dissecting the intricacies of sentence structure, word usage, and extra-textual factors—all of which contribute to the meaning the author may have intended to convey.

[11] Anthony Pagden, 'Rethinking the Linguistic Turn: Current Anxieties in Intellectual History' (1988) 49 *Journal of the History of Ideas* 519.

[12] Quentin Skinner, 'Meaning and Understanding in the History of Ideas' in James Tully (ed), *Meaning and Context: Quentin Skinner and His Critics* (Princeton: Princeton University Press, 1989) 29–67.

[13] Mark Bevir, *The Logic of the History of Ideas* (Cambridge: Cambridge University Press, 1999) 41.

[14] Gabrielle Spiegel, 'History, Historicism, and the Social Logic of the Text' in Gabrielle Spiegel (ed), *The Past as Text* (Baltimore: Johns Hopkins University Press, 2006) 3.

This approach to the study of Islamic legal history can offer and has offered fruitful insights into the history and development of Islamic law in different historical periods.[15]

This study also offers a philosophical account of various naturalistic theories in Islamic law. History is fundamentally relevant to our inquiry, but so too is legal philosophy. In order to pursue a philosophical approach without at the same time falling foul of the historical methods that are ever present in this study, the agency of any given author is noted. The methodology underlying this study presumes that the author articulated his legal philosophy in light of a jurisprudential tradition that made the underlying issue relevant, hence the use of a diachronic approach to the idea of natural law. But that jurisprudential tradition may have also served as a backdrop against which a particular author wrote, hence the focus on the theories of individual jurists writing within the tradition.[16] As such, this study incorporates both diachronic and synchronic modes of analysis.

Synchronic analysis reminds us that each jurist engages with convention individually. According to Bevir, '[w]e should be cautious...of representing tradition as an inevitable presence within all we do in case we thereby leave too slight a role for agency'.[17] A synchronic approach remains attentive to the role of agency in the way tradition is understood, 'because traditions do not fix our responses for us, they do not stand in contrast to reason'.[18] This study, however, will also situate our particular authors' arguments within a tradition that may have influenced their work or against which they may have responded. To do so, this study diachronically follows the use of certain arguments across different authors to reflect upon the traditions and theories that operated in the

[15] See eg Yasin Dutton, *The Origins of Islamic Law: The Qur'ān, the Muwaṭṭa' and Madinan 'Amal* (Surrey: Curzon, 1999); Sherman Jackson, *Islamic Law and the State: The Constitutional Jurisprudence of Shihab al-Din al-Qarafi* (Leiden: Brill, 1996); Harald Motzki, *The Origins of Islamic Jurisprudence: Meccan Fiqh Before the Classical Schools* (Leiden: Brill, 2001).

[16] As Abou El Fadl suggests, Muslim jurists were part of a corporate culture of law and legal training that did not necessarily render the discipline of law autonomous, but certainly provided a professional context in which the jurists worked and wrote. Khaled Abou El Fadl, *Rebellion and Violence in Islamic Law* (Cambridge: Cambridge University Press, 2001).

[17] Bevir, *The Logic of the History of Ideas*, 201.

[18] Bevir, *The Logic of the History of Ideas*, 223.

background and animated their arguments. By adopting a synchronic and diachronic approach, this study remains mindful of the interplay between the individual agent and the jurisprudential backdrop against which he works. As Bevir remarks:

> [P]eople always start out against the background of a tradition, traditions necessarily provide the authoritative contexts within which we exercise our reason. Equally, however, because traditions never fix limits to the conclusions people can reach, the free exercise of our reason is not undermined by the presence of an authoritative tradition.[19]

What is Natural Law?

To introduce the contents and argument of this study, an initial remark should be made about how 'natural law' is understood here, and why it is used to frame this study. The contemporary theorist of natural law, John Finnis, writes that a theory of natural law 'claims to be able to identify conditions and principles of practical right-mindedness, of good and proper order among men and in individual conduct.'[20] It is a theory that can offer a framework of analysis as well as an evaluative basis by which to distinguish good conduct from bad conduct: it 'assist[s] the practical reflections of those concerned to act.'[21]

The jurisprudence of natural law addresses a wide range of issues. Some scholars may focus on the existence of principles or goods that guide reasoning about the law, and the authority of reason to determine those principles. Within a religious context, others consider how the presence of God may contribute to a natural law philosophy. In the religious context, we should not be surprised to find that theology and legal philosophy are not such separate disciplines as to preclude their influence on each other.[22] While different legal traditions come

[19] Bevir, *The Logic of the History of Ideas*, 223.

[20] Finnis, *Natural Law and Natural Rights*, 18.

[21] Finnis, *Natural Law and Natural Rights*, 18.

[22] For basic presumptions about the kinds of theoretical issues posed by a natural law theory, see Westerman, *The Disintegration of Natural Law Theory*, 12; Grisez, *Christian Moral Principles*; Finnis, *Natural Law and Natural Rights*; Lon Fuller, *The Morality of Law* (New Haven: Yale University Press, rev edn, 1969). For a study on Jewish natural law, see David Novak, *Natural Law in Judaism* (Cambridge: Cambridge University Press, 1998).

to the topic of natural law from different conceptual vantage points, one point they seem to share is a concern for the ontological authority of reason in law. This focus on reason and its authority for normatively ordering the world is a basic question in natural law studies,[23] and is the fundamental question that animates this study.

For instance, Thomas Aquinas (d. 1274) erected a legal system of four components. At the pinnacle of Aquinas' system of law is the *Lex Aeterna*, or Eternal Law. The Eternal Law is God's law as understood in the 'mind' of God.[24] However the Eternal Law is not, as a whole, knowable by man. Rather the means by which we know God's law are through two subsidiary avenues, namely the *Lex Divina* (Divine Law) and *Lex Naturalis* (Natural Law). *Lex Divina* is generally the law as contained in scripture or revelation. The *Lex Naturalis*, on the other hand, is where we comprehend the eternal divine law through the use of reason, thereby bringing us into a relationship with the Divine. As Aquinas stated:

> [T]he light of natural reason, whereby we discern what is good and what is evil, which is the function of the natural law, is nothing else than an imprint on us of the Divine Light. It is therefore evident that the natural law is nothing else than the rational creature's participation of the eternal law.[25]

Nature provides Aquinas with a foundation for grounding the authority of natural reasoning about the Eternal Law. As Westerman has argued, Aquinas does not view God's law as a static form of precepts and codes. Rather the Eternal Law for Aquinas has more to do with the divine style: God picks a style of doing things, and adheres to it when He creates. Natural reasoning involves understanding that style and its implications for how the world is ordered: 'The eternal law is an ordering principle regulating God's creation rather than a set of coercive precepts.'[26]

[23] Westerman, *The Disintegration of Natural Law Theory*, 12. For modern accounts of natural law theory, see Finnis, *Natural Law and Natural Rights*; Grisez, *Christian Moral Principles*; Grisez and Shaw, *Fulfillment in Christ*; George, *Natural Law: Contemporary Essays*; Murphy, *Natural Law and Practical Rationality*.

[24] For the notion of the fixedness of creation and its inherent normativity in Aquinas' thought, see Lisska, *Aquinas's Theory of Natural Law*, 121–30.

[25] Aquinas, *Treatise on Law*, 15–16.

[26] Westerman, *The Disintegration of Natural Law Theory*, 29.

Notably, Anthony Lisska suggests that the authority of Aquinas' naturalistic reasoning has less to do with God than with enabling reason to move from an empirical assessment of the world to a normative evaluation that reflects the divine mind. God is important primarily for establishing existence and creation. But once creation exists, it is up to human beings, with their rational capacities, to understand the natural dispositions inherent in human nature. God simply posits existence. But our rational capacity does the work of natural lawyering.[27] As Lisska writes:

> Aquinas included the divine mind only because it provided the ultimate or capstone explanation for his ontology. God as the 'necessary being' accounts for why there is something rather than nothing. God provides the existence to the temporal essence whose structure is contingent. But an analysis of this relationship of existence dependent upon the necessary being is not itself a necessary condition for understanding the content of a temporal essence.[28]

Natural law theorists such as Aquinas tied the authority of reason to the divine mind through the medium of the created world, which is deemed to reflect the divine will or style. Their ability to develop a theory of the authority of reason depended upon fusing fact and value by rendering the divinely created world as a sufficiently objective and normative foundation for rational analysis about the norms of human behavior.

Why Natural Law?

To bridge the past and the present, this study adopts the philosophical frame of 'natural law'. But why employ 'natural law' as a thematic concept at all? There are various reasons why the concept of natural law provides an important analytic fulcrum for this study. First, it offers a philosophy of law framework for a set of questions that span both theology and law, but which are nonetheless linked. While it might be argued that this framework links distinct disciplines in the pre-modern Islamic scholarly tradition (ie theology and law), we cannot assume

[27] Lisska, *Aquinas's Theory of Natural Law*, 121.
[28] Lisska, *Aquinas's Theory of Natural Law*, 130.

that such divisions constrained the minds of our jurists. To suggest that the division of knowledge into different fields or disciplines also implies the compartmentalization of the way individual jurists' thought assumes a rigidity of the mind, and limits, if not rejects, the possibility of interdisciplinarity.

Secondly, the use of 'natural law' allows this study to illustrate the importance of a legal philosophical lens to understanding the debate at issue. The sources reviewed reflect the work of pre-modern authors who belonged to different Sunnī legal guilds and espoused theological views that spanned various schools of theology, such as the Muʿtazilite and Ashʿarite schools. But as will be illustrated below, the theological and legal affiliations of a scholar do not necessarily map onto his naturalist legal philosophy. Indeed, jurists of ambiguous theological persuasion nonetheless seem to adopt one or the other naturalist theory. Hence, to frame this study in terms of natural law permits us to emphasize the distinctiveness of legal philosophy as a frame for the intellectual debates of pre-modern Muslim jurists and theologians. Instead of identifying each jurist as a member of a particular legal or theological school, we can also appreciate their work in light of their positions on compelling and pivotal issues of legal philosophy.

Thirdly, the 'natural law' frame is used to reflect upon the authority of law in a manner that permits a conversation among scholars of different legal systems. The authority of reason is a matter of common concern to legal systems across both time and space. This study communicates across the boundaries of discipline and civilization to suggest that legal systems, religious or otherwise, cannot avoid questions about reason and authority. It is not the case that religious legal systems are characterized solely by voluntaristic authority; but neither are they so open to reasoned deliberation as to be without limits. Rather, like many legal systems, the history of Sharīʿa presents contested views about the authority of reason. In that vein, this study on Islamic natural law offers an opportunity for legal philosophers and comparative law scholars to engage with a tradition that may not be their own, and to diversify debates about law, authority, and reason in jurisprudential scholarship more generally.

Fourthly, as we will see in the case of the different Islamic natural law theories below, the authority of reason depends upon a philosophy of law in which fact and value are fused in nature, thus making nature centrally important to our analysis. Having a Creator in the background required our jurists to reflect upon the theological implications of any natural law theory. For instance, a Creator can be principally viewed as a legislator whose legislative acts define the good and the bad: X is good *because* God does X. Or the Creator can be viewed as legislating only in pursuit of the good: God does X *because* X is good. These two views of God as legislator offer distinct approaches to understanding the good, and have competing implications for a philosophy of law and the role of human reason in it. If all good is a function of God's will, then a resulting legal philosophy may limit the scope to which human beings can know the good independent of indicators from God. But if God does X because X is good, that assumes the notion of 'good' is separate and distinct from God's will on the matter. It also suggests that human beings can know the good, even if God has not provided express guidance to us about what the good is. In this latter case, we can use our reason to investigate the world around us to form principles of normative ordering that reflect what God would want for us. Consequently, to frame this study using natural law is, for the purpose of this study, to consider:

- the competing theologies of God;
- how those competing theologies of God offer distinctive understandings of the objective and normative quality of nature;
- whether and how those competing theologies and understandings of nature affect the authority of reason; and
- how methods of practical reasoning are designed to recognize and limit the use of reason in the law.

What Does Islamic Natural Law Contribute to Our Understanding of Sharīʿa and Reason?

The relationship between Sharīʿā and reason is not a topic just of recent interest. Indeed, it has been an important issue in both the pre-modern period as well as the modern one. Muslims have, throughout history, contended with the role, scope, and authority of reason in a religious tradition that is fundamentally linked to a book (the Qurʾān) that is believed to be God's word, revealed to the Prophet Muḥammad, and meant to guide humanity to salvation.[29] Adhering to and satisfying God's will is an important factor in attaining salvation. Consequently, the Qur'ān offers the most obvious source of God's will for Muslims to follow. But Muslim jurists knew that the world of lived experience cannot be and is not captured between the Qur'ān's two covers; thus they debated whether and to what extent they could build upon what they learned from the Qur'ān. The literature on legal theory (*uṣūl al-fiqh*) expounds on the ways in which Muslim jurists can extend and develop the law in light of changed circumstances, while remaining mindful of the source-texts that are deemed to represent God's will best (such as the Qur'ān and traditions of the Prophet).[30] In the modern period, much of the debate about reason has been about whether, how, and to what extent Muslims can perform *ijtihād*, or renewed interpretation, on matters already addressed by historical precedent. In both the scholarly and popular literature, the doctrine of *ijtihād* offers theorists and reformists alike an important opportunity to address the scope of moral agency, and the relationship between law, reform, and modernity.[31]

However, as noted above, a natural law inquiry frames the role of reason in a manner that is distinct from, though certainly not unrelated to, the question of *ijtihād*. Here we are interested in the ontological authority of reason in Sharīʿa or, in other words, whether and to what extent, in the absence of source-texts, reasoned deliberation about the good and the bad can assume sufficient normative authority to result in Sharīʿa norms that reflect what God desires or wills. The significance of framing this study using natural law is reflected both by contemporary Muslim and scholarly discourses on reason and Sharīʿa.

[29] eg, Q 2:1 states: 'This Book—there is no doubt it is guidance for all who are ever-mindful of God.'

[30] For scholarly treatments of Islamic legal theory, see Wael B Hallaq, *A History of Islamic Legal Theories: An Introduction to Sunnī Uṣūl al-Fiqh* (Cambridge: Cambridge University Press, 1999); Mohammad Hashim Kamali, *Principles of Islamic Jurisprudence* (3rd edn, Cambridge: Islamic Texts Society, 2003); Ṣubḥī Maḥmaṣṣānī, *Falsafat al-Tashrīʿ fī al-Islām* (3rd edn, Beirut: Dār al-ʿIlm li'l-Malāyīn, 1961).

[31] For scholarly works on *ijtihād* and the debates about whether it was forestalled or not, see Ali-Karamali and Dunne, 'The Ijtihad Controversy'. The historical validity of this alleged closure has been substantially questioned and attacked in Hallaq, 'Was the Gate of Ijtihad Closed?'. However, modern self-proclaimed reformers nonetheless consider their calls for renewed *ijtihād* to be novel and perhaps even edgy. See eg Manji, *The Trouble With Islam Today*.

Muslim Debates on Sharīʿa and Reason

This study on Islamic natural law theories arises amidst, and offers a partial corrective to, popular perceptions of Sharīʿa as legislated by God, whom the devout are bound to obey.[32] On this view reason cannot be an authoritative source for divine injunctions; at most it can confirm or corroborate what is already established by authoritative source-texts. These perceptions are neither new nor sudden; rather they have a history, which is rooted in both early theological debates and the history of legal development over centuries. Those who oppose this view are deemed heterodox, and are often labeled as modern day Muʿtazilites.[33] The Muʿtazilites are considered the early rationalists in Islam.[34] They upheld the view that God only does the good and just and avoids the evil. In other words God does X *because* X is good. By holding such a position, though, they implicitly suggested that concepts like 'good' and 'just' are virtues that are separate and distinct from God's will on any given issue. As separate and distinct from God's will, they are virtues that can be reasoned about and rationally known. But if that is the case, then it also follows that anything that we decide is good or bad would

[32] For an overview of such views and how they operate in the public sphere today, see Anver M Emon, 'Islamic Law and the Canadian Mosaic: Politics, Jurisprudence, and Multicultural Accommodation' (2008) 87 *Canadian Bar Review* 391.

[33] Richard C Martin, Mark R Woodward, and Dwi S Atmaja, *Defenders of Reason in Islam: Muʿtazilism from Medieval School to Modern Symbol* (Oxford: Oneworld Publications, 1997) 166–7. The apostasy case of Nāṣr Ḥāmid Abū Zayd, an Egyptian intellectual deemed to have apostated from Islam through his writings on the Qurʾān, is a well known case of an intellectual whose ideas were viewed by some as Muʿṭazilite or as heterodox, and thereby contrary to prevailing Islamic norms. For an overview of the relationship between intellectual freedom and apostasy cases, and the Abū Zayd case, see Baber Johansen, 'Apostasy as objective and depersonalized fact: two recent Egyptian court judgments' (2003) 70 *Social Research* 687; Susanne Olsson, 'Apostasy in Egypt: Contemporary Cases of *Ḥisbah*' (2008) 98 *The Muslim World* 95. For a comparative study of Muʿtazilite ideas and those of Abū Zayd, see Thomas Hildebrandt, 'Between Muʿtazilism and Mysticism: How much of a Muʿtazilite is Naṣr Ḥāmid Abū Zayd?' in Camilla Adang, Sabine Schmidtke, and David Sklare (eds), *A Common Rationality: Muʿtazilism in Islam and Judaism* (Würzburg: Ergon in Kommission, 2007) 495.

[34] For the history of Muʿtazilite theology, see Martin et al, *Defenders of Reason*, 25–45; W Montgomery Watt, *The Formative Period of Islamic Thought* (Oxford: Oneworld Publications, 1998) 209–52. For thematic analysis of Muʿtazilite and other theological doctrines, see Harry Austryn Wolfson, *The Philosophy of the Kalam* (Cambridge, Mass: Harvard University Press, 1976).

thereby imply that God would not act counter to that good, or in furtherance of that evil, since God only acts justly and in accordance with the good. Indeed, this suggests that we could, through our own reasoned deliberation, limit the scope of God's acts and will.[35]

Voluntarist theologians, on the other hand, were keen to uphold the omnipotence of God. They considered the Muʿtazilite position a threat to the theology of an all-powerful God. For various reasons Muʿtazilite theology lost favor in the course of Islamic intellectual history, and Voluntarist concepts have become significant theological frames for understanding God and His omnipotence.[36] Consequently, anyone who suggests today that reason has ontological authority as a source of Sharīʿa norms is deemed unpersuasive for orthodox Sunnī Muslims.[37] So, for instance, Khaled Abou El Fadl offers a philosophically oriented approach to Islam as a moral system rooted in justice.[38] But in doing so, he is immediately deemed not credible by those who consider his ideas tantamount to heterodox Muʿtazilite rationalism. As Mohammad Fadel writes in his response to Abou El Fadl:

> It is somewhat surprising, then, that Abou El Fadl would partly ground the basis for democratic life among Muslims on a heretofore discredited theological argument . . . His case would have been stronger if he had

[35] Qāḍī ʿAbd al-Jabbār, *Sharḥ al-Uṣūl al-Khamsa* (Beirut: Dār Iḥyāʾ al-Turāth al-ʿArabī, 2001) 203–7. For the debate on authorship of this treatise, see the discussion on ʿAbd al-Jabbār in Chapter II. For further discussion on the relationship between God and justice, see Martin et al, *Defenders of Reason*, 71–81.

[36] For a history of Islamic theology and on the construction of orthodoxy, see Tilman Nagel, *The History of Islamic Theology: From Muhammad to the Present* (Princeton: Markus Wiener Publishers, 2000); Oliver Leaman and Sajjad Rizvi, 'The Developed *Kalām* Tradition' in Tim Winter (ed), *The Cambridge Companion to Classical Islamic Theology* (Cambridge: Cambridge University Press, 2008) 77; Ahmed El Shamsy, 'The Social Construction of Orthodoxy' in Winter, *The Cambridge Companion to Classical Islamic Theology*, 97.

[37] This book reviews the works of authors who are often considered part of the Sunnī tradition. To examine Shīʿa legal theory on natural law was beyond the scope of this project, especially as Shīʿa jurisprudence reserves an important place for reason in the law. The author hopes that this book will inspire further research in legal philosophy, natural law, and Sharīʿa.

[38] Khaled Abou El Fadl, *Islam and the Challenge of Democracy: A Boston Review Book*, Joshua Cohen and Deborah Chasman (eds) (Princeton: Princeton University Press, 2004) 3–48.

demonstrated that democracy is consistent with either theory of the good traditionally espoused by Muslim theologians.[39]

Whether or not a scholar is explicit about his or her Muʿtazilite sensibilities, a suggestion that reason offers an important source of guidance for the modern Muslim raises suspicions of heterodoxy framed in pre-modern terms. To theorize about reason, therefore, is fraught with theological implications that demarcate not only the intellectual bounds of credible Sharīʿa-based argument, but also the political bounds of community and belonging. This is not to suggest that there is no other rationalist approach outside the Muʿtazilite model. Even Professor Fadel is keen to assert that reason has an authority that cannot be denied. For Fadel, Muslims who adhere to their religious convictions can participate in a Rawlsian overlapping consensus in a liberal public sphere.[40] His utilization of the notion of the 'reasonable' suggests that even those attempting to work within a more 'orthodox' or 'traditional' vision of Islam are nonetheless committed to finding space for reasoned deliberation.

In addition to arising amidst a popular image of Sharīʿa, this study is mindful of a tradition of Muslim reformist literature that has sought, since the late 19th century, to increase the scope of reasoned deliberation in the hope for change, development, and modernization in the Muslim world.[41] For instance, in the writings of Muḥammad ʿAbduh and Rashīd Riḍā, we find a reliance on reason and the idea of perceived goods (*maṣlaḥa*) in order to develop the Sharīʿa in light of changed historical realities. In doing so, they called for renewed interpretation and engagement with the historical legal tradition, or in other words *ijtihād*.[42] But in doing so, they could not focus on the epistemic question without acknowledging the ontological one.

[39] Mohammad H Fadel, 'Too Far From Tradition' in Abou El Fadl, *Islam and the Challenge of Democracy*, 81, 82.

[40] Mohammad Fadel, 'The True, the Good and the Reasonable: The Theological and Ethical Roots of Public Reason in Islamic Law' (2008) 21 *Canadian Journal of Law and Jurisprudence* 5.

[41] For a general overview of different modern Muslim reformists who contend with the nature and scope of reasoned deliberation, see Jasser Auda, *Maqasid al-Shariah as Philosophy of Islamic Law: A Systems Approach* (Herndon, Va: International Institute of Islamic Thought, 2008) 144–53.

[42] Hamid Enayat, *Modern Islamic Political Thought* (Austin, Tex: University of Texas Press, 1982) 46–8.

Muhammad 'Abduh (d. 1905) equated the *Shari'a* with natural law . . . and opened the door for modern jurists to use reason as a basis for legal interpretation. Pursuing this line of thought, Rashid Rida (d. 1935) might be regarded as the most effective protagonist of the use of *maslaha* as a source for legal and political reform. . . . Rida tried to re-interpret the *Shari'a* on the basis of *maslaha* . . . as the expression of public interest.[43]

These descriptive remarks are fascinating for our purpose as they raise questions about the philosophical bases by which reformists have justified the ontological authority of reason in Sharīʿa. Their questions (and especially the ambiguity of their answers) are, in part, an animating factor for this study.

The ambiguity in the response to the ontological question has continued throughout the 20th and 21st centuries. When contemporary clerics write in support of reason in Islam, they may root their conclusion in the Qurʾān itself, identifying various verses in which the Qurʾān asks the reader to think or reflect.[44] This approach to the authority of reason relies on the authority of the Qurʾān, which indeed clothes the use of reason with a type of divine authority. But the effect of this approach is to render the ontological authority of reason derivative at best. If the Qurʾānic references constitute the bases by which reason is an authoritative source of Sharīʿa, then reason does not stand as a separate and distinct source of Sharīʿa at all.

But if reason is a separate source, and the Qurʾānic references merely corroborate what we already know by reason, that begs the question: 'how do we know?' Tariq Ramadan, a European Muslim reformist, suggests that the natural world offers insights about the workings of God's will. He writes:

God always makes available to humankind tools and signs on the road that lead to recognizing Him. The first space that welcomes human beings in their quest is creation itself. It is a book . . .and all the elements that form part of it are signs that should remind the human consciousness that there exists that which is 'beyond' them. This Revelation in and through space is

[43] M Khadduri, 'Maslaha' in P Bearman, T Bianquis, CE Bosworth, E van Donzel and WP Heinrichs (eds), *Encyclopaedia of Islam, Second Edition* (Leiden: Brill, 2009) [Brill Online. University of Toronto. http://www.brillonline.nl].

[44] For an example of such a strategy, see Yusuf al-Qaradawi, *al-'Aql wa al-'Ilm fi al-Qur'ān al-Karīm* (Beirut: Mu'assasāt al-Risāla, 2001) 11–68.

wedded to Revelations in time, which, at irregular intervals, came as reminders of the origin and end of the universe and of humanity.[45]

Creation and source-texts offer two approaches to understanding the divine will. For Ramadan, both are 'texts' that must be read and reflected upon. The created world, fashioned by God, is a sign of God's will if only we would look closely. Ramadan effectively fuses fact and value in the created world, thereby rendering it a foundation for the ontological authority of reason. Ramadan offers an approach to reason's ontological authority that may be sympathetic with natural law. But depicting the natural world akin to a text raises important hermeneutic questions about the determinacy and objectivity of the law. Furthermore, the more Ramadan incorporates the human and natural sciences into legal analysis, the more he also challenges the view of law as a distinct discipline, whose efficacy in part depends upon a degree of determinacy and objectivity that may not be possible given his agenda for 'radical reform'.[46]

For the few reformist thinkers noted above, there is a clear reliance on reason as an authoritative source of Sharīʿa. They situate their arguments on a spectrum of possibilities, each of which has some basis in the vocabulary and doctrine of the Islamic legal tradition. Their positions are built upon a tradition of pre-modern legal debate about the authority of reason in Sharīʿa. Their approaches are also very much reflective of their historical moment, which some consider to be the crisis of modernity, which the Muslim world has faced with the rise of independent Muslim majority states, and the development of significant Muslim minority populations in liberal-democratic polities.[47] The reformists rely on the historical tradition to give

[45] Tariq Ramadan, *Western Muslims and the Future of Islam* (Oxford: Oxford University Press, 2004) 13.

[46] Tariq Ramadan, *Radical Reform: Islamic Ethics and Liberation* (Oxford: Oxford University Press, 2009).

[47] The 'crisis of modernity' has become a feature of much writing about the relationship between Muslims, their religious tradition, and the socio-political contexts in which they find themselves. Writing about Arab-Muslims, Haddad states that the 'impact of the power of the West has challenged to the core [their] concept of who [they] are and where [their] destiny lies.' Yvonne Yazbeck Haddad, *Contemporary Islam and the Challenge of History* (Albany: State University of New York Press, 1982) xi. For others similarly concerned with the 'crisis of modernity' for Muslims, see Bassam Tibi, *The Crisis of Modern Islam: A Preindustrial Culture in the Scientific-Technological Age*,

meaningful responses to their present context. Framing present debates with pre-modern categories situates any reformist theory within a tradition that is deemed to be a source of authority and identity. But to bring that past into the present raises concerns about how translatable the past is for those who wish to adopt it for present purposes. The past tradition was framed by jurists very much concerned with debates about theology and the implications of those debates for a theory of law. Modern reformists, though, have very different concerns. To rely on past traditions without duly attending to what they signified in the past ignores the historical significance of the internal debates, and how that historical significance may adversely affect the interests of contemporary reformists. This study focuses on the pre-modern debates to understand a world of law and philosophy different from our own. However, it remains ever mindful of how that past still animates the present.

Scholarly Debates on Sharīʿa and Reason

The scholarly literature on Islamic law reflects different approaches to the place of reason in the law. In the aggregate, it conveys an openness to the ontological question that underlies this study. Certainly Muslim jurists of the pre-modern world emphasized the role of foundational text and close adherence to its terms as a means for legitimating their juristic analyses.[48] But as recent scholarship

Judith von Sivers (trans) (Salt Lake City: University of Utah Press, 1988); Fazlur Rahman, *Islam and Modernity: Transformation of an Intellectual Tradition* (Chicago: University of Chicago Press, 1982); Mohammad Arkoun, *Rethinking Islam: Common Questions, Uncommon Answers*, Robert D Lee (trans) (Boulder, Colo: Westview Press, 1994); Abdelwahab el-Affendi (ed), *Rethinking Islam and Modernity* (London: The Islamic Foundation, 2001). In his recent book, Wael Hallaq addresses the crisis of modernity, and the impact of the modern state system on the nature and function of Islamic law. Hallaq, *Shari'a: Theory, Practice, Transformations.*

[48] Asaf AA Fyzee, *Outlines of Muhammadan Law* (3rd edn, Oxford: Oxford University Press, 1964) 78–9; Noel J Coulson, *A History of Islamic Law* (1964; reprint, Edinburgh: Edinburgh University Press, 1997) 76; Bernard G Weiss, *The Spirit of Islamic Law* (Athens, Ga: University of Georgia Press, 1998) 38–65. This emphasis on foundational text will be illustrated in Chapter III. Studies of Islamic legal theory illustrate the priority given to literalist readings by reference to the interpretive preference for the apparent meaning (*ẓāhir*) of words over the allegorical or metaphorical meaning (*majāz*). For a treatment on such rules of interpretation, see Mohammad Hashim Kamali, *Principles of Islamic Jurisprudence* (3rd edn, Cambridge: Islamic Text Society, 2003) 117–66.

suggests, fidelity to the text does not preclude the interpretive license and agency that is generally a feature of mature legal systems, despite the rarefied image of Sharīʿa that often predominates in the popular imagination.[49] Contemporary analyses of Islamic law and legal theory emphasize that pre-modern Muslim jurists utilized discretion in adjudicating cases,[50] theorized about interpretative agency,[51] articulated theories of legal authority amidst difference and dispute,[52] and designed doctrines that reflect contextual factors of varying sorts.[53] Mohammad Hashim Kamali's survey of the principles of Islamic jurisprudence offers the closest thing in English to a textbook on the modes and types of legal reasoning in Islamic law.[54] Yasin Dutton's work on the early *Muwaṭṭāʾ* of Mālik b. Anas argues that the origins of Islamic law were not merely textual, and reflect an implicit non-textual discourse about the early practice of the Prophet, his companions and successors.[55] Studies on the *fatwā* and the resolution of cases offer a window into various historical moments, and show how the nature of legal decision must take into account the context and subjectivity of the adjudicator who makes decisions in light of both text and context.[56] This is not to suggest that all Sharīʿa reasoning is to be rendered a function of pure context, discretion or even expediency.[57] Those who have described

[49] For a discussion of this concept of Islamic law, see Anver M Emon, 'Conceiving Islamic Law in a Pluralist Society: History, Politics and Multicultural Jurisprudence' [2006] *Singapore Journal of Legal Studies* 331; Emon, 'Islamic Law and the Canadian Mosaic.'

[50] Leslie Peirce, *Morality Tales: Law and Gender in the Ottoman Court of Aintab* (Berkeley: University of California Press, 2003); David S Powers, *Law, Society and Culture in the Maghrib, 1300–1500* (Cambridge: Cambridge University Press, 2002).

[51] Khaled Abou El Fadl, *Speaking in God's Name: Islamic Law, Authority and Women* (Oxford: Oneworld Publications, 2001); Muhammad Khalid Masud, *Shatibi's Philosophy of Islamic Law* (Islamabad: Islamic Research Institute, 1995); Hallaq, *A History of Islamic Legal Theories*; Wael Hallaq, *Authority, Continuity and Change in Islamic Law* (Cambridge: Cambridge University Press, 2001).

[52] Abou El Fadl, *Rebellion and Violence.*

[53] Dutton, *The Origins of Islamic Law.*

[54] Mohammad Hashim Kamali, *Principles of Islamic Jurisprudence* (3rd edn, Cambridge: Islamic Texts Society, 2005).

[55] Dutton, *The Origins of Islamic Law.*

[56] Muhammad Khalid Masud, Brinkley Messick, and David S Powers, *Islamic Legal Interpretation: Muftis and Their Fatwas* (Cambridge, Mass: Harvard University Press, 1996); Powers, *Law, Society and Culture in the Maghrib*; Peirce, *Morality Tales.*

[57] Such an unflattering view of Islamic law and legal reasoning was held by US Supreme Court Justice, Felix Frankfurter, in *Terminiello v Chicago*, 337 US 1, 11; 69 S Ct 894, 899 (1949).

Islamic legal adjudication in an anthropological key, for instance, have met criticism from those who see in Islamic legal reasoning a mode of justice that is disciplined by reason, and yet open to the complexity of lived experience upon which the law is often called to adjudicate.[58]

Notably, some in the field of Islamic law and history have remarked that there is no natural law tradition in Islam.[59] For instance, Patricia Crone writes that when pre-modern Sunnī Muslims debated the philosophical question concerning situations where there is no revelation on a matter (*qabla wurūd al-sharʿ*) they indulged in a thought experiment about human nature as if it were stripped of divine guidance. According to Crone, in Islamic law no one has the right to create obligations that invoke the divine. That is God's job alone, and humans cannot speak on behalf of Him. While humans can create their own laws, such laws have no bearing on other-worldly salvation.[60] In a sense, Crone and others are right. The prevailing Sunnī position, as expressed in pre-modern treatises on legal theory (*uṣūl al-fiqh*), holds that where there is no scripture on a matter, one is left in a state of suspended judgment (*tawaqquf*); there is no epistemically coherent way to determine the divine law on that matter, and consequently no one is in a sufficient epistemic position to attribute to God a ruling of any normative force.[61] Reason does not assume any ontological authority akin to that of

[58] Lawrence Rosen has written extensively in the field of Islamic law and anthropology. See *The anthropology of justice: Law as culture in Islamic society* (1989; reprint, Cambridge: Cambridge University Press, 1990); *The Justice of Islam: Comparative Perspectives on Islamic Law and Society* (Oxford: Oxford University Press, 2000). For those who have criticized Rosen for not sufficiently accounting for the disciplined nature of legal reasoning, see Powers, *Law, Society and Culture*, 23–52; Khaled Abou El Fadl, 'Islamic Law and Ambivalent Scholarship [A Review of Lawrence Rosen, *The Justice of Islam: Comparative Perspectives on Islamic Law and Society* (Oxford: Oxford University Press, 2000)]' (2002) 100 *Michigan Law Review* 1421.

[59] George Makdisi, *Ibn ʿAqil: Religion and Culture in Classical Islam* (Edinburgh: Edinburgh University Press, 1997) 130; Patricia Crone, *God's Rule: Government and Islam: Six Centuries of Medieval Islamic Political Thought* (New York: Columbia University Press, 2004) 263–4. Notably, the Shīʿite tradition considers reason to be a source of law. However, to investigate the full extent of the debate in the Shīʿite tradition is beyond the scope of this study. For discussions about the debates on the use of reason in Shīʿite jurisprudence, see Robert Gleave, *Inevitable Doubt: Two Theories of Shīʿi Jurisprudence* (Leiden: Brill, 2000).

[60] Crone, *God's Rule*, 263–4.

[61] For the discussion on this point, see Chapter III.

scripture to justify using it as a basis for determining and constructing obligations that emanate from the divine.

This study, however, shows that Muslim jurists recognized to a certain extent that reason must have ontological authority for Sharīʿa purposes. Pre-modern Sunnī Muslim jurists struggled to understand Sharīʿa conceptually in light of their debates on nature and reason. To narrow the scope of this study, it focuses on juristic debates about the ontological authority of reason in situations where there is no scriptural or revelatory text.[62] Jurists framed their debate on this question by reflecting upon whether their use of reason (*ʿaql*) alone could be the basis for knowing the good (*ḥusn*) and the bad (*qubḥ*), and thereby legitimately justify correlating obligations and prohibitions under Sharīʿa law, where there is no scriptural source-text. For the purpose of this study the use of 'scriptural' or 'revelatory' is meant to signify foundational 'source-texts' of religious belief and practice, such as the Qur'ān and oral traditions of the Prophet, which in the aggregate constitute a corpus of evidence that stands outside and separate from the individual.[63]

The debate on the ontological authority of reason required jurists to incorporate fundamental theological premises in their jurisprudence. They theorized about nature and reason amidst competing theological commitments about the authority and omnipotence of God. For them, nature is the link between the divine will and human reason. They viewed nature as the product of God's purposive creation for the benefit of humanity. As such, nature's goodness is tied to God's omnipotence, purposiveness, and either *justice* or *grace* upon humanity. As a divine good, nature constitutes a body of facts that we can investigate. Using our reason, we can make conclusions about both the good (*ḥusn*) and the bad (*qubḥ*) in empirical terms. But because the empirical world is infused with a divine, purposeful,

[62] An English source on Islamic natural law offers a broad-based approach to the role of nature in Islamic intellectual history: A Ezzati, *Islam and Natural Law* (London: ICAS Press, 2002). In doing so, though, the author does not offer an account of Islamic natural law that resonates with the debates that fall more generally within the field of legal philosophy.

[63] This definition of revelation and/or scripture is inspired by Robert M Adam, 'Introduction' to Immanuel Kant, *Religion within the Boundaries of Mere Reason and Other Writings*, Allen Wood and George di Giovanni (trans) (1998; reprint, Cambridge: Cambridge University Press, 2006) xxxi.

deliberate good, our reasoned conclusions about the empirical good are infused with normative content stemming from the divine creative will. In other words, the 'is' becomes the 'ought'. Pre-modern Muslim jurists argued that because nature is created by God and thereby reflects His goodness, nature is also good, and thereby is fused with both fact and value. This fusion opens the way for reasoned observations of nature to transform into norms governing our conduct.

At the heart of these pre-modern debates are the terms of art *ḥusn* and *qubḥ*, which mean good and bad, respectively.[64] To focus on the debates around these two terms will situate us within the particularity of the Islamic legal tradition, while maintaining our interest in natural law as a philosophical frame of inquiry. The two terms are antonyms of each other, as indicated by the pre-modern lexicographer Ibn Manẓūr (d. 711/1311).[65] According to Ibn Manẓūr, the term *qubḥ* can be defined as an absence or diminution of *ḥusn* (*naqd-al-ḥusn*), while *ḥusn* is the opposite of *qubḥ*, as well as the diminution of *qubḥ* (*al-ḥusn ḍiddu al-qubḥ wa naqduhu*).[66] In Sunnī legal theory these terms of art capture a debate about whether conceptions of the good and the bad (and thereby obligation and prohibition) are rationally determinable, or whether everything that is good or bad in the world is the product of a divine legislative will.[67]

Kevin Reinhart has offered an important study of these terms, and their implication for the more general debate on *qabla wurūd al-sharʿ*, which he calls the 'before revelation complex'. For Reinhart, the debates on the 'before revelation complex' involve discussions about whether acts not addressed by scripture are presumptively

[64] EW Lane, *Arabic-English Lexicon* (Cambridge: Islamic Texts Society, 1984) 1:570, 2:2479.

[65] Throughout the work, the Islamic *hijra* date is provided alongside the common era date based on the Gregorian calendar.

[66] Abū al-Faḍl Jamāl al-Dīn Muḥammad b. Makram Ibn Manẓūr, *Lisān al-ʿArab* (6th edn, Beirut: Dār al-Ṣadr, 1997) 2:552, 13:114.

[67] Fazlur Rahman, 'Law and Ethics in Islam' in Richard G Hovannisian (ed), *Ethics in Islam* (Malibu, Calif: Undena Publications, 1985) 3–15, is sensitive to the connection between this moral question and the law generally. On the connection between this debate and jurisprudence, see also George Makdisi, 'Ethics in Islamic Traditionalist Doctrine' in Hovannisian, *Ethics in Islam*, 47–63, 50. However, Makdisi argues that Islamic law is mainly characterized by voluntarism. Makdisi also treats this issue in his biography of the 6th/12th century jurist, Ibn ʿAqīl Makdisi *Ibn ʿAqil*, 97–130.

prohibited, permitted, or in a state of indecision. Reinhart writes that the specific questions Muslim jurists addressed in this debate were really indirect mechanisms by which they could ask epistemologically difficult questions about moral valuation that are otherwise too unnerving to deal with directly. He states:

> [W]hen someone first posed this problem in debate it was eagerly seized upon and elaborated, we suppose, because through it Muslim intellectuals could examine notions too amorphous and sometimes too disturbing or unnerving to state baldly. Perhaps, also, through these 'thought experiments' they could discuss issues too profound to think about directly.[68]

This is not to suggest that the pre-modern debate was a mere façade by which Muslim jurists asked difficult theoretical questions about rational moral evaluation without doing so directly. On the contrary, Reinhart suggests that the hypotheticals were meant to have some theoretical bite. He writes:

> When Muslim scholars in the foreground were asking about acts before Revelation, I believe they were also reflecting upon important epistemological questions in the background. They were asking about the importance of Revelational knowledge over against other sources of knowledge; they were asking, What constitutes religious knowledge?; they were also asking questions about moral categorization and its relation to being itself: Does the goodness of gratitude or the badness of a lie come from some characteristic innate to the nature of gratitude and prevarication?...They asked also, What is it that makes something good? Does its goodness reside in the structure of the created world or in the ungrounded determination of God?[69]

Ḥusn and *qubḥ*, as terms of art, offered jurists a vocabulary by which to address the nature of knowledge, and the relationship between knowledge, reason, and authority. As will be shown below, these terms and the 'complex' within which they fell are philosophically significant for understanding the ontological authority of reason in Sharīʿa. Consequently they present the uniquely Islamic starting point for addressing the existence and contours of Islamic natural law theories.

[68] Kevin Reinhart, *Before Revelation: The Boundaries of Muslim Moral Thought* (Albany: SUNY Press, 1995) 4.

[69] Reinhart, *Before Revelation*, 5.

Islamic Natural Law Theories: An Overview

Not all who read this book may come to it as a specialist in pre-modern Islamic law or history, and so may benefit from this brief overview of the study. Likewise, students and specialists in the field may find a general outline of the argument useful as they work through the detailed debates of each jurist. This study focuses on debates that center around the Arabic words *ḥusn* and *qubḥ*. These two terms mean *good* and *bad*, respectively. They feature centrally in a pre-modern debate in Islamic legal philosophy about the authority of reason to make ethical decisions and transform them into Sharīʿa obligations. Muslim jurists questioned the authority of reason to constitute obligations in situations where no source-text exists to justify a particular legal conclusion, or as they would say: *min qabla wurūd al-sharʿ*.[70] When viewed from the lens of legal philosophy, and more specifically natural law jurisprudence, this phrase raises the question of whether human moral inquiry into the good (*ḥusn*) and the bad (*qubḥ*) can be an authoritative basis for asserting a rule of law consonant with the divine will when source-texts are silent. While one refrain in Muslim apologetic literature often holds that there is no issue unaddressed by a source-text in Islamic law, pre-modern Muslim jurists clearly disagreed. This is not to suggest that this debate ignores the existence of source-texts. Rather it arguably recognizes that source-texts are finite, and that sometimes we require an alternative authority for the law, such as reason.

Not surprisingly, jurists disagreed about the authority of reason on grounds spanning the fields of theology and legal theory. Competing theologies about the omnipotence of God affected how pre-modern jurists conceived of the authority of reason. Their different theological starting points contributed to two models of natural law theory, hereinafter called Hard Natural Law and Soft Natural Law. Hard Natural Law theorists relied on the theological presumption that God only does what is good: God wants X *because* X is good. From this starting theological presumption, they developed natural law theories by which they granted ontological authority to reason

[70] For further insight on this issue, see Reinhart, *Before Revelation*.

in Sharīʿa by linking the divine will and human reason through the medium of nature. Soft Natural Law theorists started from the contrary Voluntarist theological position: X is good *because* God wants X. They held that goodness and Sharīʿa norms were two different matters. Reason can certainly determine what is good or bad. But that rational conclusion cannot assume the authority of a Sharīʿa norm. Despite their Voluntarist critique of Hard Natural Law, Soft Natural Law theorists nonetheless recognized that in some cases there is no source-text to guide us in understanding the Sharīʿa. In some cases, we would need to rely on an alternative authority to generate norms to order our affairs.

The distinct theological starting points lead jurists of both camps to different theories about the authority of reason in the law. Despite their theological differences, though, this study will show that the different natural law theories that ultimately resulted actually share much in common. Jurists of different theological camps did not deny the fact that a philosophy of law must make room for reasoned deliberation. To do so, jurists of both camps ultimately relied on nature as a link between the authority of the divine will and the authority of reason, which allows us to frame their legal philosophies using natural law. The remainder of this chapter will summarize how they understood the link between God, nature, and reason, and developed competing theories to limit the potential for idiosyncrasy and abuse of discretion.

Theory I: Hard Natural Law

The first pre-modern theory of natural law, hereinafter called Hard Natural Law, is reflected in the works of al-Jaṣṣāṣ, and the Baṣran Muʿtazilites al-Qāḍī ʿAbd al-Jabbār and Abū al-Ḥusayn al-Baṣrī. It is built upon theological first principles about God and nature. Hard Natural Law jurists espoused as a theological first principle that God only does good and is incapable of doing any evil. Consequently, according to Hard Natural Law adherents, when God created the world, He intended to benefit humanity. God would not have created the world to benefit God's self since God requires no such benefit. Nor would God create it in order to cause pain and suffering for others regardless of their behavior, since that would be unfair and unjust to those adversely affected. As God is only just, they held that creation must therefore pose a benefit to others. From this proposition, they thereby held that we can discern these benefits through the use of our reason and thereby develop norms of behavior whose normative authority is based on the divine creative will, which purposely created the benefits in the first place. Hard naturalists fused the value arising from God's justice and will with the facts of a natural order to invest nature with both objectivity and normative value.

A significant theological implication of Hard Natural Law theory is whether human beings can, through their rational analysis into the good and the bad, create norms of behavior that God not only would, but indeed must, punish and reward. This proposition raised theological concerns because of the implication it had for the theology of God's omnipotence. If God is truly omnipotent, how could He essentially be bound by human reasoning to reward or punish certain conduct that people designate as obligatory and prohibited (*wājib* and *maḥẓūr*)? To make their argument, Hard Naturalists upheld the theology of a just God, and of a nature in which God's will and human reason can be linked. Nature is objectively good for humanity given the assumption of a just Creator that only does the good and needs nothing. Consequently, Hard Naturalists argued that one could rationally deduce the good from nature, and transform that finding into a normative Sharīʿa value since the empirical goodness of nature embodies the purposeful intent of God. For the Hard Naturalists al-Jaṣṣāṣ (d. 370/981), Qāḍī ʿAbd al-Jabbār (d. 415/1025) and Abū al-Ḥusayn al-Baṣrī (d. 436/1044) the fusion of fact and value is a central feature of their natural law theory, and is expressed as the presumption of permissibility (*ibāḥa*). In the absence of evidence to the contrary, all things are good and at a base level legally permissible, with no consequence one way or another.

Hard Natural Law theorists fused fact and value in nature. In doing so they held that human beings can reason about the good and the bad (*ḥusn, qubḥ*) by observing the natural world, and that their initially empirical assessments transform into normative ones. They argued that the normative content of empirical assessments is founded upon the fusion of fact and value, by which nature is invested with a presumptive normativity that stems from God's purposeful creation of nature for human benefit. Rational determinations of the good and the bad, based on natural observations, transform into divine obligation because of the fusion of fact and value. Once an act is deemed good on a rational basis, it can be obligatory to perform that act, with liability for punishment in the Hereafter in the event of omission. Unlike their Soft Natural Law opponents, the Hard Naturalists relied on a view of nature that is constant and determinate. This feature of constancy in their conception of nature is why this study calls their version of natural law 'hard'.

The Voluntarist Critique of Hard Natural Law

Voluntarist jurists were concerned about the theological implications of Hard Natural Law. They argued that the implication of Hard Naturalism is not only that God cannot do evil, but also that God would be obliged to reward or punish someone because of a reasoned determination we make. This implication challenged the assumption of God's omnipotence. Voluntarist jurists adopted the theology of an omnipotent God who is not subjected to reasoned determinations about the good and the bad. Indeed, these concepts have no meaning without God's deliberate decision: X is good *because* God wants X. Anything else would seem to constrain God's infinite power. Voluntarist jurists were concerned that if the Sharīʿa were susceptible to conclusions from reason alone, then effectively human beings could hold God obliged to enforce rules that arise purely out of human determinations without reference to God's will. God's judgment, therefore, would be contingent on the results of human rational inquiry.[71] This possibility challenges the theological premise of an all-powerful God subservient to no one.

Voluntarists argued that one must investigate and analyze source-texts with divine authority to determine obligations and prohibitions that reflect the divine will. Indeed for Voluntarist jurists,

[71] George F Hourani, 'Two Theories of Value in Medieval Islam' (1960) 50 *Muslim World* 269, 276–7.

'"good" and "right" and similar terms have no meaning other than "that which God wills": thus God makes things good or right for us by His decision that they should be so.'[72] Richard Frank remarks that for Voluntarists, 'the ontological reference of "bad" is God's prohibition. These valuations are true of actions only by the giving of the law (*bish-shar'*) and not by the mind's intuitive judgment... so that "he who does not validly know the law does not validly know that a bad action is bad."'[73] In other words, one must wait for divinely inspired source-texts (*sharʿ*) before making any Sharīʿa determination. In the absence of *sharʿ*, Voluntarists generally held that there is no divine obligation on the matter, and that one is left in a state of suspended judgment (*tawaqquf*).

This is not to suggest that they avoided determining the value of acts on which scripture is silent. They admitted that humans can use their reason to understand creation and create a moral ordering of things. Human beings can assess the good and the bad as empirical matters, and can assert cultural or moral truths about the good and the bad. But those truths cannot be considered obligations emanating from the divine. For instance the Shafiʿite-Ashʿarite jurist al-Juwaynī (d. 478/1085) recognized that people constantly make judgments about how best to avoid harm (*ijtināb al-mahālik*) and enjoy various benefits in nature (*ibtidār al-manāfiʿ*).[74] But making moral determinations of the good and the bad is entirely different from identifying a ruling of God (*ḥukm Allāh*). Whether something is obligatory or prohibited depends on whether God has provided a sanction for violating the given norm. Without a sanction, one cannot meaningfully speak of obligations and prohibitions.[75] *Ḥusn* and *qubḥ* are ethical terms of art, but these terms do not contribute content to the Sharīʿa. While Hard Naturalists assured themselves that eternal happiness (*al-saʿādat al-ukhrawiyya*) could be achieved

[72] Hourani, 'Two Theories of Value,' 270. See also Sherman A Jackson, 'The Alchemy of Domination? Some Ashʿarite Responses to Muʿtazilite Ethics,' (1999) 31 *International Journal of Middle East Studies* 185.

[73] Richard M Frank, 'Moral Obligation in Classical Muslim Theology' (1983) 11 *Journal of Religious Ethics* 204 (citation omitted).

[74] Abū al-Maʿālī al-Juwaynī, *al-Burhān fī Uṣūl al-Fiqh*, Ṣalāḥ b. Muḥammad b. ʿAwīḍa (ed) (Beirut: Dār al-Kutub al-ʿIlmiyya, 1997) 1:10.

[75] Al-Juwaynī, *al-Burhān*, 1:10.

through a rational engagement with reality in the pursuit of a good (*maṣlaḥa*), Voluntarists doubted whether that nexus offers any insight into the divine will. As Hourani writes: '[i]t is possible to some extent to discover by empirical reason what produces happiness in an earthly society, and to see the causal relation between the means and the end. But where the goal is happiness in an afterlife...there is no intelligible relation between the cause (certain kinds of action) and the effect (the reward of bliss in the next life),' since the implication of our acts in this world on our salvation in the Hereafter is something only God can know.[76] Reason has no authority to resolve or decide upon such matters.

The Voluntarists issued their critique of Hard Naturalism on two grounds. First, they argued that nature is not sufficiently determinative, objective, or foundational to ground the authority of reason: fact is not fused with value. Their opposition to any fusion of fact and value is based on Q. 17:15, which states: 'We do not punish until We send a messenger.' This verse enshrines the idea that divine sanction requires an express statement of will, not a reasoned inquiry into the good and the bad. To reason from nature, they argued, assumes too much of both God and the human capacity to know the divine will. For instance, the 11th century jurist Ibn Ḥazm, never one to mince words, argued that the Hard Naturalists' fusion of fact and value in nature was 'plain pomposity' (*makābirat al-iyān*).[77] By their very nature, human beings are prone to sexual licentiousness, drunken debauchery, and lapses in religious observance. These are all potentially natural dispositions, he noted, all of which God prohibits expressly. Consequently, one cannot argue from the facts of nature to moral norms and obligations with the imprint of the divine.

Secondly, while they accepted the fact that human beings make rational moral judgments all the time, those determinations cannot assume the normative authority of a divine rule whereby God is bound by human reason to reward or punish. For nature to be a bounty and source of goodness, one had to assume that God only

[76] Hourani, 'Two Theories of Value,' 273.

[77] Abū Muḥammad Ibn Ḥazm, *al-Iḥkām fī Uṣūl al-Aḥkām* (Cairo: Dār al-Ḥadīth, 1984) 1:54.

does the good, seeking to benefit humanity.[78] Voluntarist jurists rejected this theology of God, especially since it potentially undermines God's omnipotence. If God can only do the good for humanity's benefit, and human reason can decide what is good, then effectively humans can require God to reward and punish certain behavior. This possibility undermined, for the Voluntarists, the idea that God was beyond any limits. Jurists such as Abū Isḥāq al-Shīrāzī (d. 476/1083) argued vociferously that God is not limited in any way. Rather God does as He wishes and rules as He desires (*yaf'alu Allāh ma yashā' wa yaḥkumu ma yurīdu*).[79]

For Voluntarist jurists, where no source-text addresses an issue, no one can assert a divine rule of law. Voluntarist jurists did not deny that a rule of God exists; they argued instead that humans are not in an epistemic position to determine what the law is.[80] Consequently in situations where there is no source-text, Voluntarist jurists held that the divine law is in a state of deferred judgment (*tawaqquf*, *waqf*), such that one cannot authoritatively assert a rule of obligation or prohibition.[81]

Hard Naturalists countered, however, that the position of deferred judgment (*tawaqquf*) is substantively no different than their presumption of permissibility. Both positions imply that one suffers no consequence for acting.[82] But Voluntarists countered that Hard Natural Law depends on an affirmative rational assumption of

[78] For Hard Naturalist sources relying on this assumption, see Abū Bakr al-Jaṣṣāṣ, *Uṣūl al-Jaṣṣāṣ: al-Fuṣūl fī al-Uṣūl*, Muḥammad Muḥammad Tāmir (ed), 2 vols (Beirut: Dār al-Kutub al-ʿIlmiyya, 2000) 2:100; Abū al-Ḥusayn Muḥammad b. ʿAlī b. al-Ṭayyib al-Baṣrī, *al-Muʿtamad fī Uṣūl al-Fiqh* (Beirut: Dār al-Kutub al-ʿIlmiyya, n.d.) 2:320.

[79] Abū Isḥāq al-Shīrāzī, *Sharḥ al-Lumʿa*, ʿAbd al-Majīd Turkī (ed) (Beirut: Dār al-Gharb al-Islāmī, 1988) 2:983–4.

[80] On human epistemic weakness, see Abū ʿAbd Allāh Muḥammad b. Maḥmūd b. ʿAbbād al-Aṣfahānī, *al-Kāshif ʿan al-Maḥṣūl fī ʿIlm al-Uṣūl*, ʿĀdil Aḥmad ʿAbd al-Mawjūd and ʿAlī Muḥammad Muʿawwaḍ (eds) (Beirut: Dār al-Kutub al-ʿIlmiyya, 1998) 1:370-1.

[81] Al-Khaṭīb al-Baghdādi, *Kitāb al-Faqīh wa al-Mutafaqqih* (n.p.: Maṭbaʿat al-Imtiyāz, 1977) 192–4; Ibn Ḥazm, *Iḥkām*, 1:52; Abū al-Muẓaffar al-Samʿānī, *Qawāṭiʿ al-Adilla fī al-Uṣūl*, Muḥammad Ḥasan Muḥammad Ḥasan Ismāʿīl al-Shāfiʿī (ed) (Beirut: Dār al-Kutub al-ʿIlmiyya, 1997) 2:46–7, 52; Abū Isḥāq al-Shīrāzī, *Sharḥ al-Lumʿa*, 2:977; Tāj al-Dīn ʿAbd al-Raḥmān b. Ibrāhīm Ibn al-Farikān, *Sharḥ al-Waraqāt*, Sārah Shāfī al-Hājirī (ed) (Beirut: Dār al-Bashā'ir al-Islāmiyya, 2001) 347–50, stated that this position was adopted by the majority of Ashʿarites.

[82] Abū Bakr al-Jaṣṣāṣ, *Uṣūl al-Jaṣṣāṣ*, 2:103.

the fusion of fact and value in nature, and thereby the goodness that underlies the legal category of the permissible (*ḥalāl, mubāḥ*). The Voluntarist position of *tawaqquf* or suspended judgment makes no such rationalist assumption. It only asserts the absence of an authoritative source-text that could justify finding an obligation.[83]

Voluntarists acknowledged that when source-texts are silent, some mode of analysis is required to ensure that we can still order our lives. It is one thing to suspend judgment, but another to suggest that no liability follows by acting one way or another. To respond to this second concern, Voluntarists relied on the rational presumption of *istiṣḥāb al-ḥāl*, or the presumption of continuity, whereby they argued that where no scripture governs a case, no liability is imposed for acting as one wishes. This is a rational presumption that does not amount to an affirmative rational assertion of legal value. For Voluntarists, the presumption of continuity involves the use of reason only to the extent that it is utilized epistemically to determine whether any scripture exists that governs the given situation. Reason has no ontological authority in Sharīʿa. A rational conclusion about the good and the bad is not infused with normative power. Where there is no authoritative source-text there is no law. Fundamentally the presumption of continuity does not violate the principle that obligation must come from an express legislative will.

Theory II: Soft Natural Law

As much as they rejected Hard Natural Law, Voluntarists were not so jurisprudentially naïve as to assume that sufficient source-texts exist to address every potential legal issue. Certainly issues would arise for which no source-text provides guidance. Simply to rely on the presumption of continuity or the suspension of judgment offers little comfort to those of us keen to order our affairs normatively. To suspend Sharīʿa judgment in these cases is tantamount to

[83] Abū al-Walīd al-Bājī, *Iḥkām al-Fuṣūl fī Aḥkām al-Uṣūl*, ʿAbd al-Majīd Turkī (ed) (2nd edn, Beirut: Dār al-Gharb al-Islāmī, 1995) 2:689; Ibn Ḥazm, *Iḥkām*, 1:56; Abū Ḥāmid Muḥmmad b. Muḥammad al-Ghazālī, *al-Mustaṣfā min ʿIlm al-Uṣūl*, Ibrāhīm Muḥammad Ramaḍān (ed) (Beirut: Dār al-Arqam, n.d.) 1:133; al-Samʿāni, *Qawāṭiʿ al-Adilla*, 2:52, al-Shīrāzī, *Sharḥ al-Lumʿa*, 2:979–80.

limiting the capacity of Sharīʿa to order normatively the complexity of lived experience. The Voluntarists' response to this situation illustrates how they balanced their theological commitment to God's omnipotence with the need to endow reason with sufficient authority to extend the Sharīʿa.

Voluntarists developed what is herein called Soft Natural Law. Soft Natural Law theories rely on a conception of nature that, just as for the Hard Naturalists, fuses fact and value: nature is deemed beneficial for human beings. But the benefit that nature provides is not a consequence of God's eternal goodness and His inability to do evil. Rather, nature is a constant good only because of God's grace (*faḍl, tafaḍḍul*).[84] An empirical investigation into nature reveals that the created world poses various benefits to human existence. This evidence of goodness indicates, for Voluntarist Soft Naturalists, that God created the world for the purpose of supporting, maintaining, and preserving the interests of people. But God does so purely out of His grace, which is subject to change if God so desires. The argument of grace both allows for the fusion of fact and value in nature—thus rendering natural reason authoritative—and preserves a theological commitment to God's omnipotence, since God can alter His grace as He sees fit. For Soft Naturalist jurists, God need not have provided any guidance through His creation of nature. But since He did, out of His grace, humans can rely upon it. But they do so not because of some theological assumption about the limits of God's power. Instead, we can reason about the good and the bad as a basis for the law only because of God's purposive, merciful, and gracious creation of our ability to discern such things from His creation—which God can alter at any time. While both Hard and Soft Naturalists fused fact and value in nature, the Soft Naturalists

[84] The technical terms of *faḍl* and *tafaḍḍul* are the key term of art for the Voluntarist naturalist theory, which also distinguished it from Hard Naturalism. For other Voluntarist examples, see Fakhr al-Dīn al-Rāzī, *al-Maḥṣūl fī ʿIlm Uṣūl al-Fiqh*, Ṭaha Jābir Fayyāḍ al-ʿAlwāni (ed), (3rd edn, Beirut: Mu'assasat al-Risāla, 1997) 5:176; Shihāb al-Dīn al-Qarāfī, *Nafā'is al-Uṣūl fī Sharḥ al-Maḥṣūl*, Muḥammad ʿAbd al-Qādir ʿAṭā (ed) (Beirut: Dār al-Kutub al-ʿIlmiyya, 2000) 4:642; Najm al-Dīn al-Ṭūfī, '*al-Ḥadīth al-Thānī wa'l-Thalāthūn,*' in Muṣṭafā Zayd, *al-Maṣlaḥa fī al-Tashrīʿ al-Islāmī wa Najm al-Dīn al-Ṭūfī* (2nd edn, n.p.: Dār al-Fikr al-'Arabī," 1964), 213; Abū Isḥāq al-Shatibi, *al-Muwāfaqāt fī Uṣul al-Sharīʿa*, ʿAbd Allāh Darāz et al (eds), 2 vols (Beirut: Dār al-Kutub al-ʿIlmiyya, n.d.) 2:131.

argued that its constancy is subject to a divine purposiveness that can be changed at God's discretion. Nature, as it exists, is certainly a source of the good. But it is not an unchangeable, indubitable good. This theologically-based contingency of nature's constant goodness is the reason why this study considers this second natural law model to be soft. Despite the contingency in nature, the theory of God's grace suggests that Soft Naturalists fused fact and value in nature to render reason an ontologically authoritative source of Sharīʿa norms, where source-texts are otherwise silent.

Soft Natural Law and Practical Reasoning

Of crucial significance—not to mention some degree of irony—is the fact that both Hard and Soft Natural Law jurists fused fact and value in nature to render reason an authoritative source of Sharīʿa norms. In the end, both considered nature objective and distinct from the individual observing what it can and does 'say'. Despite their differing theologies of God, the two groups of natural law jurists have much in common, from the perspective of legal philosophy.

This irony though is not as poignant as it may first seem. Certainly the ontological authority of reason is a shared feature of both Hard and Soft Natural Law. But Soft Naturalist jurists did not discard their concerns about the implications of reason's authority in the law. Consequently, we see them limiting the scope of reasoned deliberation in the law by developing highly structured methodologies of legal analysis and inquiry. Soft Natural Law jurists designed various theories of practical reasoning, many of which revolve around the term *maṣlaḥa* or a perceived good, and frame practical reasoning as an enterprise that aspires to fulfill basic purposes of the law, or what are called *maqāṣid al-sharīʿa*. As will be discussed below, Soft Naturalist jurists generally held that the purpose of the Sharīʿa is to preserve five fundamental values: life, lineage, property, mind, and religion. Any rule that is not fundamentally premised or justified by reference to an authoritative source, such as the Qurʾān or a *ḥadīth* of the Prophet, must satisfy one or more of these fundamental values.

As these values are highly abstract, jurists recognized the importance of arguing to a particular legal ruling via a legal principle of the good or *maṣlaḥa*, in light of these abstract, fundamental values. What is *maṣlaḥa*? In the context of Soft Naturalist practical reasoning, *maṣlaḥa* is a legal term of art that has to do with a perceived general good that speaks to the perfection of a polity, both at the individual and general levels.[85] For instance, an oft-cited early example of a rule pursuant to *maṣlaḥa* is provided by a story about the second caliph ʿUmar b. al-Khaṭṭāb (r. 634–644 CE), who suspended the corporal punishment for theft in a time of famine. The Qurʾān stipulates that the convicted thief must suffer the amputation of his hand.[86] Despite the source-text's prohibition against theft, famine presented a substantive public interest that affected how ʿUmar would apply and enforce the law.[87] Perhaps his ruling was exceptional. Or perhaps the conditions that render theft punishable are deemed not to exist in a case of famine. In either case, though, jurists contended with arguments based on both source-texts and reasoned deliberation about the wellbeing of the polity. In the pre-modern literature, Muslim jurists debated the relevance, authority, and significance of *maṣlaḥa* for legal reasoning.

Not all *maṣlaḥa*-based arguments are authoritative. Indeed, those that contravene an authoritative source-text must fail for a lack of authority. And yet, even this limiting factor does not always preclude a ruling on the basis of *maṣlaḥa*. In the absence of a source-text, a *maṣlaḥa*-based argument could justify a rule of law.[88]

[85] For general studies on *maṣlaḥa*, see Yūsuf Ḥāmid al-ʿĀlim, *al-Maqāṣid al-ʿĀmma li al-Sharīʿa al-Islāmiyya* (Herndon, Va: International Institute of Islamic Thought, 1991); Ḥusayn Ḥāmid Ḥassān, *Naẓariyyat al-Maṣlaḥa fī al-Fiqh al-Islāmī* (Cairo: Dār al-Nahḍa al-ʿArabiyya, 1971); Muṣṭafā Zayd, *al-Maṣlaḥa fī al-Tashrīʿ al-Islāmī wa Najm al-Dīn al-Ṭūfī* (2nd edn, Cairo: Dār al-Fikr al-ʿArabī, 1964); Muhammad Khaled Masud, *Islamic Legal Philosophy: A Study of Abū Isḥāq al-Shāṭibī's Life and Thought* (Delhi: International Islamic Publishers, 1989) 2, 150; for studies on the concept of *maṣlaḥa*, see Kamali, *Principles of Islamic Jurisprudence*, 351–68; Ihsan Baghby, 'Utility in Classical Islamic Law: The Concept of "Maslahah" in 'Usul al-Fiqh" (PhD dissertation, University of Michigan, 1986) 3; M Khadduri, 'Maṣlaḥa' in *Encyclopaedia of Islam, Second Edition.*

[86] Qurʾān 5:38.

[87] Ibn Qayyim al-Jawziyya, *Iʿlām al-Muwaqqiʿīn ʿan Rabb al-ʿĀlamīn*, ʿAbd al-Raḥmān al-Wakīl (ed) (Cairo: Maktabat Ibn Taymiyya, n.d.), 3:14–15.

[88] Muḥammad Abū Zahra, *Uṣūl al-Fiqh* (Cairo: Dār al-Fikr al-ʿArabī, 1957) 293; Zayd, *al-Maṣlaḥa fī al-Tashrīʿ al-Islāmī*, 33.

How jurists defined *maṣlaḥa* is not an easy issue to survey. Indeed, this study is not designed to offer an answer to that question. Rather, it illustrates how Soft Naturalists used concepts such as *maqāṣid al-sharīʿa* and *maṣlaḥa* to develop a theory of practical reasoning by which they could recognize *and* limit the authority of reason in the law.

This section began by noting the irony that despite their difference, the Hard and Soft Naturalists both fused fact and value in nature to provide a philosophical foundation for the ontological authority of reason in Sharīʿa. However, the Soft Naturalists' model of practical reasoning illustrates how they developed an epistemology of inquiry that is designed, in large part, to limit the scope of reasoned deliberation. This douses the poignancy of the irony. With one gesture, Soft Naturalists granted reason ontological authority, but with another they limited its scope of operation in the law.

The pre-modern move to limit the scope of reason raises the specter of a second irony that brings us to modern day reform movements in the Muslim world. For many 20th and 21st century Muslim reformers, the related concepts of *maqāṣid al-sharīʿa* and *maṣlaḥa* offer a mechanism of practical reasoning that is rooted in the pre-modern Islamic tradition *and* provides an interpretative model for responding to the challenges of modernity. For them, *maqāṣid* and *maṣlaḥa* are conceptual opportunities for enhancing the scope of reason amidst an inherited tradition of legal doctrine that is often considered an obstacle to ongoing development.[89] Spanning the globe from Indonesia to the Arab world, Muslim reformists have adopted these concepts to call for reform in the Sharīʿa tradition.[90] Indeed, even in the realm of Muslim civil

[89] Muṣṭafā Zayd argues that *maṣlaḥa*-based reasoning offers an important framework for practical reasoning that was used by pre-modern jurists and can continue to be used today, especially as many circumstances of the modern world have no prior precedent in authoritative source texts or otherwise. Zayd, *al-Maṣlaḥa fī al-Tashrīʿ al-Islāmī*, 28–32.

[90] Mujiburrahman, 'Islam and Politics in Indonesia: the political thought of Abdurrahman Wahid' (1999) 10 *Islam and Christian-Muslim Relations* 339, 348; Michael Mumīsa, *Islamic Law: Theory and Interpretation* (Beltsville, Md: Amana Publications, 2002) 163–4; Fathi Osman, 'Islam and Human Rights: The Challenge to Muslims and the World' in El-Affendi, *Rethinking Islam and Modernity*, 27, 38–42. Indeed Muslim institutes have commissioned translations of Arabic sources that address these concepts. The effort has resulted in an increase in English language sources, which

society, we find these concepts animating how Muslims organize and contribute to the world stage. For instance, the Cordoba Initiative, with offices in New York City and Kuala Lumpur, is spearheading the development of a 'Sharia Index Project'. The proposed Sharīʿa Index offers a standard for evaluating the Islamicity of a Muslim state. The values that animate the Index are drawn directly from the concept *maqāṣid al-Sharīʿa*.[91] Gender justice groups such as *Sisters in Islam* and *Women Living Under Muslim Laws* utilize the language of *maqāṣid* on their websites to legitimate their calls for legal reform to promote gender equality in Muslim lands.[92]

If we read the Soft Naturalists' model of practical reasoning as a response to Hard Naturalism, we cannot help but recognize their use of *maqāṣid al-sharīʿa* and *maṣlaḥa* as devices expressly designed to limit the operation of reason in the law. *Maqāṣid al-sharīʿa* and *maṣlaḥa* were developed by pre-modern Soft Naturalists as a check on the scope of reason, despite their naturalist theory that recognized its authority in the law in the first place. Modern reformists see these concepts as enhancing the authority of reasoned deliberation amidst an inherited tradition of *fiqh* that dominates the discourse on Islamic law. This second irony lies in the distance between the animating principles of the Soft Naturalists, and those of modern reformers. The Soft Naturalists were concerned with

are aimed to inspire innovative thinking about Islam and its legal history. See eg the two works published by the International Institute of Islamic Thought (IIIT): Muhammad al-Tahir Ibn Ashur, *Treatise on Maqāṣid al-Sharīʿa*, Mohamed el-Tahir el-Masawi (trans) (London: International Institute for Islamic Thought, 2006); Ahmad al-Raysuni, *Imam al-Shatibi's Theory of the Higher Objectives and Intents of Islamic Law*, Nancy Roberts (trans) (London: International Institute of Islamic Thought, 2005). More recently, IIIT published the following English monograph: Jasser Auda, *Maqasid al-Shariah as Philosophy of Islamic Law* (London: International Institute of Islamic Thought, 2008).

[91] For the website, visit <http://www.cordobainitiative.org/?q=content/shariah-index-project>.

[92] eg, Women Living Under Muslim Laws offers the following *maqāṣid*-based definition of Islamic feminism: 'Islamic feminism aims to recover and implement the fundamental objectives (maqasid) of Islam: social justice and the equality of all Muslims, including gender equality' <http://www.wluml.org/english/newsfulltxt.shtml?cmd[157]=x-157-547094>.

For the Sisters in Islam website and publications, visit <http://www.sistersinislam.org.my>.

theological first principles and the imperatives of jurisprudence. Soft Naturalists were wary of any jurisprudence that might impinge on God's omnipotence. And yet they could not ignore the jurisprudential imperative of having to adjudicate where source-texts are lacking. Their legal philosophy recognized the ontological authority of reason; but in doing so, Soft Naturalists limited the extent to which reason is an indubitable authority. God's grace is an important feature in both rendering reason authoritative, and ensuring its authority is contingent on the divine will. Likewise the model of practical reasoning ensures the primacy of God's express will, and so limits the scope over which reasoned deliberation can operate. For modern reformers, the concerns arising over reasoned deliberation have less to do with theological first principles. For them, the significance of debates about reason have to do with the challenge of modernity, the modern state system, and the image of Sharīʿa as a system of rules that many believe impede development at the individual, regional, national, and transnational levels.

After Islamic Natural Law

This study focuses on the pre-modern in order to situate the particular debates on natural law in the intellectual milieus in which they were developed. But, the two ironies of Islamic natural law take us from the pre-modern to the modern period. There is little doubt that Sharīʿa remains a vibrant discourse for Muslims the world over. Whether in popular discourses, political contests,[93] or scholarly debate, Sharīʿa invokes considerable response in the world today. However, what it may have meant centuries ago is one thing; what it means today is different. Thinking philosophically about Sharīʿa without recourse to history will more often than not gloss over the particularities that animated the pre-modern theoretical discourse to begin with.

By identifying the ironies, we are in a better position to understand the significance of the pre-modern debates, and the various

[93] The political significance of Sharīʿa is evident in the way it has become a point of multicultural debate in polities ranging from Canada to the Philippines. See Emon, 'Canadian Mosaic'; Emon, 'Techniques and Limits of Rights Reasoning'.

camps that were formed from and by the debates. Those camps, whether defined by theological school or legal guild, offer important indices of how a particular jurist might think about an issue. The ironies also alert us to the importance of metaphysics to pre-modern jurists, and the relationship of metaphysics to their respective theologies of God and their theories of natural law. While we can demarcate fields of thought along disciplinary lines, that does not mean such fields of thought cannot penetrate one another. Indeed, theology and Sharīʿa are brought together through the lens of natural law; they are in large part brought together because of the metaphysics that animates their jurisprudence—a metaphysics that can be traced to how we understand God and nature.

The ironies, though, show that the fusion of fact and value can have the effect of preserving the status quo. If what exists is also what ought to be, then it is not clear how Islamic natural law provides a mechanism of fostering change. It can certainly aid in the development of new laws where source-texts are silent. But the more source-texts contribute to authoritative precedents, the less room for employing the *maqāṣid-maṣlaḥa* model of analysis. Indeed to use the *maqāṣid-maṣlaḥa* model expansively in order to foster change may actually require a rejection of various parts of the inherited tradition of Sharīʿa. To seek change through *maqāṣid* in the modern day, it would seem, begs a preliminary question of what constitutes the relevant sources of Sharīʿa that control and limit the scope of reasoned deliberation in the law.

The ironies suggest that this study of Islamic natural law theories is simply a starting point for those keen to understand the dynamics of legal philosophy within a Sharīʿa framework. Certainly many might find the metaphysics of Islamic natural law unconvincing. They might find the fusion of fact and value far too stagnating. They may find the *maqāṣid-maṣlaḥa* model of practical reasoning far too formalistic to account for the complexity of modern life. Yet such critiques are not unique to Islamic law. Legal systems across the world suffer from similar limitations. Perhaps that simply suggests such limits are characteristic of legal systems generally. Aristotle, when writing about justice, was mindful of both the formality of the law, and the need to provide more case-specific analysis in situations where legal formality may cause substantive injustice.

Sometimes a judge must look to the equities of a case to render a justice that is not fully captured by the formal legal system. This is not to suggest that the resort to equity indicates a failure of the justice system. Both the formality of the law and the equitable inquiry contribute to the fulfillment of justice. The essential nature of the equitable is that 'it is a rectification of the law where the law is defective because of its generality.'[94] Likewise, Balakrishnan Rajagopal, writing about international law, remarks that law 'needs to establish its own field of autonomy only by simplifying and excluding much of actual reality... indeed, each time law comes into contact with "reality", it struggles to reflect it, even as it maintains its distance from it to show that as "law", it is different from the "reality" and can therefore constrain it.'[95] Islamic natural law and the *maqāṣid-maṣlaḥa* model of practical reasoning may be designed to respond to the natural world, the world of human experience. But their metaphysics and formality may have the effect of covering over more of the world than reflecting it.

[94] Aristotle, *Nichomachean Ethics*, Harris Rackham (trans) (Hertfordshire: Wordsworth, 1996) 134.

[95] Balakrishnan Rajagopal, *International Law from Below: Development, Social Movements, and Third World Resistance* (Cambridge: Cambridge University Press, 2003) 65.

II

Hard Natural Law

This chapter addresses what this study calls Hard Natural Law. The three authors addressed below adopt parallel approaches to Hard Natural Law jurisprudence in their theoretical discussions on rational deliberation about the good and the bad (*ḥusn, qubḥ*). At a general level, their concern is whether empirical evaluations of the good and the bad can lead to Sharīʿa norms, whose authority participates in or draws upon the authority of the Divine Will. Their theoretical approaches show how nature provides the foundation for the authority of reason as a source of Sharīʿa. Hard Naturalist jurists such as al-Jaṣṣāṣ, Qāḍī ʿAbd al-Jabbār, and Abū al-Ḥusayn al-Baṣrī fused fact and value in nature, and situated their use of reason within a natural teleology directed to the telos of human fulfillment in both this world and the Hereafter. This study calls their version 'hard' because their conception of nature as a bounty to humanity is fixed and not vulnerable to a divine 'change of mind'. This is distinct from the 'Soft Naturalists', as will be shown in Chapter IV, who also fused fact and value in nature, but rendered the goodness of nature vulnerable to a change in the 'divine mind'.

Generally under Hard Natural Law, fact and value are fused in nature, thereby rendering nature a normative foundation for reasoned deliberation about the good and the bad and, by implication, for Sharīʿa obligations and prohibitions. Hard Natural Law jurists presumed that nature is deliberately created by a just God who creates the world to benefit humanity.[1] They justified their presumption by

[1] See eg the writers, Abū Bakr al-Jaṣṣāṣ, *Uṣūl al-Jaṣṣāṣ: al-Fuṣūl fī al-Uṣūl*, Muḥammad Muḥammad Tāmir (ed), 2 vols (Beirut: Dār al-Kutub al-ʿIlmiyya, 2000) 2:100; al-Qāḍī ʿAbd al-Jabbār, *Kitāb al-Majmūʿ fī al-Muḥīṭ bi al-Taklīf*, Yan Peters (ed), 3 vols (Beirut: Dār al-Mashriq, 1999) 2:175; Abū al-Ḥusayn Muḥammad b. ʿAlī b. al-Ṭayyib al-Baṣrī;, *al-Muʿtamad fī Uṣūl al-Fiqh* (Beirut: Dār al-Kutub al-ʿIlmiyya, n.d.) 2:320.

referring to the Qur'ānic verse that states: '[God] created for you [mankind] all that is in the earth.'[2] Hard Naturalist jurists denied that God would create the world with no purpose whatsoever, concluding that this would be tantamount to an act of futility (*ʿabath*), which is incongruous with their theology of a just God. They also denied that creation is designed to cause harm without posing any benefit at all, because such a result would render God unjust and obscene (*aqbaḥ*). Consequently, creation must be for the purpose of bestowing an affirmative benefit. But upon whom? It could not be for God since, theologically speaking, God is beyond such needs. The conclusion they reached is that creation must be for the benefit of people (*li manāfiʿ al-mukallafīn*). This theology of God fuses fact and value in nature, and thereby renders nature a foundation for reasoned deliberation about the good, the bad, the obligatory and the prohibited, with an authority that stems from God's will.[3]

[2] Qur'ān, 2:29. In recounting the Hard Naturalist position, jurists of both naturalist persuasions would cite this and other Qur'ānic verses. See Abū Bakr Muḥammad b. Aḥmad al-Samarqandī, *Mīzān al-Uṣūl*, ʿAbd al-Mālik ʿAbd al-Raḥmān al-Saʿdī (ed) (n.p.: Maṭbaʿa al-Khulūd, 1987) 1:316–17, who cites the above quoted verse. Other jurists refer to different Qur'ānic verses to represent the same argument; Abū Isḥāq al-Shīrāzī, *Sharḥ al-Lumʿa*, ʿAbd al-Majīd Turkī (ed) (Beirut: Dār al-Gharb al-Islāmī, 1988) 2:981–2, who refers to Qur'ān, 7:32, which states 'Say to those who prohibit the adornments of God, which He provided for His servants, and the good things of sustenance.'

[3] Al-Jaṣṣāṣ, *Uṣūl al-Jaṣṣāṣ*, 2:100. For a similar argument by another Hard Naturalist jurist, see Abū al-Ḥusayn al-Baṣrī, *al-Muʿtamad fī Uṣūl al-Fiqh*, 2:320. The Hard Naturalists' opponents also characterized the naturalistic argument in similar fashion, using terms such as *intifāʿ*, *manfaʿa, nafʿ*, *gharaḍ* and *fā'ida* to capture the notion of creation purposely being for the benefit of humanity. See eg, Abū al-Ḥasan ʿAlī b. ʿUmar b. al-Qaṣṣār (d. 397/1007), *al-Muqaddima fī al-Uṣūl*, Muḥammad b. al-Ḥusayn al-Sulaymānī (ed) (Beirut: Dār al-Gharb al-Islāmī, 1996) 154; al-Khaṭīb al-Baghdādī (d. 463/1072), *Kitāb al-Faqīh wa al-Mutafaqqih* (n.p.: Maṭbaʿat al-Imtiyāz, 1977) 192–4; Abū al-Walīd al-Bājī (d. 474/1081), *Iḥkām al-Fuṣūl fī Aḥkām al-Uṣūl*, ʿAbd al-Majīd Turkī (ed) (Beirut: Dār al-Gharb al-Islāmī, 1995) 2:689–90; Abū Isḥāq al-Shīrāzī (d. 476/1083), *Sharḥ al-Lumʿa*, 2:982; al-Samʿānī (d. 489/1096), *Qawāṭiʿ al-Adilla*, 2:48–9; al-Samarqandī (d. 540/1145), *Mīzān al-Uṣūl*, 1:317; Fakhr al-Dīn al-Rāzī (d. 606/1209), *al-Maḥṣūl fī ʿIlm Uṣūl al-Fiqh*, Ṭaha Jābir al-ʿAlwāni (ed) (3rd edn, Beirut: Mu'assasat al-Risāla, 1997) 1:127–8, 149; Abū ʿAbd Allāh Muḥammad b. Maḥmūd b. ʿAbbād al-Aṣfahānī (d. 653/1255), *al-Kāshif ʿan al-Maḥṣūl fī ʿIlm al-Uṣūl*, ʿĀdil Aḥmad ʿAbd al-Mawjūd and ʿAlī Muḥammad Muʿawwaḍ (eds) (Beirut: Dār al-Kutub al-ʿIlmiyya, 1998) 1:359, 381; Shihāb al-Dīn al-Qarāfī (d. 684/1285), *Nafā'is al-Uṣūl fī Sharḥ al-Maḥṣūl*, Muḥammad ʿAbd al-Qādir ʿAṭā (ed) (Beirut: Dār al-Kutub al-ʿIlmiyya, 2000) 1:138–9, 163; Tāj al-Dīn ʿAbd al-Raḥmān b. Ibrāhīm Ibn al-Farikān (d. 690/1291), *Sharḥ al-Waraqāt*, Sārah Shāfī al-Hājirī (ed) (Beirut: Dār al-Bashā'ir al-Islāmiyya, 2001) 350–2.

Hard Natural Law jurisprudence involves two profound steps, both of which are premised on the above theological argument about God and its implications for Sharīʿa analysis. The Hard Naturalists first argued that embedded in each aspect of the created world are characteristics (*wajh*) that reflect its underlying nature. These characteristics are objective, empirical qualities that we can objectively assess and characterize as being good or bad. Secondly, they held that we can derive Sharīʿa legal values from this objective evaluation of an act because God created nature with the express purpose (*gharaḍ*) of benefiting mankind. All acts are part of God's creation and, therefore, all acts embody a positive normativity imposed by the creative and purposeful divine. This view of reality combines both fact and value. Nature is not simply a body of facts that can coldly and objectively be observed and analyzed. Rather, implicit in nature is a divinely inspired presumptive positive value that animates a naturalistic jurisprudence.

For Hard Naturalists, all acts are presumptively permissible (*mubāḥ*) unless proven otherwise. Permissibility in this sense is a positive good, and as such embodies an affirmative normative content. The presumption of permissibility (*ibāḥa*) is the theoretical device by which the Hard Naturalists fused fact and value to create a starting point for a natural law inquiry. God's purposefulness in creating nature as a benefit for people is the basis for a naturalist presumption from which inquiries into Sharīʿa obligations start. As such, one can move from an observation of nature to an ultimate determination of a Sharīʿa obligation and prohibition in a manner that is both objective and normative. This rational, naturalistic presumption offers a way to overcome the logical gap between the empiricism of nature and the normativity of obligation or, in other words, between the 'is' and the 'ought'.

On this naturalistic basis, Hard Naturalist jurists would often go even further and argue that in some cases they could assert a positive obligation (*wājib*), as opposed to a mere permission to commit an act without liability. To illustrate their argument, Hard Naturalists relied on a standard hypothetical of thanking the benefactor (*shukr al-munʿim*).[4] They asked whether thanking one's benefactor (in particular, God) is obligatory as a matter of reason. Rhetorically this hypothetical is powerful because it suggests that anyone who denies that thanking the benefactor is obligatory prior to the existence of revelation is ungrateful for the bounties God bestows upon him (*kufrān al-niʿma*). The argument for the obligation of thanking the benefactor varies, from asserting it as a universal principle[5] to arguing that it poses no harm, to the fact that at the very least it allows one to obviate the possibility of punishment for failure to thank.[6]

Al-Qarāfī, although adopting what we call Soft Natural Law, provided a summary of how Hard Naturalists grounded obligations in an investigation into nature. He wrote about how they organized acts around the five categories of obligation, or the *al-aḥkām al-khamsa*. Where an act concerns a pure or dominant benefit (*maṣlaḥa khāliṣa aw rājiḥa*), we can reasonably discern that God desires us to

[4] For Hard Naturalist discussions of this hypothetical, see al-Qāḍī ʿAbd al-Jabbār al-Asadābādī, *al-Mughnī*, Ṭaha Ḥusayn (ed), 16 vols (Cairo: Wizārat al-Thaqāfa wa-al-Irshād al-Qawmī, al-Idārah al-ʿĀmma lil-Thaqāfa, n.d.), *al-Sharʿiyyāt*: 141, who argued that even if God were to prohibit one from thanking Him, it would not be prohibited because of the pre-existing knowledge of it being obligatory based on its inherent characteristics that are rationally ascertainable. See also Qāḍī ʿAbd al-Jabbār, *Sharḥ al-Uṣūl al-Khamsa* (Beirut: Dār Iḥyāʾ al-Turāth al-ʿArabī, 2001) 45. Abū Bakr al-Jaṣṣāṣ, *Uṣūl al-Jaṣṣāṣ: al-Fuṣūl fī al-Uṣūl*, Muḥammad Muḥammad Tāmir (ed), 2 vols (Beirut: Dār al-Kutub al-ʿIlmiyya, 2000) 2:100, argued that thanking the benefactor is among those obligations that are universally known by reason, and never alter despite changes in circumstances. This hypothetical is also discussed by Soft Naturalists in their critique of Hard Naturalism. See Abū Ḥāmid Muḥammad b. Muḥammad al-Ghazālī, *al-Mustasfā min ʿIlm al-Uṣūl*, Ibrāhīm Muḥammad Ramaḍān (ed) (Beirut: Dār al-Arqam, n.d.) 1:146, who argues that reason cannot be the basis for the obligation of thanking the benefactor. Al-Samarqandī, *Mīzān al-Uṣūl*, 1:292, said that obligations like thanking the benefactor fall into the category of things that are good in themselves and can be known by reason without reference to scripture. See also Abū ʿAlī al-Shāshī, *Uṣūl al-Shāshī* (Beirut: Dār al-Kitāb al-ʿArabī, 1982) 142, who held that thanking the benefactor is one of those things that are universally good in themselves (*ḥusn bi nafsihi*) and must be satisfied without exception (*lā yasquṭu illā bi al-idāʿ*). Interestingly, Ibn Ḥazm argued that some of those who adopted the presumption that all things are prohibited (*maḥzūr*) except otherwise provided, excepted thanking the benefactor from this presumption. Abū Muḥammad Ibn Ḥazm, *al-Iḥkām fī Uṣūl al-Aḥkām* (Cairo: Dār al-Ḥadīth, 1984) 1:52.

[5] Al-Jaṣṣāṣ, *Uṣūl al-Jaṣṣāṣ*, 2:100; al-Shāshī, *Uṣūl al-Shāshī*, 142.

[6] See Fakhr al-Dīn al-Rāzī, *al-Maḥṣūl*, 1:147–57, who responds to these points.

perform the act. If an act involves a pure or dominant act of harm (*al-mafsada al-khāliṣa aw al-rājiḥa*), we can reasonably presume that God wants it to be omitted. If an act is free from both *maṣlaḥa* and *mafsada*, or if both balance each other out in a single act, the act is deemed permissible (*mubāḥ*).

Acts that are purely good or bad, al-Qarāfī held, are further delineated into different legal categories. Where an act poses a pure or dominant benefit (*maṣlaḥa*), and involves a matter of limited significance (*al-martaba al-daniyya*), the act is only recommended (*nadb*), whereby one receives a reward for committing it, but no consequences arise from omitting it. If the significance of the act is high (*al-martaba al-ʿulyā*), the act is considered obligatory (*wujūb*). On the other hand, if the act involves a pure or dominant harm or *mafsada*, and the act is of limited significance, the act is reprehensible (*karāha*), where one is rewarded for omitting it, but no consequences follow from committing it. If the significance is high, then the act is outright prohibited (*muḥarram*).[7] This description, albeit from a Soft Naturalist opponent, illustrates how one can move from a rational investigation into the circumstances and context of the good and bad to a determination of obligation and prohibition.

Hard Naturalist jurists offered different theoretical approaches for their jurisprudence, as illustrated by the three case studies below. But the thread that unites them is that they fused fact and value in

[7] Al-Qarāfī, *Nafāʾis al-Uṣūl*, 1:138–9. Al-Qarāfī took pains to describe the Muʿtazilite view accurately and in fact castigated those who, in their opposition to the Muʿtazilites, oversimplified or misrepresented their theories. Al-Qarāfī, *Nafāʾis al-Uṣūl*, 1:140. He even argued that given the Muʿtazilite's premises, their naturalistic arguments are in fact coherent. Consequently, al-Qarāfī spent much of his analysis attacking the premises upon which the Muʿtazilites rely. So, for instance, he wrote that the Muʿtazilites rely on the notion of *maṣlaḥa* to ground their obligations in both objectivity and normativity. However they also rely on scripture as a basis for obligations. Al-Qarāfī indicated that it is possible that scripture may prohibit something that is rationally considered a *maṣlaḥa*, and as such the Muʿtazilī argument suffered from contradiction. Al-Qarāfī, *Nafāʾis al-Uṣūl*, 1:138–9. Furthermore, al-Qarāfī argued that while the terms *ḥusn* and *qubḥ* may anchor God's actions to a prevailing *maṣlaḥa* in theory, it is not necessarily the case that human rational speculation can identify what that *maṣlaḥa* is in any given case. Al-Qarāfī, *Nafāʾis al-Uṣūl*, 1:148–9. Consequently, he later held that the *ḥusn* and *qubḥ* do not capture the *maṣlaḥa* or *mafsada* of an act, but rather reflect God's determination of punishment and reward. Al-Qarāfī, *Nafāʾis al-Uṣūl*, 1:152.

nature through the presumption of permissibility. For them, nature becomes both the objective and normative basis for assessing the good and bad, and thereby for creating Sharīʿa obligations.

The Presumption of Permissibility in the Hard Natural Law of Abū Bakr al-Jaṣṣāṣ (d. 370/981)

At the heart of Hard Natural Law jurisprudence is the presumption of permissibility (*ibāḥa*). This principle reflects the idea that all of creation is primordially a positive good that human beings can make use of, without worrying about limitations, prohibitions, or other restraints on use. The importance of this presumption or principle is that it constitutes the jurisprudential mode by which fact and value are fused in nature. This principle, as we will see, becomes a central factor for rendering reason an authoritative source of law.

To illustrate how the principle operates, we will begin our discussion of Hard Natural Law with the work of Abū Bakr al-Jaṣṣāṣ, a Ḥanafī jurist from Baghdad. According to the biographical tradition, al-Jaṣṣāṣ was a highly regarded Ḥanafī scholar who assumed the leadership of his legal school (ie *madhhab*) in Baghdad.[8] He seems to have avoided entanglements with legal adjudication since it is reported that he refused offers to be chief *qāḍī* of Baghdad.[9]

[8] Abū al-Faraj ʿAbd al-Raḥmān b. ʿAlī b. Muḥammad b. al-Jawzī, *al-Muntaẓam fī Taʾrīkh al-Mulūk wa al-Umam*, Muḥammad ʿAbd al-Qādir ʿAṭā and Muṣṭafā ʿAbd al-Qadr ʿAṭā (eds) (Beirut: Dār al-Kutub al-ʿIlmiyya, n.d.) 14:277; Abū Bakr Aḥmad b. ʿAlī al-Khaṭīb al-Baghdādī, *Taʾrīkh Baghdād*, Muṣṭafā ʿAbd al-Qādir ʿAṭā (ed) (Beirut: Dār al-Kutub al-ʿIlmiyya, 1997) 5:72; Abū al-Falāḥ ʿAbd al-Ḥayy b. al-ʿImād, *Shadharāt al-Dhahab fī Akhbār man Dhahab* (Beirut: Dār al-Kutub al-ʿIlmiyya, n.d.) 3:71; Shams al-Dīn Muḥammad b. Aḥmad ʿUthmān al-Dhahabī, *Siyar Aʿlām al-Nubalāʾ*, Shuʿayb al-Arnaʾūt and Akram al-Būshi (eds) (Beirut: Muʾassasat al-Risāla, 1986) 16:340–1; Shams al-Dīn Muḥammad b. Aḥmad ʿUthmān al-Dhahabī, *al-ʿIbar fī Khabar man Ghabar*, Abū Ḥājir Muḥammad al-Saʿīd b. Basyūnī Zaghlūl (ed) (Beirut: Dār al-Kutub al-ʿIlmiyya, n.d.) 2:133–4; Khayr al-Dīn al-Ziriklī, *al- Aʿlām* (12th edn, Beirut: Dār al-ʿIlm li al-Malayīn, 1997) 1:171.

[9] Abū al-Faraj ʿAbd al-Raḥmān b. ʿAlī b. Muḥammad Ibn al-Jawzī, *al-Muntaẓam fī Taʾrīkh al-Mulūk wa al-Umam*, Muḥammad ʿAbd al-Qādir ʿAṭā and Muṣṭafā ʿAbd al-Qadr ʿAṭā (eds) (Beirut: Dār al-Kutub al-ʿIlmiyya, n.d.) 14:277; al-Khaṭīb al-Baghdādī, *Taʾrīkh Baghdād*, 5:72; Ibn al-ʿImād, *Shadharāt al-Dhahab*, 3:71; al-Dhahabī, *al-ʿIbar*,

Al-Jaṣṣāṣ lived in Baghdad, the capital of the ʿAbbāsid caliphate, during the 4th/10th century, when the Twelver-Shiʿite Buwayhids assumed control of the city. The Buwayhids reigned as a minority community of Shiʿites and seem to have used their power to expand the boundaries of the prevailing intellectual milieu.[10] This is particularly important in the case of al-Jaṣṣāṣ, whose intellectual predispositions are not entirely clear. In particular, the biographical literature is unclear about his theological affiliation. Reinhart denies that al-Jaṣṣāṣ was a Muʿtazilite theologian, or held views associated with the Muʿtazilites. The various biographical dictionaries Reinhart relies on indeed leave that question ambiguous.[11] But in his *Siyar*, al-Dhahabī wrote that al-Jaṣṣāṣ may have had Muʿtazilite leanings (*qīla kāna yamīlu ilā al-iʿtizāl*).[12] This does not necessarily mean al-Jaṣṣāṣ was Muʿtazilite, but it certainly raises doubts about our ability to categorize him neatly with respect to a particular historical school of theology.

This ambiguity in al-Jaṣṣāṣ' theological adherence provides an opportunity to illustrate how the lens of legal philosophy offers an important frame for this debate on legal authority, and enhances our appreciation of al-Jaṣṣāṣ' intellectual diversity and contribution. The focus on natural law provides an additional mode of analysis for understanding the theoretical richness offered by authors such as al-Jaṣṣāṣ, whose ideas may transcend categories of identity deeply rooted in Islamic intellectual history.

Given the way al-Jaṣṣāṣ formulated the discussion on *ḥusn* and *qubḥ*, what seems to be at stake is the authority to make determinations of obligation with a divine imprint. Specifically, he characterized the debate as pertaining to 'the legal rulings on the

2:134. Al-Dhahabī, *Siyar Aʿlām al-Nubalāʾ*, 16:340, reports that al-Jaṣṣāṣ was nearly monastic (*manzilat al-ruhbān*) in his circumstances and behavior.

[10] See Joel L Kraemer, *Humanism in the Renaissance of Islam: The Cultural Revival During the Buyid Age* (2nd edn, Leiden: Brill, 1992).

[11] Kevin Reinhart, *Before Revelation: The Boundaries of Muslim Moral Thought* (Albany: SUNY Press, 1995) 198 nn 35–45 and accompanying text. Notably, Reinhart does not reference al-Dhahabī's text, noted below.

[12] Al-Dhahabī, *Siyar Aʿlām al-Nubalāʾ*, 16:341. See also Nabil Shehaby, 'The Influence of Stoic Logic on al-Jassas's Legal Theory' in John Emery Murdoch and Edith Dudley Sylla (eds), *The Cultural Context of Medieval Learning* (Boston: D Reidel Publishing Co, 1975) 61, 73.

acts of one who is subjected to obligation' (*ahkam af'āl al-mukallaf*).[13] In other words, the debate concerns how we evaluate the legal significance of acts performed by those who are of the age and capacity to be considered subject to the law. According to al-Jaṣṣāṣ, acts in general can be classified into three possible categories: permissible (*mubāḥ*), obligatory (*wājib*), and prohibited (*maḥẓūr*). Each category of acts is described in accordance with the consequences, punitive or otherwise, that result from committing such acts. For example, an act that is permissible is one where the actor is neither rewarded for committing the act nor punished for omitting the act in the Hereafter. An act that is obligatory is one that the actor is rewarded for committing and punished for omitting, and conversely, an act that is prohibited is one for which the actor is punished for committing and rewarded for omitting.[14]

Al-Jaṣṣāṣ, though, was principally interested in how to evaluate the legal significance of acts not addressed by scripture. On this matter he reported that some jurists held such acts to be presumptively permissible unless otherwise specified by reason as either bad (*qubḥ*) or obligatory (*wujūb*). Others argued that all acts are presumptively prohibited unless specified otherwise by reason. Al-Jaṣṣāṣ analyzed the issue by distinguishing between universal values and others that are subject to change. He said that prior to the existence of revelation, an act may be obligatory (*wājib*) as long as the value of the act never changes. *Wājib*, in this case, applies to acts that, on the basis of reason, are understood as obligatory in all circumstances, such as having faith in God (*imān*), thanking the benefactor (*shukr al-mun'im*), and pursuing fairness (*inṣāf*).[15] Likewise, matters may rationally be deemed to be prohibited, as long as they are universally and unalterably evil, such as oppression and disbelief in God. Specifically he said: '[Among the acts known before revelation] is what is bad in itself (*qabīḥ li nafsihi*) and prohibited, and does not change and alter from its state (*ḥālihi*).'[16] Al-Jaṣṣāṣ had in mind universal Sharī'a values that do not change and are not subject to a case by case analysis. Whether obligatory or

[13] Abū Bakr Aḥmad b. 'Alī al-Jaṣṣāṣ, *Uṣūl al-Jaṣṣāṣ: al-Fuṣūl fī al-Uṣūl*, Muḥammad Muḥammad Tāmir (ed) (Beirut: Dār al-Kutub al-'Ilmiyya, 2000), 2:99.

[14] Al-Jaṣṣāṣ, *Uṣūl al-Jaṣṣāṣ*, 2:99.

[15] Al-Jaṣṣāṣ, *Uṣūl al-Jaṣṣāṣ*, 2:100.

[16] Al-Jaṣṣāṣ, *Uṣūl al-Jaṣṣāṣ*, 2:100.

prohibited, these are acts whose universal normative standing is made possible on the basis of reason.

Reason can also contribute to more context-sensitive determinations of obligation. According to al-Jaṣṣāṣ, there are acts that change their Sharīʿa value with regard to their circumstances. On a purely reasoned basis, we may determine these acts to be permissible, prohibited, or obligatory pursuant to the benefits and harms arising from the acts in question.[17] Importantly, whatever is not addressed by scripture and is not among the universal values is *presumptively permissible if the act poses a greater benefit than harm.*[18]

Al-Jaṣṣāṣ justified this presumption of permissibility on the basis of his theology of God and its implication on the fusion of fact and value in creation. He wrote that God could have created nature for four possible reasons.

- God may have created it to benefit no one in particular. But this is foolhardy and a waste, according to al-Jaṣṣāṣ (*ʿabath wa safah*).[19]
- God may have created nature to cause injury and not to bestow benefit (*khalaqahā li yaḍurra bihā min ghayri nafʿ*).[20] According to al-Jaṣṣāṣ, such a proposition would be abominable and detestable (*ashnaʿ wa aqbaḥ*).[21]
- God may have created nature and all of creation to benefit God. But that is theologically impossible since God is not affected by benefits (*manāfiʿ*) or harms (*muḍārr*).[22]
- The last possibility, and the one endorsed by al-Jaṣṣāṣ, is that God created nature to benefit people (*annahu khalaqahā li manāfiʿ al-mukallafīn*).[23]

Because creation exists for the advantage of humanity, then all acts (which are a part of creation) are presumptively beneficial for people (*makhlūqatun li manāfiʿ al-mukallafīn*).[24] The terms for 'benefit'

[17] ʿAlā ḥasab mā yataʿallaqu bi fiʿlihi min manāfiʿ al-mukallafīn wa maḍarrihim. Al-Jaṣṣāṣ, *Uṣūl al-Jaṣṣāṣ*, 2:100.
[18] Lam yakun fīhi ḍarr aktharu mimmā yujtalabu bi fiʿlihi min al-nafʿ. Al-Jaṣṣāṣ, *Uṣūl al-Jaṣṣāṣ*, 2:100.
[19] Al-Jaṣṣāṣ, *Uṣūl al-Jaṣṣāṣ*, 2:100.
[20] Al-Jaṣṣāṣ, *Uṣūl al-Jaṣṣāṣ*, 2:100.
[21] Al-Jaṣṣāṣ, *Uṣūl al-Jaṣṣāṣ*, 2:100.
[22] Al-Jaṣṣāṣ, *Uṣūl al-Jaṣṣāṣ*, 2:100.
[23] Al-Jaṣṣāṣ, *Uṣūl al-Jaṣṣāṣ*, 2:100.
[24] Al-Jaṣṣāṣ, *Uṣūl al-Jaṣṣāṣ*, 2:100.

and 'harm' (*manāfi*ʿ, *naf*ʿ, *maḍarr*, *ḍarr*) are technical terms of art that fuse fact and value. The benefit and harm here, though, are not purely empirical qualities; they embody the normativity of the divine will. In other words, the idea of a nature purposefully created by God reflects both the objective existence of the world, and the normative content embedded in the world, given the divine imprint on creation. The idea that God would create nature for human benefit speaks to how al-Jaṣṣāṣ united both fact and value, thereby making nature a basis for his philosophy of law.

To suggest that God's creation of nature implies a presumption contrary to permissibility would be demeaning to God, according to al-Jaṣṣāṣ. By fusing fact and value in nature, al-Jaṣṣāṣ argued against those who held that nature is not objective, determinate, or necessarily beneficial. Al-Jaṣṣāṣ' view of nature involves a set of theological assumptions about God and nature as expressed in the notion of benefit (*manāfi*ʿ, *intifā*ʿ). Al-Jaṣṣāṣ was adamant that embedded in nature is an unflinching affirmative benefit for people. He said: 'it is necessary that there be benefit [*intifā*ʿ] in such an act in any way [such benefit] may come.'[25] By so holding, al-Jaṣṣāṣ preserved nature as an empirical base while also infusing into nature a normative foundation to justify and legitimate reasoned determinations of obligations and prohibitions.

In some cases, al-Jaṣṣāṣ recognized the existence of universal obligations and prohibitions. At a minimum, though, acts are permissible in that all of creation is normatively created for human fulfillment, even though the act presents no additional quality of obligation or prohibition, punishment or reward. At all times, though, he started from a view of God and nature that allowed him to fuse fact and value in the created world to render reason an authoritative source of law.

For al-Jaṣṣāṣ, whether we rationally assert universal or contingent legal values, we will rely on a naturalistic foundation to justify our Sharīʿa determinations. Al-Jaṣṣāṣ' natural law jurisprudence is built on his presumption of permissibility, which (1) relies on the empiricism of nature for an objective basis for reasoned deliberation, and (2) provides a normative foundation for obligation by fusing the

[25] Wajaba an yakūna lahum al-intifāʿ bihā ʿalā ayyi wajh ya'tī lahum dhālik minhā. Al-Jaṣṣāṣ, *Uṣūl al-Jaṣṣāṣ*, 2:100.

facts of nature with a divinely inspired normativity. This presumption is not unique to al-Jaṣṣāṣ' Hard Naturalism. As will be seen below, it is a key component for other Hard Naturalist jurists, thereby offering an appropriate focus for our inquiry into the authority of reason as a source of Sharīʿa norms.

The Hard Natural Law of Qāḍī ʿAbd al-Jabbār (d. 414 or 415/1025)

Al-Qāḍī ʿAbd al-Jabbār was born into a poor family in Asadābād, where he began his life as a student of Islamic thought. From a theological perspective, he was originally Ashʿarite at this early stage in his life. Like many other students, he traveled to continue his studies with well-respected scholars. Of special note is the fact that he traveled to Baṣra, among other places. At this time, Baṣra was an important cultural centre of the Buwayhid Empire and of Muʿtazilite learning. In the mid-10th century it was conquered by the Buwayhid Muʿizz al-Dawla who set up his central capital in Baghdad while delegating his son, al-Ḥabashī, to govern Baṣra. Historians have indicated that al-Ḥabashī was keenly interested in cultural and intellectual learning, and developed a library with thousands of volumes. Importantly, Baṣra was home to a Muʿtazilite library. Historians suggest that during his stay in Baṣra, ʿAbd al-Jabbār abandoned his earlier Ashʿarite commitments and became a Muʿtazilite theologian. Because of his learning and extensive writing, he earned the reputation of being the leading exponent of the Baṣran Muʿtazilites, and is considered to have written the foundational texts for the later period of the intellectual movement.[26]

[26] Margaretha T Heemskerk, *Suffering in the Muʿtazilite Theology: ʿAbd al-Jabbār's Teaching on Pain and Divine Justice* (Leiden: Brill, 2000) 37–41. For entries on ʿAbd al-Jabbār in pre-modern biographical dictionaries *(ṭabaqāt)* and more recent accounts, see al-Khaṭīb al-Baghdādī, *Ta'rīkh Baghdād*, 11:114–6; Tāj al-Dīn Abū Naṣr ʿAbd al-Wahhāb. ʿAlī b. ʿAbd al-Kāfī al-Subkī, *Ṭabaqāt al-Shāfiʿiyya al-Kubrā* (Beirut: Dār al-Kutub al-ʿIlmiyya, 1999) 3:116–17; Ṣalāḥ al-Dīn Khalīl Aybak al-Ṣafadī, *Kitāb al-Wāfī bi al-Wafayāt*, Ayman Fu'ād Sayyid (ed) (Stuttgart: Franz Steiner, 1991) 18:31–4; Ibn al-ʿImād, *Shadharāt al-Dhahab*, 3:202–3; al-Dhahabī, *Siyar Aʿlām al-Nubalā'*, 17:244–5; al-Ziriklī, *al-Aʿlām*, 3:273–4; SM Stern, 'ʿAbd al-DJabbār' in HAR Gibb et al (eds), *Encyclopaedia of Islam* (2nd edn, Leiden: Brill, 1960–) 1:59.

ʿAbd al-Jabbār was certainly an important writer within the Muʿtazilite tradition. However, as Heemskerk has noted, not all texts attributed to him were necessarily authored by him. For instance, the work *Sharḥ al-Uṣūl al-Khamsa* was originally thought to have been ʿAbd al-Jabbār's work, as dictated by his student Mānkdīm. Heemskerk relates, though, that Mānkdīm may have done more than merely dictate the work; he offers in the extant text a critical paraphrase of a work by ʿAbd al-Jabbār that is no longer extant. Likewise, the work entitled *al-Majmūʿ fī al-Muḥīṭ bi al-Taklīf*[27] was initially ascribed to the pen of ʿAbd al-Jabbār but later shown to be a paraphrase by his student Ibn Mattawayh (d. 469/1076). Heemskerk, following the advice of Gimaret, advises that since the two texts above are critical paraphrases of ʿAbd al-Jabbār's work, they should be used with caution when articulating the views of ʿAbd al-Jabbār. On the other hand, the *Mughnī*[28] need not be viewed with the same caution. Using various literary analyses, Heemskerk argues that ʿAbd al-Jabbār dictated the work, and is very much the author of the *Mughnī* that has survived and been ascribed to him.[29] For these reasons and the particular interest in the views of ʿAbd al-Jabbār, this study will focus on the views expressed in *al-Mughnī*.[30]

ʿAbd al-Jabbār developed a Hard Natural Law theory that relies on certain key terms, which contribute to a general theory of natural law. In particular, he built his theory around certain key terms of art, namely: sustenance (*rizq*), obligation (*taklīf*), divine assistance (*lutf*), legal theory (*al-sharʿiyyāt*), and justice (*al-taʿdīl wa'l-tajwīr*). Generally, his theory can be summarized as follows. God provides

[27] ʿAbd al-Jabbār, and al-Ḥasan b. Aḥmad b. Mattawayh, *Majmūʿ fī al-Muḥīṭ bi al-Taklīf* (Beirut: al-Maṭbaʿa al-Kāthūlīkiyya, 1965).

[28] ʿAbd al-Jabbār al-Asadābādī, *al-Mughnī*.

[29] Heemskerk, *Suffering*, 2–9. For more on these works, see George F Hourani, 'The Rationalist Ethics of ʿAbd al-Jabbār' in SM Stern et al (eds), *Islamic Philosophy and the Classical Tradition: Essays Presented by his friends and pupils to Richard Walzer on his Seventieth Birthday* (Oxford: Bruno Cassirer, 1972) 105, 105–6; Stern, 'ʿAbd al-Jabbār', 1:59.

[30] When citing to a volume of *al-Mughnī*, all volume references will be to the topic-title of the volume, rather than following the custom of referring to the volume number. The version of *al-Mughnī* used for this study did not use numbers to indicate the volume, although some other versions may do so. I am adopting this mode of citation to ensure readers can effectively locate the material cited.

human beings with sustenance or *rizq*, which is an empirically verifiable good that sustains human life, as a matter of *fact*. Importantly, since *rizq* is bestowed by God, it offers a basis for fusing fact and value in nature, and the sustenance it provides. At the most primordial level of existence, *rizq* is normatively good and thereby 'permissible' to all, especially since ʿAbd al-Jabbār theologically held that God only does the good (*annahu taʿālā lā yafʿalu illā al-ḥasan*).[31] All things in the world, including acts by human beings, are fundamentally part of God's creation. Therefore at a primordial level, they reflect God's goodness, unless source-texts indicate otherwise. Consequently, according to ʿAbd al-Jabbār, human acts are, from a legal perspective, presumptively permissible to commit, unless proven otherwise. Permissibility or *ibāḥa*, according to ʿAbd al-Jabbār, signifies an act for which one is neither blamed nor rewarded. On first impression, an act that involves neither reward nor blame may seem value neutral. However, according to ʿAbd al-Jabbār, among the different categories of affirmatively good acts are those which do not invoke blame on someone (*annahu mimmā lā yastaḥaqqu bihi al-dhamm ʿalā wajh fa yakūna ḥasan*).[32] Since permissible acts involve no blame, ʿAbd al-Jabbār asserted that permissibility presents a base level of goodness (*fa ammā al-mubāḥ fa huwa kulluhu ḥasan lā ṣiffa lahu zāʾida ʿalā ḥasanihi*), which permits him to assert the presumptive goodness of creation.[33] ʿAbd al-Jabbār fused fact and value in nature, akin to al-Jaṣṣāṣ, by considering the primordial state of all *rizq* to be permissible, and thereby good.

As indicated above, ʿAbd al-Jabbār's naturalist thesis relies in part on the theological premise that God cannot do anything other than the just or good, thereby creating the necessary condition for the presumption of permissibility. He said that God's acts all pose some

[31] ʿAbd al-Jabbār, *al-Mughnī*, al-Taʿdīl 1: 3. For more on Muʿtazilite approaches to God's justice, see Richard Frank, 'Can God do what is wrong?' in Tamar Rudavsky (ed), *Divine Omniscience and Omnipotence in Medieval Philosophy: Islamic, Jewish and Christian Perspectives* (Boston: D Reidel Publishing Co, 1985) 69; idem., 'The Autonomy of the Human Agent in the Teaching of ʿAbd al-Ǧabbar' (1982) 95 *Le Muséon: Revue d'Études Orientales* 323; Michael Schwarz, 'The Qāḍī ʿAbd al- Ǧabbār's Refutation of the Ašʿarite Doctrine of 'Acquisition' (kasb)' (1976) 6 *Israel Oriental Studies* 229.

[32] ʿAbd al-Jabbār, *al-Mughnī*, al-Taʿdīl:7.

[33] ʿAbd al-Jabbār, *al-Mughnī*, al-Taʿdīl:31.

sort of benefit (*naf*ʿ).[34] That benefit is not for God, but rather aids someone else. If God were to create something that benefits no one, He would act foolishly and futilely (*ʿabath*).[35] Since God cannot commit a futile or foolhardy act, given the theological view of God's goodness, it follows for ʿAbd al-Jabbār that all of God's acts are righteous, benevolent, and intended to benefit humanity (*kawn jamīʿ afʿālihi iḥsān wa tafaḍḍul*).[36]

Importantly, permissibility is only the first step of ʿAbd al-Jabbār's naturalistic reasoning. The invocation of *rizq* is merely the starting point in a larger discussion on the nature of law and legal ordering. For instance, while the *rizq* in the world may initially be available to all to use, it is subjected to some form of distribution in the interest of ordering society. *Rizq* considered in a primordial sense prior to distribution presents the initial state of nature's factual and normative good. Upon its distribution, entitlements arise by which someone can claim a certain *rizq* to the exclusion of others: with distribution comes a regime of obligations and prohibitions. Using property as an analogy to develop his natural law theory, ʿAbd al-Jabbār illustrated how one can reason from a primordial state of a generally normative creation to a subsequent state of law and order on naturalistic grounds.

ʿAbd al-Jabbār, though, was aware that mere distribution would not always lead to a just distribution. Some might claim more *rizq* out of greed or coercive force. The distribution process itself must be subjected to some mode of reasoning to ensure a just outcome. Consequently, ʿAbd al-Jabbār embedded his conception of *rizq* within a teleology characterized by the term *lutf*. *Lutf* reflects the divinely created dispositions of human beings that direct humans to the good. This is not to say that all people will do the good all the time. Nonetheless, humans ought to pursue a distribution of the *rizq* by taking into consideration their dispositions or *lutf*, all of which are created by God and form the basis of a divinely created natural teleology that justifies, authorizes, and guides naturalistic reasoning.

[34] ʿAbd al-Jabbār, *al-Mughnī*, al-Taʿdīl:34.
[35] ʿAbd al-Jabbār, *al-Mughnī*, al-Taʿdīl:34.
[36] ʿAbd al-Jabbār, *al-Mughnī*, al-Taʿdīl:34.

The Theory of *Rizq*: Fusing Fact and Value

One of ʿAbd al-Jabbār's key terms of art for his natural law theory is *rizq*, which reflects a benefit that people can lawfully enjoy (*mā yantafiʿu bihi*).[37] *Rizq* invokes both the empirical facts of nature and its presumptive normative value. ʿAbd al-Jabbār stated that *rizq* is something that is not created for its own sake, but rather for the benefit of someone else (*lā budda min kawnihi rizqan li al-ghayr*).[38] *Rizq* benefits all of humanity (*jumlat al-ʿibād*) since, at the most primordial level, God does not designate a particular *rizq* for a particular person (*lahum an yantafiʿū bihi min ghayr takhṣīṣ*).[39] In this sense, drinking water or eating fish from the sea is presumptively permissible for all. Such things are 'sustenance for all, and no one can be independent from them. Consequently, one who uses them instinctively [is entitled] to benefit from them, and [doing so] is good (*ḥasan*).'[40] ʿAbd al-Jabbār said that God did not initially create nature's bounties to benefit some people over others. God initially created all things to facilitate life in general (*li manāfiʿ al-ḥayy*).[41] This presumptive initial state of nature does not change, even in those cases where certain things are later distributed or claimed for the benefit of a certain group over others. Certainly, rational animals who partake of nature subsequently distribute goods among themselves.[42] If X owns a piece of property, he is entitled to enjoy it to the exclusion of others; Y cannot use the property except with X's permission. But prior to this distribution, God's *rizq* is permissible for all—whether rational or non-rational animals—and no one has an ontological priority to prevent another from enjoying it.[43]

The presumption of permissibility, which arises out of the theory of *rizq*, is the means by which ʿAbd al-Jabbār fused fact and value in his natural law theory. Presumptively, things 'are created for

[37] Muḥibb al-Dīn Abū Fayḍ Muḥammad Murtaḍā al-Ḥusayni al-Zabīdī, *Tāj al-ʿArūs min Jawāhir al-Qāmūs*, ʿAlī Shīrī (ed), 20 vols (Beirut: Dār al-Fikr, 1994) 13:162.
[38] ʿAbd al-Jabbār, *al-Mughnī*, al-Taklīf:27.
[39] ʿAbd al-Jabbār, *al-Mughnī*, al-Taklīf:27.
[40] ʿAbd al-Jabbār, *al-Mughnī*, al-Taklīf:27.
[41] ʿAbd al-Jabbār, *al-Mughnī*, al-Taklīf:27.
[42] ʿAbd al-Jabbār, *al-Mughnī*, al-Taklīf:27, 30.
[43] ʿAbd al-Jabbār, *al-Mughnī*, al-Taklīf:27, 30.

[humanity] to enjoy and they are sustenance for them [all] from this perspective' (*an takūna makhlūqa li yantafiʿū bihā fa takūnu rizq lahum min hādha al-wajh*).[44] Because creation is a boon for humanity from a just and willing Creator, creation embodies an affirmative normative value that entitles people to use their reason to order their affairs, based on the benefits they perceive. Permissibility here is the theoretical means by which ʿAbd al-Jabbār fused fact and value to create a naturalistic foundation for rational speculation. By rooting his approach to a purposeful creation of nature, he provides a normative, naturalistic foundation as an initial starting point for legal reasoning.

ʿAbd al-Jabbār recognized that a natural law theory must move from global permissibility to a legal order that protects a range of interests. Hence, while he theorized that 'we know through reason that we can utilize everything that benefits us,' he nonetheless limited the scope of acting on the basis of permissibility to instances where 'there is neither temporal nor eternal harm imposed on us for doing so, nor on someone else.'[45] We know the beneficial quality will always exist. Hence, the harm inquiry does not challenge the initial presumption that there is sustenance in fact (*lā fī kawnihi rizqan fī al-ḥaqīqa*). Rather, the second level of inquiry takes into account the cost of enjoyment.[46] If there is harm in acting in a certain way, then on purely rational grounds we should avoid doing so. He wrote: 'It is established as a matter of reason that avoiding harm in a manner that is known with certainty or probability to avoid [that harm] is obligatory' (*qad thabata bi al-ʿaql anna al-taḥarruz min al-maḍārr bi al-wajh alladhī yuʿlamu aw yuẓannu annahu muḥraz bihi minhā wājib*).[47] In other words, where X can avoid harm, X must do so. But if the act poses no harm to anyone, the act remains permissible.

Additionally, ʿAbd al-Jabbār utilized the harm principle to account for and minimize the normative implications of factual indeterminacy in the created world. ʿAbd al-Jabbār was aware that

[44] ʿAbd al-Jabbār, *al-Mughnī*, al-Taklīf:27.
[45] ʿAbd al-Jabbār, *al-Mughnī*, al-Taklīf:33.
[46] ʿAbd al-Jabbār, *al-Mughnī*, al-Taklīf:33.
[47] ʿAbd al-Jabbār, *al-Mughnī*, al-Taklīf:43.

no act poses a pure harm or a pure benefit. All activities have a mixture of both. Instead, he held that seeking benefits (*iltimās al-manāfiʿ*) in which no one else is harmed or injured, whether in this life or the Hereafter, is by definition good (*ḥasan*), even if in seeking out the benefit one must undertake some hardship (*al-amr al-shāqq*).[48] He stated: 'If... in the preponderance of X's opinion (*ghalaba fī ẓannihi*) when X undertakes some acts to obtain the *rizq*, [and] enjoy it while experiencing some hardship, [his undertaking] is necessarily good.'[49] In other words, those acts posing a harm should be avoided. But no good can be achieved without some expenditure of energy or exertion. In this latter sense, ʿAbd al-Jabbār recognized the factual indeterminacy of the good, and used the harm principle to provide some guidance to reasoned deliberation about the good. There is not always going to be a pure benefit without hardship. But the determinacy of the good to be pursued is understood in a way that accounts for hardship and difficulty.

In addition to the harm principle, ʿAbd al-Jabbār invoked a 'claim principle' to contribute further to the ordering of the world and goods. For instance, suppose Zayd is permitted to make use of a *rizq* without causing harm, and he thereby makes a claim on it. According to ʿAbd al-Jabbār, Zayd becomes the owner of it (*ṣāra mālikan lahu*) and no one can undermine his ownership in that regard.[50] Suddenly, what is initially permissible for all becomes subjected to a subsequent distribution process that restricts the scope of people's behavior. Property ownership is the result of a process by which creation is distributed among people, and from which rights and entitlements are created. For example if X possesses a gift, then as against all others X reasonably becomes the one most entitled to it (*ṣāra amlak bihi*).[51] ʿAbd al-Jabbār used the claim principle to explain the distinction between his presumptive state of creation, where everything is permissible for everyone, and the later developments of obligations and prohibitions reflecting the incorporation of the claim and harm principles. Property law offers a

[48] ʿAbd al-Jabbār, *al-Mughnī*, al-Taklīf:43–4.
[49] ʿAbd al-Jabbār, *al-Mughnī*, al-Taklīf:44.
[50] ʿAbd al-Jabbār, *al-Mughnī*, al-Taklīf:34.
[51] ʿAbd al-Jabbār, *al-Mughnī*, al-Taklīf:34.

jurisprudential analogy by which ʿAbd al-Jabbār illustrated how a naturalistic theory of obligation starts from a presumption of the normativity of nature, and proceeds to the determination of obligations and prohibitions that arise once a system of ownership is in place. The rational principles that effectuate, uphold, and enforce any distribution contribute to a legal system of obligations and prohibitions. Obligations and prohibitions thereby reflect assessments of the interests and stakes of different people in the *rizq*, which they have utilized to pursue the good. But just because we can now make determinations of obligation and prohibition does not mean that the initial presumption about the *rizq* is invalid.

For ʿAbd al-Jabbār, wherever we find *rizq*, we can locate the normative beginnings of a legal order. He wrote: 'If the *rizq* is for someone, then it is necessary that anyone who obstructs him from enjoying it be blamed.'[52] To illustrate his point, ʿAbd al-Jabbār referred to a prophetic discussion about a woman who starves a cat. She prevents it from enjoying what is permissible for it, and as such she is not only blamed but also is put in hell for doing so (*madhmūma mustaḥaqqa li al-nār*).[53] For ʿAbd al-Jabbār's analysis to work, he must consider the cat entitled to certain goods, thereby rendering the woman's obstruction wrongful. ʿAbd al-Jabbār's theory initially requires the presumption of permissibility to fuse fact and value. Having jumped that theoretical hurdle, ʿAbd al-Jabbār could thereby proceed to the next stage of his theory in which he recognized a system of rights and entitlements, with legal consequences.

Human Dispositions (*Lutf*) and the Construction of a Natural Teleology

To develop his natural law theory further, ʿAbd al-Jabbār argued that human beings are invested with a kind of guidance that allows them to understand the beneficial nature of the *rizq* and the order that should arise once it is distributed. To do so, he introduced the concept of *lutf*. Heemskerk states that '[a] *lutf*... motivates

[52] ʿAbd al-Jabbār, *al-Mughnī*, al-Taklīf:35.

[53] ʿAbd al-Jabbār, *al-Mughnī*, al-Taklīf:35. For the *ḥadīth*, see Ibn al-Jawzī, *Kitāb Aḥkām al-Nisāʾ* (Beirut: Manshūrāt al-Maktaba al-ʿAṣriyya, 1981) 372.

someone to perform an act; it is not the motive itself...[T]he *lutf* does not cause an act, but it urges someone to perform it. It is possible that someone knows a *lutf* but does not choose to do that which the *lutf* motivates him to do.'[54] In ʿAbd al-Jabbār's theory of Hard Natural Law, *lutf* is a term of art that reflects the God-given human dispositional traits or motivations that propel us toward the good and keep us away from evil.[55] The *lutf* guides us in matters of obligation (*lutf fī al-taklīf*)[56] and constitutes a type of 'divine assistance that motivates the agent to choose obedience and abstain from transgression'.[57] ʿAbd al-Jabbār wrote that the *lutf* 'beckons [one] (*yadʿū*) to an act of obedience (*fiʿl al-ṭāʿa*)'.[58] In short, the *lutf* is a dispositional trait that directs us to the good. By itself, it does not determine action, but rather represents humanity's divinely created innate sense of the good.

Although the *lutf* resides in humans, it is endowed by God. To explain, ʿAbd al-Jabbār related a tradition that states that God has bestowed divine guidance on humanity by sending the prophets and the law they brought, 'even though some of that [law] was from the prophets'.[59] God may be removed from the direct articulation of the law. But when prophets articulated the law in their own terms, they did so on the authority of God, who sent them as divine guidance to pronounce the law for their respective communities. Although the prophets articulate the law, their inspiration is from God since the prophets are His *lutf* to humanity. ʿAbd al-Jabbār suggested that like prophets, human dispositions are bestowed by God on humans to indicate the good. God may not speak to us directly. But by knowing that the *lutf* exists and observing its dispositional content, we can know and pursue what pleases God and thereby conform to His will.[60] Indeed, we can rely on the *lutf* for insights into right conduct in conformity with the divine will

[54] Heemskerk, *Suffering*, 148–50.

[55] Binyamin Abrahamov, 'ʿAbd al-Jabbār's Theory of Divine Assistance (*Lutf*)' (1993) 16 *Jerusalem Studies in Arabic and Islam* 41, 43.

[56] ʿAbd al-Jabbār, *al-Mughnī*, al-Taklīf:46.

[57] Abrahamov, 'ʿAbd al-Jabbār's Theory,' 43.

[58] ʿAbd al-Jabbār, *al-Mughnī*, al-Luṭf:9.

[59] ʿAbd al-Jabbār, *al-Mughnī*, al-Luṭf:10.

[60] ʿAbd al-Jabbār, *al-Mughnī*, al-Luṭf:10.

because, as ʿAbd al-Jabbār was keen to remind us, God only creates the good and is not capable of creating evil.[61] The goodness inherent in the *lutf*, which stems from the goodness of God, contributes to the normative value of the choices we make on the basis of the *lutf*. With the *lutf*, we are guided, indirectly nonetheless, by the divine; our choices reflect the nature of that guidance.

When we follow the directives of our *lutf*, there is a correspondence between the *lutf* and the manifestation of the act. ʿAbd al-Jabbār called this correspondence *tawfīq*. Likewise, when the *lutf* prevents one from committing an act of evil, this correspondence between the *lutf* and the omission is called *ʿiṣma* or a state of being free from sin.[62] The problem with this designation, as ʿAbd al-Jabbār noted, is that many theologians argued that only the prophets are sinless, while the Shiʿites also held their infallible *imāms* to be sinless. How can ordinary humans be sinless too? ʿAbd al-Jabbār did not believe that ordinary people are sinless. They may be endowed with *lutf* and thus have dispositions toward the good and away from evil; but they may not adhere to those dispositions in their actual behavior. Rather the *lutf* 'contributes to the doing of good, but does not indicate that the individual actually does good because of it' (*li annahu yufīdu fiʿl al-ṣalāḥ bihi wa lā yufīdu anna al-mukallaf qad ṣalaḥa bi dhālik*).[63] ʿAbd al-Jabbār consequently admitted that while all people are endowed with *lutf*, not all may in fact experience *tawfīq* or *ʿiṣma*.

We may not always follow the guidance of our *lutf*, but nonetheless it is part of our natural constitution. And that is all ʿAbd al-Jabbār required to render reason an authoritative source of Sharīʿa. Theorizing at a general level (*ʿalā jihat al-tawassuʿ*), ʿAbd al-Jabbār held that we benefit from divine assistance, and thereby have the ability to embark on a course of behavior that either corresponds with the good or avoids the evil.[64] The *lutf* represents the potentiality in human nature to engage in morally righteous thought and conduct. That potentiality may not always result in specific moral

[61] ʿAbd al-Jabbār, *al-Mughnī*, al-Luṭf:10; al-Taklīf:58.

[62] ʿAbd al-Jabbār, *al-Mughnī*, al-Luṭf:15. See also the definition of *lutf* provided by Ibn Manẓūr, *Lisān al-ʿArab* (6th edn, Beirut: Dār al-Ṣadr, 1997) 9:316.

[63] ʿAbd al-Jabbār, *al-Mughnī*, al-Luṭf:20.

[64] ʿAbd al-Jabbār, *al-Mughnī*, al-Luṭf:15–16.

action, but the possibility that it might is all that ʿAbd al-Jabbār required to situate the telos of his natural law theory. Despite human imperfection, the *lutf* nonetheless exists as part of our nature, which we can look to for guidance as to God's will:

> God, being [perfectly] knowledgeable and in no need of assistance... simply commits the obligatory and avoids evil [without considering consequences]... As such, God is not in need of any assistance. God establishes divine assistance for others, and not Himself.... [Consequently] it is necessary for one to have the *lutf* so that he can avoid harm to himself... If he were not to [avoid harm], he would deserve punishment where he chooses the evil and avoids the obligatory. The *lutf* thereby determines that one [should] not act in such a manner, thereby removing punishment from oneself while [doing] what earns him reward.[65]

What makes a *lutf* indicative of the good and of obligation is that the *lutf* directs us to achieve the good for ourselves and avoid harm to ourselves, if only we would take notice of it.

Importantly, the good to which the *lutf* guides us is not instrumental, but rather contributes to our self-fulfillment. Self-fulfillment lies at the heart of ʿAbd al-Jabbār's theory of obligation. God does not obligate us to perform an act to benefit someone else. According to ʿAbd al-Jabbār, God knows that 'it is not obligatory on Zayd to bring about goods (*iltimās al-maṣāliḥ*) for someone else or to avoid harms (*dafʿ al-maḍārr*) on someone else.'[66] The obliging force of the *lutf* is based on the fact that obligations and prohibitions are designed to help us seek the telos of our own self-fulfillment. The consequences of an act are not irrelevant to ʿAbd al-Jabbār's analysis (for example, the harm principle). But his natural law theory is not based on a strictly utilitarian calculus about maximizing the good for the largest number of people. It is better viewed as a natural teleology, in which fact and value are fused in order to endow human reason with the authority to set us, individually and collectively, on a course of action aimed at self-fulfillment and social perfection.

For example, he stated that the prophets fulfill their obligations by spreading and effectuating God's message (*adāʾ al-risāla*).[67] In

[65] ʿAbd al-Jabbār, *al-Mughnī*, al-Taklīf:89.
[66] ʿAbd al-Jabbār, *al-Mughnī*, al-Luṭf:46.
[67] ʿAbd al-Jabbār, *al-Mughnī*, al-Luṭf:46.

doing so, they certainly benefit the religious community. But that does not change the fact that there is a benefit for the prophets as well (*ṣalāḥ li al-muʾdī*). Indeed, the benefit for the prophets is what makes the requirement to spread God's message obligatory to begin with. This benefit constitutes the *lutf* for the prophets that makes obligation on them possible and good. So while in the prophets' deeds lies a benefit for others, the prophets' obligations to perform their deeds are meaningful because underlying their actions is a benefit that contributes to their own self-fulfillment.[68]

ʿAbd al-Jabbār's Hard Naturalism involves key terms such as *rizq* and *lutf*, both of which are meaningful conceptually as long as we accept a just God who can commit no evil. Indeed, if God commits an act without intending to do good, then God acts senselessly (*ʿābith*). As senselessness is a form of evil, ʿAbd al-Jabbār concluded that God can only bring about the good. 'God most high created creation to benefit [humanity]. It is not permitted that He created what can bestow a benefit, except that He intended to bestow a benefit. If [things] were otherwise, then [creation] would be useless, which is not permitted [of God].'[69] Elsewhere, he wrote: 'There is no escaping the fact that [God] created people to benefit them and created the inanimate world as a means to instill benefit.'[70] The benefits of creation are captured by the term *rizq*, which offers ʿAbd al-Jabbār the necessary term of art to fuse fact and value, and thereby allow him to reason from the *rizq* to the good and the obligatory.

The *lutf* or dispositional quality in human nature certainly offers a guide to all of us who wish to understand the will of God. The imperative to understand the *lutf* and follow its guidance is based on the fact that it guides us to self-fulfillment. For ʿAbd al-Jabbār, benefit is not calculated in utilitarian or consequentialist fashion. The benefit is designed to promote self-fulfillment, which makes obligation both justified and meaningful in ʿAbd al-Jabbār's Hard Natural Law theory. ʿAbd al-Jabbār did not suggest that we always will know and follow our *lutf*. But he did not need to offer such a

[68] ʿAbd al-Jabbār, *al-Mughnī*, al-Luṭf:46.
[69] ʿAbd al-Jabbār, *al-Mughnī*, al-Sharʿiyyāt:146–7.
[70] ʿAbd al-Jabbār, *al-Mughnī*, al-Taklīf:64.

thesis to philosophize about the ontological authority of reason in the law. The mere possibility that we can reason to the good and the bad using our divinely endowed *lutf* is all that he needed to formulate his naturalist thesis about reason and the telos of Sharīʿa.

Desire and Natural Reasoning

To bring his theory to a close, ʿAbd al-Jabbār tied his theory of *lutf* to human desires, which might seem paradoxical given his interest in a theory of natural reasoning that avoids the pitfalls of idiosyncrasy and indeterminacy in the natural world. But as he could not escape the implications of subjectivity in reasoned inquiry, he arguably had to theorize about the relationship between God and desire in order to articulate his theory of the authority of reason. According to ʿAbd al-Jabbār, '[t]he first thing that is good from God is that He initially created life (*khalq ḥayy*) and desires (*khalq al-shahwa*) to experience existence in the [various] ways one appreciates and enjoys it' (*li mudrak mawjūd ʿala wajh yudrikuhu fa yaltadhdhu bihi*).[71] A person must have and rely upon his desire, otherwise no enjoyment of creation would be possible.[72] Certainly we could know and experience creation purely with our senses. But without desire, how could we speak meaningfully of tendencies, leanings, or dispositions? The senses provide an empirical basis for knowing the world; but desire contributes to a normative ordering of that world in light of one's preference for one thing over another (*li nayl mā yudriku bi [al-ḥawāss]*).[73] In fact, ʿAbd al-Jabbār said God would be unjust if He failed to create our desires, but nonetheless expected us to know and appreciate the obligation of obedience to Him: 'It is not good [for God] to create the senses except by including the creation of the desires (*khalq al-shahwa*) to create dispositional leanings where there is no obligor (*li nayl al-mudrakāt bihā matā lam yakun mukallif*).'[74]

Senses alone can only offer a description of the world. But desire makes our tendencies, preferences, and leanings possible, especially

[71] ʿAbd al-Jabbār, *al-Mughnī*, al-Taklīf:72.
[72] ʿAbd al-Jabbār, *al-Mughnī*, al-Taklīf:73.
[73] ʿAbd al-Jabbār, *al-Mughnī*, al-Taklīf:77.
[74] ʿAbd al-Jabbār, *al-Mughnī*, al-Taklīf:77.

in those cases where there is no authority dictating how we should or should not behave. In other words, in the absence of source-texts, we are left to our own devices to decide upon our course of conduct. Our senses can offer a factual accounting of the benefits and harms of acting one way or another. But without desires or tendencies, any choice we might make would lack the kind of normative content that makes choice morally and legally meaningful. For ʿAbd al-Jabbār, human desires therefore create an initial starting point for natural law reasoning about obligation.

The importance of human desires, though, is not designed to render the law vulnerable to idiosyncratic whimsy or reducible to a pure subjectivist thesis of legal reasoning. Rather, the desire element embraces the moral agency of the individual. ʿAbd al-Jabbār recognized that our desires are not always for the good. He was also aware that not all goods are necessarily what we may desire. Furthermore, some goods that we desire may involve pain and harm (*alam*).[75] In other words, the good may involve hardship and pain that will no doubt run against our personal preferences, but nonetheless is still good and so must be pursued. In these cases, it would be a mistake to consider the hardship as normatively bad. Rather, the hardship may be part of what is required to obtain the good.[76] Indeed, without effort and hardship, the concept of obligation has little meaning for ʿAbd al-Jabbār. For example, he wrote that 'if one of us wants something from someone else, which is described as an obligation, yet he wants from [the latter] something that does not entail a hardship (*mashaqqa*) such as eating something good, it is not characterized as an [obligation].'[77] Importantly, the very idea of hardship is meaningful in part because ʿAbd al-Jabbār incorporated desire in his jurisprudence in a way that is tied to the wisdom of creation, and not to the idiosyncrasy of human whimsy.

For instance, suppose someone must be punished (*al-ʿiqāb*).[78] The punishment can be good if one deserves to be punished (*li kawnihi mustaḥaqqan*).[79] Where punishment is deserved, it is by

[75] ʿAbd al-Jabbār, *al-Mughnī*, al-Taklīf:85.
[76] ʿAbd al-Jabbār, *al-Mughnī*, al-Taklīf:85, 86.
[77] ʿAbd al-Jabbār, *al-Mughnī*, al-Taklīf:294.
[78] ʿAbd al-Jabbār, *al-Mughnī*, al-Taklīf:85.
[79] ʿAbd al-Jabbār, *al-Mughnī*, al-Taklīf:85.

definition good despite the pain it causes. The punishment is certainly not desirable from the criminal's perspective: he does not enjoy the pain. But the suffering of deserved punishment is nonetheless a good because of a system of entitlements and responsibility that speaks to the divine will.[80] Hence the normative quality of desire is embedded within a larger inquiry into the wisdom of the natural order of things. The normative role of desire in ʿAbd al-Jabbār's Hard Natural Law theory permits a jurisprudence that incorporates the humanistic and the divine in a manner that renders the law as neither idiosyncratic nor so objectively determined as to preclude moral agency.

Our desires and *lutf* are tools that allow us to understand the wisdom in creation, of which we are a part. ʿAbd al-Jabbār used the term *ʿilla* to capture the idea of wisdom in creation. *ʿIlla* refers to the circumstantial context of the wisdom that makes creation good (*wajh al-ḥikma alladhī lahu ḥasuna minhi al-khalq*).[81] In other words, the *ʿilla* captures the circumstances that are susceptible to human rational inquiry, and which demonstrate the purposefulness and beneficial quality of creation. The *ʿilla* operates in ʿAbd al-Jabbār's natural law theory as a focal point of rational deliberation in order to prevent human desire from becoming so self-referential as to lose its connection to the larger natural world. Indeed, even God recognizes that knowing the circumstances surrounding an act is necessary to know its normative quality: 'God's knowledge of the goodness of the thing leads to His choice of it.'[82] To illustrate his point, ʿAbd al-Jabbār wrote: 'it would not be good for God to obligate Zayd to stand or sit, as He obligates the return of bailments (*radd al-wadīʿa*), fairness (*inṣāf*), and thanking the benefactor (*shukr al-munʿim*) when there is no good (*maṣlaḥa*) in [standing or sitting].'[83] The obligation to stand or sit in this statement offers no apparent benefit or purpose tied to self-fulfillment, unlike other acts that offer a benefit. Consequently, the good of any given act will depend on the circumstances that render it good.[84]

[80] ʿAbd al-Jabbār, *al-Mughnī*, al-Taklīf:85.
[81] ʿAbd al-Jabbār, *al-Mughnī*, al-Taklīf:92.
[82] ʿAbd al-Jabbār, *al-Mughnī*, al-Taklīf:96.
[83] ʿAbd al-Jabbār, *al-Mughnī*, al-Taklīf:149.
[84] ʿAbd al-Jabbār, *al-Mughnī*, al-Taklīf:149.

Of course, recourse to the context and circumstances of a good may insert a degree of indeterminacy into our inquiry into the natural world. While nature provides an objective foundation for reasoned deliberation, as opposed to mere human whimsy, it is not necessarily determinate. Furthermore, human beings, given their limited abilities, are in a weak epistemic position to know with certainty the full context of any given act. However ʿAbd al-Jabbār did not require certainty in one's knowledge of the circumstances of an act. Rather, as ʿAbd al-Jabbār stated, 'Any act of ours is good on the basis of the preponderance of opinion' (*wa kullu fiʿl yaḥsunu minnā li ghalabat al-ẓann*).[85] Presumably, only God has perfect knowledge. Humans on the other hand are fallible: their determinations are neither certain nor unambiguous. Nevertheless, a naturalistic decision beset by some factual uncertainty is still authoritative and valid. For instance, ʿAbd al-Jabbār said that on the basis of the preponderance of opinion (*ghalabat al-ẓann*) one can know the goodness of business and trade (*ḥusn al-tijāra*) and other such activities.[86] 'We recognize [that] the basis for its goodness is something that is possible, namely profit (*ribḥ*).'[87] The possibility of profit makes trade a good activity. Actual profit in any given case is not certain or guaranteed. But the mere factual possibility of it renders any particular engagement in trade presumptively good as a normative matter.

But, as indicated above, just because God may put a disposition in people and may want someone to behave in a certain way does not mean that the individual will in fact behave in that way. He may act contrary to God's wishes. This possibility raises yet another feature of the interaction between reason, desire and moral agency, namely the individual's will (*irāda*). The *irāda* involves a determination of a particular course of conduct and a choice to act in that manner.[88] Individuals create a will to action by investigating

[85] ʿAbd al-Jabbār, *al-Mughnī*, al-Taklīf:89.

[86] ʿAbd al-Jabbār, *al-Mughnī*, al-Taklīf:90.

[87] ʿAbd al-Jabbār, *al-Mughnī*, al-Taklīf:90.

[88] ʿAbd al-Jabbār, *al-Mughnī*, al-Taklīf:159. Just because someone can act contrary to God's wishes does not diminish God's omnipotence. Rather, God can want one to be obedient and have faith even though He also knows that some people will not do so. For example, a father may want his son to act in a certain way, but may learn that his son refuses to do so. Whether his son abides by the father's wishes or not has no bearing on the fact that the father still has a specific desire. ʿAbd al-Jabbār, *al-Mughnī*,

the *rizq* of creation in light of their *lutf*, desires, and the context-bound benefits of the natural world (*maṣlaḥa*), to reach a preponderance of opinion (*ghalabat al-ẓann*) concerning the proper course of conduct. This will or intent is formed in conjunction with the individual's power and capacity (*tamkīn*) to engage in a process of analysis. This human capacity depends on those instrumentalities (*al-ʿudad wa al-ālāt*) that are necessary to make moral inquiry possible, namely the capacity to reason.[89] This capacity, combined with the *lutf*, is what empowers and enables an individual to form a specific will. The *lutf* and the capacity to reason are both from God, and an individual utilizes both to create a will to act rightly or wrongly. God instills in one whom He knows will disbelieve the same *lutf* and capacity as He grants to another whom He knows will believe.[90] A person will utilize both to investigate a situation and decide whether it poses a benefit. His assessment, although subject to epistemological frailties (ie *ẓann*), will nonetheless present sufficiently authoritative knowledge by which he can validly act. As ʿAbd al-Jabbār stated: '*Ẓann* can be a circumstance establishing the goodness of acts' (*inna al-ẓann qad yakūnu wajhan li ḥasan al-fiʿl*).[91]

Reasoning to Obligations from a Just God

ʿAbd al-Jabbār's natural law theory utilizes key conceptual terms to link the divine will and human moral agency in a manner that justifies the authority of reason as a source of Sharīʿa obligation (*taklīf*). His theory is premised upon recognizing that God's obligations are not always express, but sometimes require us to reason about the divine will. He stated:

> [God] wants [people to do] acts, which He informs them [directly] (*ʿarrafahum*) are obligatory or recommended, or erects evidence (*dallahum*) of that [fact]. It is not taboo to know that [God] wants that, whether from the perspective of reason (*jihat al-ʿaql*) or... from the perspective of

al-Taklīf:160. In the same way, God may have a desire even though God knows, given His ubiquitousness, that individuals will not fulfill that divine desire.

[89] ʿAbd al-Jabbār, *al-Mughnī*, al-Taklīf:292.
[90] ʿAbd al-Jabbār, *al-Mughnī*, al-Taklīf:265.
[91] ʿAbd al-Jabbār, *al-Mughnī*, al-Taklīf:268.

transmitted knowledge (*jihat al-sam*ʿ). Because of that, it is said that God most high obligates from both aspects together.[92]

For ʿAbd al-Jabbār, obligation requires an obligor who, for ʿAbd al-Jabbār, is a just God who avoids all evil, and would not impose harm without reason or justification. A valid obligation requires one who is obligated (*mukallaf*), namely one who is endowed with *lutf*, and not coerced against his will either to commit or omit the act (*rafʿ al-mawāniʿ wa wujūh al-iljāʾ*).[93] The obligee must have the capacity to investigate and choose his course of conduct freely; this requirement therefore leads us to consider the role of reason as a source of obligation.[94] It may not be the only source, but it is an important one.

Because his Hard Naturalism is designed to grant authority to natural reasoning, ʿAbd al-Jabbār did not require that all obligations be expressly commanded. Express commands (*amr*) are surely the most obvious form (*al-aẓhar*) of command, by which an obligor's intent can be known.[95] But it is not the only form. As an example, ʿAbd al-Jabbar posited a hypothetical about a master and his slave. 'The master can be described as obligating his slave if [the master] instructs [the slave] (*afhamahu*) by indicators (*bi al-ishāra*) that he desires [the slave] to act, just as [the master] is described [as obligating the slave] when he commands [the slave explicitly].'[96] Those indicators may be less than express, without diminishing or negating the existence of an obligation. When the commands are not express, ʿAbd al-Jabbār's Hard Naturalism assumes that a just God would nonetheless communicate His will somehow. This communicative process is what ʿAbd al-Jabbār called *taʿrīf*, namely instructing or informing. The obligor must inform (*taʿrīf*) the obligee of the obligation. An obligee can investigate the circumstances to determine if he has implicitly or explicitly been informed of an obligation.

But what counts as a valid indicator of the divine will? Perhaps all we need to do is assess the circumstances of benefit, harm, and hardship without really inquiring into whether God desires humans

[92] ʿAbd al-Jabbār, *al-Mughnī*, al-Taklīf:299.
[93] ʿAbd al-Jabbār, *al-Mughnī*, al-Taklīf:292.
[94] ʿAbd al-Jabbār, *al-Mughnī*, al-Taklīf:292.
[95] ʿAbd al-Jabbār, *al-Mughnī*, al-Taklīf:295.
[96] ʿAbd al-Jabbār, *al-Mughnī*, al-Taklīf:295.

to commit a certain act or not. In other words, while we may not know God's will with certainty, we can investigate empirical indications of hardship. But by focusing our investigation on the empirical reality of hardship or *mashaqqa*, are we effectively marginalizing the role of the divine intent in our analytic process? If this were the case, we would effectively divorce God's will from grounding the normative authority of any naturalistic rational inquiry. But as we know from above, God's intent is ever-present in creation, given ʿAbd al-Jabbār's concept of *rizq*, *lutf*, and *tamkīn*, which links our desires and our rational capacities to a divinely created world. For ʿAbd al-Jabbār, we do not simply investigate the factual existence of hardship and benefit in the world, and render our findings as law. Rather, obligation depends upon certain premises about God's creative power and just character. Our knowledge of obligation depends on whether God has perfected our reason and erected indicators of His will (*ikmāl al-ʿaql wa naṣb al-adilla*). In other words, humans must have the necessary capacity, and God must, as a matter of justice, provide sufficient evidence for us to investigate.

For example, suppose a slave knows his master is thirsty, and as a result gives him water. The master makes no indication that he desires water; rather the slave takes it upon himself to bring water to his master. The slave's act in this case is not the hardship that makes obligation meaningful. The hardship of obligation arises only once a will to impose the hardship on the slave exists. Consequently, if the master desires the slave to do so, the basis for obligation now exists. But mere intent is not enough. To obligate his slave, the master must do something that constitutes communication or *taʿrīf* (*mā yaqūmu maqām al-taʿrīf*) before an obligation can arise.[97]

To understand what God makes clear to people through *taʿrīf*, the individual not only must be endowed with certain faculties (*alāt*) to determine the normative quality of an act, but must also act from a position of knowledge. 'Just as the individual (*mukallaf*) needs to have the capacity of bringing about an act through his own faculties (*qudra*) and instrumentalities (*al-ālāt*) in order for an obligation on him to be valid, he also needs to be knowledgeable

[97] ʿAbd al-Jabbār, *al-Mughnī*, al-Taklīf:299.

(*ʿālim*) of his obligations and their characteristics.'[98] Yet knowledge of obligations is different in kind from knowledge of their underlying circumstances. One may be in an epistemically weak position to assert with confidence the full factual details of a situation, but that does not prevent one from making normative determinations of obligation. ʿAbd al-Jabbār's theory of legal authority accounts for epistemic weakness without sacrificing the authority of reasoned deliberation about obligation.

> The preponderance of opinion (*ghalabat al-ẓann*) assumes the position of knowledge (*maqām al-ʿilm*) as a method of knowing the evil of something, its goodness, and its obligation. As for its assuming the position of knowledge concerning the underlying facts of an act, that is not appropriate.[99]

In other words, the preponderance of opinion cannot assert with absolute certainty knowledge about the empirical facts of an act, as the factual context of an act may be far beyond the scope of one's rational faculties to comprehend fully. Assessments of moral value and obligation are substantively different from empirical assessments, and as such while one may not be able to determine the concrete details of an act, one can, in the absence of contrary evidence, posit norms to guide human conduct.

For example, ʿAbd al-Jabbār wrote about how Muslims face the Kaʿba during prayer (*qibla*). Even if one is out of sight from the Kaʿba, he must still pray facing it. But the direction of the Kaʿba is uncertain (*maẓnūnā*), despite the fact that the obligation of facing it is clear and certain (*wujūb al-tawajjuh ilayhā maʿlūm*). There may be differing opinions on the direction of the Kaʿba, but the obligation to face it is clear and unambiguous.[100] In this way, we can assert the normative value of an act without knowing the full context and concrete details of that act. A person's epistemic weakness is not a reason for denying him the ability to assert obligations on naturalistic grounds. The point for ʿAbd al-Jabbār is not to know the full details of an act, but rather to be reasonably convinced that a certain course of conduct will gain the actor some benefit or avoid

[98] ʿAbd al-Jabbār, *al-Mughnī*, al-Taklīf:371.
[99] ʿAbd al-Jabbār, *al-Mughnī*, al-Taklīf:373.
[100] ʿAbd al-Jabbār, *al-Mughnī*, al-Taklīf:374.

harm. 'It is rationally established that avoiding probable harm (*al-maḍārr al-maẓnūna*) is obligatory (*wājib*), just as [it is] obligatory to avoid certain harm (*al-maḍārr al-maʿlūma*). There is no difference in our knowledge of obligations to avoid [harm], whether [it is] reached by probability or certainty (*ḥuṣūl al-ẓann wa al-ʿilm*).'[101]

His concepts of *rizq*, *lutf*, and *ʿilla* offer a framework that recognizes the authority of reason, and accounts for our inevitable fallibility amidst a theology of a just God. He stated:

> The individual needs reason because by it he knows much of what he is obligated [to do], such as the obligation of returning bailments (*radd al-wadīʿa*) and thanking the benefactor (*shukr al-munʿim*), as well as the evil of oppression (*qubḥ al-ẓulm*), and the good of kindness (*ḥusn al-iḥsān*). He reaches through [reason] knowledge of all that he is obligated to do, through the method of investigation (*al-istidlāl*) into the scriptural and rational [bases for obligation]. It is not permitted that he investigate evidence (*adilla*) except with a fully formed rational faculty (*kāmil al-ʿaql*) and knowledge of evidence (*ʿālim al-adilla*)...He needs [reason] to execute all the [obligatory] acts, since if he is not a rational being, he cannot know the circumstances of acts whereby he receives reward or punishment [for committing them].[102]

For ʿAbd al-Jabbār, reason is an essential element for constructing obligations. In some cases it operates by itself, and in other cases, it evaluates an act in conjunction with scriptural texts. The scope he granted reason for making normative evaluations was rather broad, but did not encompass all moral determinations. He stated:

> With perfected reason (*kamāl al-ʿaql*) one knows some evils (*baʿḍ al-muqabbaḥāt*), some of the good (*baʿḍ al-muḥassanāt*), and some obligations (*baʿḍ al-wājibāt*). He knows the evil of oppression, ingratitude, and of deceit that poses no benefit or repels no harm. He knows the good of generosity (*ḥusn al-iḥsān*) and graciousness (*tafaḍḍul*). He knows the obligation to thank the benefactor, to return bailments when asked, and to act righteously (*al-inṣāf*). He knows that it is good to blame [one] for [committing] evil where there is no obstruction [from doing the good], and the good of blaming [one] for avoiding obligations where there is nothing impeding [their fulfillment]. It is necessary to attain this knowledge because if it were not attained, the

[101] ʿAbd al-Jabbār, *al-Mughnī*, al-Taklīf:374.
[102] ʿAbd al-Jabbār, *al-Mughnī*, al-Taklīf:375.

individual would not fear of failing to investigate (*al-naẓar*), since obligation is founded upon [this knowledge]. Knowledge of justice is not possible without it because when he does not know the difference between the good and the bad, he cannot immunize the eternal divine from evil and attribute to Him the good. Much of the divine assistance (*al-alṭāf*) and social goods (*al-maṣāliḥ*) cannot be realized without [this rationally based knowledge]. He cannot legitimately know the remaining evil deeds, whether known through reason or scripture, except by attaining this knowledge.[103]

Reason therefore plays a significant role in moving from an assessment of the *lutf* and the benefits of nature to a reasoned conclusion about right human conduct and obligation. Obligations therefore are not simply contingent on express commands and prohibitions by the divine lawgiver. Yet, reason does not operate in a vacuum. The meaningfulness of Sharīʿa obligations is premised on a just God who provides sufficient evidence for us to understand the obligations we must observe. As ʿAbd al-Jabbār said, 'it is not possible to say that God most high obligates us with acts of worship but does not inform us (*lā yuʿarrifunā*) of His intentions for them. That would be an obligation that is not possible to satisfy' (*taklīf mā lā yuṭāqu*).[104]

God must erect indicators of His will to communicate with His creation. Often God may do so through express text, which ʿAbd al-Jabbār called *khiṭāb*.[105] That communication serves as evidence (*dalāla*) for us by which people investigate and arrive at knowledge of God's will and requirements.[106] The *khiṭāb* contributes to the evidentiary base that individuals must investigate (*taqwiyya ḥāl al-dalāla*).[107]

But express source-texts are not the only means of informing humanity.[108] Whether God legislates expressly or by creating naturalistic indicators, the result is the same. One can determine Sharīʿa values, whether by reference to express scripture or by rationally investigating the circumstances that render something good or bad. Those circumstances are constant parts of the natural order that God

[103] ʿAbd al-Jabbār, *al-Mughnī*, al-Taklīf:384.
[104] ʿAbd al-Jabbār, *al-Mughnī*, al-Sharʿiyyāt:10.
[105] ʿAbd al-Jabbār, *al-Mughnī*, al-Sharʿiyyāt:12.
[106] ʿAbd al-Jabbār, *al-Mughnī*, al-Sharʿiyyāt:12.
[107] ʿAbd al-Jabbār, *al-Mughnī*, al-Sharʿiyyāt:12.
[108] ʿAbd al-Jabbār, *al-Mughnī*, al-Sharʿiyyāt:141.

has created. In fact, those circumstances are so embedded in the natural order that ʿAbd al-Jabbār went so far as to suggest that not even God can alter the moral valuation of something after He has created the necessary circumstances that give the act a specific normative value. He wrote: 'If God most high prohibited gratitude (*shukr al-niʿma*) it would not become prohibited because of the prior knowledge of its obligatory nature' (*fa law annahu taʿālā harrama shukr al-niʿma mā kāna yaṣīru muḥarraman li taqaddum al-maʿrifa bi wujūbihi*).[109] This is not to suggest that God's prohibition might not have some effect. Rather, ʿAbd al-Jabbār's point suggests that presuming the authority of rational determinations is not invalid just because in some cases the reasoned conclusion is rebutted by an express decree. As ʿAbd al-Jabbār stated: 'even if the prohibition came from God, the prior knowledge would not be affected just as the knowledge that foodstuffs are the property of Zayd does not affect the prior knowledge that it is [in a presumptive state] of permissibility' (*wa law kāna al-taḥrīm yaḥṣilu min qablihi la kāna taqaddum al-maʿrifa lā yuʾaththaru fī dhālik, kamā lā yuʾaththiru taqaddum al-maʿrifa bi anna al-ṭaʿām milk li zayd fī annahu yaṣīru mubāḥ bi ibāḥatihi*).[110]

With this statement, we come full circle to the presumption of permissibility. The *rizq* of creation contributes to the presumption of the primordial permissibility of all things. Through his theory of *rizq*, ʿAbd al-Jabbār fused fact and value to create nature as both an empirical and normative good. As creation gets distributed, a system of rights and entitlements subsequently arises that leads to determinations of obligation and prohibition. Despite this, however, the initial presumption is not invalid or defeated. Rather, it provides the foundation for ʿAbd al-Jabbār's naturalism. The primordial state of things is fundamentally infused with a positive normative value regardless of any subsequent ordainments that arise thereafter. The initial presumption of permissibility is not invalidated because subsequent divine commands might counter it.

The need to engage in naturalistic reasoning is essential for ʿAbd al-Jabbār, and is a path to obligation that is presumed to be authoritative unless otherwise specified. Consequently, unless there

[109] ʿAbd al-Jabbār, *al-Mughnī*, al-Sharʿiyyāt:141.
[110] ʿAbd al-Jabbār, *al-Mughnī*, al-Sharʿiyyāt:141.

are express indicators to the contrary, one can rationally investigate the circumstances of nature to establish the normative value of an act because of a natural teleology that links desires, dispositions, and the created world to the divine will. Natural teleology links the empirical to the normative because the created world embodies the goodness of God in the form of human dispositions and the presumptively beneficial quality of nature.

The Natural Law Epistemology of Abū al-Ḥusayn al-Baṣrī (d. 436/1044)

As the previous sections illustrate, Islamic Hard Natural Law fuses fact and value in nature, using the presumption of permissibility, in order to grant authority to human reason. ʿAbd al-Jabbār's Hard Natural Law certainly reflects a philosophically nuanced jurisprudence that relies on certain theological premises to make the model work. The Hard Naturalist Abū al-Ḥusayn al-Baṣrī also recognized the significance of fusing fact and value in nature. But while ʿAbd al-Jabbār's theory is highly philosophical, al-Baṣrī's emphasized the methodology of practical reasoning in Hard Natural Law.

Abū al-Ḥusayn al-Baṣrī was a Muʿtazilite jurist born in Baṣra, but who spent much of his life in Baghdad.[111] Nonetheless, he is linked to the Baṣran school of Muʿtazilites, and studied under the guidance

[111] For biographical accounts of his life, see generally Abū al-Fidāʾ Ismāʿīl b. Kathīr, *al-Bidāya wa al-Nihāya*, ʿAbd al-Raḥmān al-Lawqī and Muḥammad Ghāzī Bayḍūn (eds) (Beirut: Dār al-Maʿrifa, 1996) 11–12:504–5; Ibn al-Jawzī, *al-Muntaẓam*, 15:300; Abū al-ʿAbbās Aḥmad b. Muḥammad b. Ibrāhīm b. Abī Bakr b. Khallikān, *Wafayyāt al-Aʿyān wa Anbāʾ Abnāʾ al-Zamān*, Yūsuf ʿAlī Ṭawīl and Maryam Qāsim Ṭawīl (eds) (Beirut: Dār al-Kutub al-ʿIlmiyya, 1998) 4:99; Aḥmad b. Yahyā b. al-Murtaḍā, *Kitāb Ṭabaqāt al-Muʿtazila* (Beirut: al-Maṭbaʿa al-Kāthūlikiyya, 1961) 118–19; Ibn ʿImād, *Shadharāt al-Dhahab*, 3:259; al-Dhahabī, *Siyar Aʿlām al-Nubalāʾ*, 17:587; al-Khaṭīb al-Baghdādī, *Taʾrīkh Baghdād*, 3:314–5; al-Ṣafadī, *al-Wāfī bi al-Wafayāt*, 4:125. Al-Baṣrī is often criticized in the *ṭabaqāt* or biographical literature for only narrating one *ḥadīth*, which apparently was quite popular among the Muʿtazilites. According to this *ḥadīth*, Muḥammad is reported to have said: what is known of the discourse of the first prophet (ie Adam) is that if one feels no shame, he should do as he desires (*idhā lam tastaḥyī fa aṣnaʿ mā shiʾta*). Notably, the Shāfiʿī biographer Shams al-Dīn al-Dhahabī (d. 748/1374) chastised al-Baṣrī for introducing innovations (*bidaʿ*) into the religious tradition. Al-Dhahabī, *Siyar Aʿlām al-Nubalāʾ*, 17:587.

of Qāḍī ʿAbd al-Jabbār, discussed above. Notably, though, Gimaret indicates that despite his affiliation with the Baṣran school, Abū al-Ḥusayn 'must be considered a dissident, perhaps a heterodox, member, for he disagreed with its masters on a number of significant issues'.[112] While Gimaret's discussion concentrates on theological points on which Abū al-Ḥusayn differed from the masters of his school of theology (*kalām*), the point Gimaret makes is important as we consider the jurisprudential dimensions of the various authors we have encountered. The dynamic nature of intellectual thought may render any attempt to strictly categorize a jurist-theologian a difficult matter. Indeed, the more we consider the ambiguity of al-Jaṣṣāṣ' leanings toward Muʿtazilite thought, ʿAbd al-Jabbār's shift from Ashʿarite to Muʿtazilite thinking, and now Abū al-Ḥusayn al-Baṣrī's complex identity as a dissident Baṣran Muʿtazilite, the more we will need additional modes of inquiry, such as a philosophy of law approach, from which we have chosen natural law as a frame for our inquiry.

In this section, we will examine al-Baṣrī's *al-Muʿtamad fī Uṣūl al-Fiqh*. His work was an important contribution to the field of legal theory (*uṣūl al-fiqh*), which even the later Ashʿarite jurist and theologian Fakhr al-Dīn al-Rāzī (d. 606/1209), whose work we will see in Chapters III and IV, relied upon to write his own monumental treatise on the topic entitled *al-Maḥṣūl*.[113] Al-Baṣrī intended his *al-Muʿtamad* to be an exposition on how to deduce the law from authoritative proof texts (*al-adilla al-sharʿiyya*). When he outlined the book's organization, he admitted that discussions on rational presumptions such as the presumption of permissibility should occur early in the book. But since he wrote the book with a focus on the methods of deriving laws from scriptural proofs, the discussion on rational presumptions occurs later in the book.[114] In other

[112] D Gimaret, 'Abu'l-Ḥosayn al-Baṣrī' in *Encyclopedia Iranica* (London: Routledge, 1983) 1:322.

[113] In fact, al-Rāzī specifically refutes Abū al-Ḥusayn al-Baṣrī's position on *ḥusn* and *qubḥ*. Fakhr al-Dīn al-Rāzī, *al-Maḥṣūl fī ʿIlm Uṣūl al-Fiqh*, 1:105–9. For a similar critique of al-Baṣrī, see the commentaries on al-Rāzī's work by the following: Al-Aṣfahānī, *al-Kāshif ʿan al-Maḥṣūl*, 1:253–8; al-Qarāfī, *Nafāʾis al-Uṣūl*, 1:98–106.

[114] Abū al-Ḥusayn Muḥammad b. ʿAlī b. al-Ṭayyib al-Baṣrī, *al-Muʿtamad fī Uṣūl al-Fiqh* (Beirut: Dār al-Kutub al-ʿIlmiyya, n.d.) 1:8–9.

words, while he recognized the presumption as an analytic starting point, he relegated it to a later section because of his epistemic focus. With this epistemic focus, he argued that while reason has the authority to determine the law, it does not do so in a vacuum or without limits. Like ʿAbd al-Jabbār, al-Baṣrī adopted the presumption of permissibility to justify philosophically the authority of reason in the law. But his epistemic focus is meant to emphasize that naturalistic reasoning offers one form of normative authority whose weight will vary in light of existing source-texts and precedent.

Ḥusn and *Qubḥ* as a Discourse on Obligation

For al-Baṣrī, the debates on *ḥusn* and *qubḥ* are about the authority of human reason to determine Sharīʿa obligations. But this way of framing the significance of both terms begs a question about the definition of obligation. When he wrote about legal categorization, he offered a legal typology of acts that reflects his larger concern with the nature and shades of obligation. For instance, he said that on the basis of reason or scriptural authority (*ʿaql, samʿ*), acts can be good (*ḥusn*), bad (*qubḥ*), obligatory, or prohibited.[115] Furthermore, for an obligation to be meaningful at all depends on the capacity of individuals both to understand what they must do and to have the ability to perform the act in question. When someone is asleep, insane, or below the age of majority, he is not culpable for any acts he commits since he does not have the capacity to know the consequence of his actions. He is neither blamed nor praised for his behavior (*lā yatawajjahu naḥū fāʿilihā dhamm wa lā madḥ*)[116] since under the law he is not under any obligation (*taklīf*).[117]

To be obligated to perform an act, one must have both the capacity to perform the act (*al-qādir ʿalayhi*) and the capacity to know what the act entails (*al-mutamakkin min al-ʿilm bihi*).[118] Consequently a bad act (*qabīḥ*) is one that should be avoided by those who have the capacity to choose their behavior and know

[115] Abū al-Ḥusayn al-Baṣrī, *al-Muʿtamad,* 1:334.
[116] Abū al-Ḥusayn al-Baṣrī, *al-Muʿtamad,* 1:335.
[117] Abū al-Ḥusayn al-Baṣrī, *al-Muʿtamad,* 1:335.
[118] Abū al-Ḥusayn al-Baṣrī, *al-Muʿtamad,* 1:335.

what it involves. If someone decides to act badly, he deserves the resulting blame (*istiḥqāq al-dhamm*).[119] Acts that are bad or *qabīḥ* are divided into various categories and subcategories, as follows:[120]

- major bad acts (*kabīr*): acts that are sanctioned with punishment that exceeds any level of reward or praise one might otherwise receive:
    - acts that involve significant punishment (*ʿiqāb ʿaẓīm*), such as for acts of disbelief (*kufr*);
    - acts that involve something less than the above level of punishment, as in the case of causing corruption (*fisq*);[121]
- minor bad acts (*ṣaghīr*): acts for which the punishment and blame (*ʿiqābuhu wa dhammuhu*) do not exceed the reward (*thawāb*) and praise (*madḥ)* the actor receives when performing them.[122]

Al-Baṣrī noted that the jurists of Iraq divided bad acts into various categories: (1) prohibited acts (*al-muḥarram*); (2) reprehensible acts (*al-makrūh*); (3) those which are best to avoid (*mā al-awlā an lā yufʿala*); and (4) acts for which there is no consequence (*lā baʾs bi fiʿlihi*).[123]

The term *ḥasan* or good is applied to acts that should be performed on condition that the actor has the full capacity and knowledge to do so.[124] Good acts are divided into two categories. The first category involves acts that invoke praise. Such acts may require affirmative actions that garner praise, and whose omission may in some cases require sanction (eg *nadb, wājib*).[125] The second are acts that are permissible or *mubāḥ*, according to al-Baṣrī.[126]

[119] Abū al-Ḥusayn al-Baṣrī, *al-Muʿtamad*, 1:335.
[120] Abū al-Ḥusayn al-Baṣrī, *al-Muʿtamad*, 1:335.
[121] Abū al-Ḥusayn al-Baṣrī, *al-Muʿtamad*, 1:335.
[122] Abū al-Ḥusayn al-Baṣrī, *al-Muʿtamad*, 1:335.
[123] Abū al-Ḥusayn al-Baṣrī, *al-Muʿtamad*, 1:335.
[124] Abū al-Ḥusayn al-Baṣrī, *al-Muʿtamad*, 1:335.
[125] Abū al-Ḥusayn al-Baṣrī, *al-Muʿtamad*, 1:336. Al-Baṣrī further subdivided these categories. For instance, he distinguished between those obligatory duties (*wājib*) that fall on the individual qua individual (*al-wājib ʿalā al-aʿyān*), and those that fall on the individual as part of a communal obligation that can be satisfied if others perform the duty, such as participating in jihād (*al-wājibāt ʿalā al-kifāya*). Abū al-Ḥusayn al-Baṣrī, *al-Muʿtamad*, 1:336.
[126] Abū al-Ḥusayn al-Baṣrī, *al-Muʿtamad*, 1:335.

Adopting the principle of permissibility, al-Baṣrī held that an act that is permissible is affirmatively good, as opposed to being value neutral.[127] Importantly, these categories and labels of the good and the bad are important to consider because they are characteristically Sharīʿa terms of art that capture the way in which jurists designated whether an act is obligatory, prohibited, recommended, reprehensible or permissible under the Sharīʿa.

There is no doubt that God's will (and thereby theology generally) is very much part of the background to al-Baṣrī's model of Hard Natural Law, thereby indicating the relationship between his Hard Natural Law theory and Sharīʿa obligations. For instance, al-Baṣrī considered bad acts to constitute sinful acts (*maʿṣiyya*) that God dislikes (*annahu fiʿl yakrahuhu Allāh*).[128] Al-Baṣrī also described bad acts as those which customarily imply that God rejects them using indicators of divine prohibition (*nahy*) or threat (*waʿīd*).[129] A bad act may also be called *muḥarram*, which reflects God's repudiation of the act, whether through a threat or prohibition (*bi al-waʿīd wa al-nahy*).[130] Indeed, a bad act is not just bad on purely rational grounds. It is bad because of a quality that runs contrary to the divine will.

Likewise, al-Baṣrī held that good acts cannot be understood without an implicit reference to the divine will. For example, an act that is permissible reflects 'the removal of prohibition (*ḥaẓr*) and impediments (*manʿ*) [established via] deterrent mechanisms, threats or other means'.[131] To suggest an act involves no divine prohibition does not mean there is an absence of divine will. Rather the absence

[127] Notably, this positive valuation of permissible acts is a central feature in al-Baṣrī's natural teleology, and thus links his Hard Naturalism to the theories of Hard Naturalism espoused by al-Jaṣṣāṣ and ʿAbd al-Jabbār.

[128] Abū al-Ḥusayn al-Baṣrī, *al-Muʿtamad*, 1:336.

[129] Abū al-Ḥusayn al-Baṣrī, *al-Muʿtamad*, 1:337.

[130] Abū al-Ḥusayn al-Baṣrī, *al-Muʿtamad*, 1:337. Al-Baṣrī refers to other terms to reflect the centrality of God's will in denoting an act as bad. For instance, *dhanb* or sin connotes that an act is *qabīḥ* or bad. It is an act for which one receives blame (*muʾākhadha*) or punishment (*ʿuqūba*). Yet another term that is often used to capture the idea behind the notion of *qabīh* is makrūh or reprehensible. This is an act that customarily indicates God's displeasure and dislike. And finally, the terms *mazjūr ʿanhu* (deterred from) or *mutawaʿʿad ʿalayhi* (threatened against) also denote God's desire to ensure that such acts are avoided. Abū al-Ḥusayn al-Baṣrī, *al-Muʿtamad*, 1:337.

[131] Abū al-Ḥusayn al-Baṣrī, *al-Muʿtamad*, 1:337.

of punishment illustrates the presence of the divine will in affirming the goodness of permissible acts. Judgments about the good and the bad are not merely human assessments but reflect the will of God.

The above discussion is essential for understanding what al-Baṣrī meant when he utilized terms such as *ḥusn* and *qubḥ*. He did not invoke some abstract notion of the good and the bad that reflects purely rational inquiries. Rather, terms like *ḥusn* and *qubḥ* are theoretically used to recognize and legitimate the use of naturalistic reasoning as an instrument for understanding the divine will.

Theology, Permissibility, and the Authority of Natural Reason

Having established the significance of the divine will in his theoretical framework, al-Baṣrī described the qualities of human nature that make reasoned deliberation about the good and bad possible:

> [E]ach capable person (*kullu qādir*), who rational people would recognize as capable and discerning (*qādir mumayyiz*), is able to bring acts into being (*yaqduru ʿalā ījād al-afʿāl*) according to each perspective, whether bad, good, obligatory, or something else. We permit each capable person to act pursuant to the good, except where God and His Messenger instruct against performing the act.[132]

If we know the difference between the good and the bad, and we have the ability to act pursuant to our knowledge of the difference, then we are presumptively permitted to act pursuant to the good that we know and identify. But where there is express legislation to the contrary, our reasoned conclusions must give way.

But what does it mean to know and distinguish between the good and the bad? Al-Baṣrī said that both scripture and reason can determine the quality of an act as obligatory, prohibited, recommended, reprehensible, or permissible.[133] Reason is authoritative because the presumption of permissibility offers the necessary foundation for its authority to determine the good and the bad (*ḥasan, qabīḥ*). Just as in the case of al-Jaṣṣāṣ and ʿAbd al-Jabbār, al-Baṣrī's discussion on permissibility is a theoretical technique used to fuse fact and value.

[132] Abū al-Ḥusayn al-Baṣrī, *al-Muʿtamad*, 1:342.
[133] Abū al-Ḥusayn al-Baṣrī, *al-Muʿtamad*, 1:341.

To render all things presumptively permissible is to invest nature with a normative value that allows one to move from empirical assessments of the good to normative evaluations as an initial starting point in any legal analysis. As his discussion in this vein is important for understanding his natural law theory, it is translated in full below:

God, most high, created tastes in things (*al-ṭuʿūm fī al-ajsām*), despite being able to refrain from creating them in such a manner. It is established that in doing so, He had a specific purpose. If [He did not], then [the creation of tastes] would be futile (*ʿabath*). It is impossible that the purpose [in creating them] would be to grant [God] a benefit or repel harm [from Him] since those do not apply to Him. It is not possible that [the creation of tastes] involves a harm imposed on someone else, since there may not be harm in them. Rather they are only harmful once one knows and experiences them (*innamā tuḍirru bi idrākihā*). [That implies that] experiencing the [tastes] is permissible. It is not good that [God's] purpose would be purely to harm someone who does not deserve to be harmed (*lā yastaḥaqqu al- iḍrār*). It is necessary that the purpose underlying the experience of [the created tastes] is to render a benefit for someone else. [He gains this benefit] by directly experiencing [the tastes], or by avoiding them where their nature poses a corruption. [In either case] he earns a reward (*thawāb*) for experiencing them (*bi idrākihā*). [He benefits] by investigating [the nature of the tastes]. And in that lies the [primordial] permissibility of experiencing them (*fī dhālik ibāḥa idrākihā*). One earns reward by avoiding [the savory items *only after* his] soul beckons [him] to experience them. Consequently, his experience of them exists *prior* [to his avoidance]. Likewise, he can investigate [the savory tastes] only when they are actually known. Knowledge of them rests on actually experiencing them. God most high did not create knowledge of them in us without [reference to our] experience. It is therefore true that there is no advantage in [tastes] unless benefiting from them is [primordially] permissible. That shows that God erects as a matter of reason the permissibility of benefiting from those things to achieve knowledge of the tastes in them.[134]

For al-Baṣrī, the authority of reason to assess the normative value of an act depends upon an initial, primordial fusion of fact and value in a world created by God. God creates taste (*al-ṭuʿūm*) amidst the possibility of not creating it at all. For al-Baṣrī, such a creative act could only occur from the purposeful direction (*gharaḍ*) of the divine.[135] If there were no purposefulness in taste, then creating it

[134] Abū al-Ḥusayn al-Baṣrī, *al-Muʿtamad*, 2:320 (emphasis added).
[135] Abū al-Ḥusayn al-Baṣrī, *al-Muʿtamad*, 2:320.

would have been a waste (*ʿabath*), which would run contrary to his theology of a just God. Al-Baṣrī argued that God did not create taste to avoid harm or engender benefit for Himself as these are things that do not affect Him. Perhaps God created taste to harm someone else. However al-Baṣrī said that it would not be good if God's purpose was purely to cause harm to someone who did not deserve it. Further, he queried how we could ever know of any harm unless we first had a chance to taste the food. It may be that the savory quality of food does not involve any harm (*qad lā yakūnu fihā ḍarar*).[136] It can only cause harm once one initially knows and experiences the nature of the foodstuffs at a primordial moment of existence. Consequently, it follows for al-Baṣrī that the divine purpose (*gharaḍ*) of allowing us to recognize and understand the nature of taste at some primordial moment is to create a benefit for those other than God (*fa wajaba an yakūna al-gharaḍ bi idrākihā nafʿ yaʿūdu ilā ghayrihi*).[137] Certainly after experiencing such tastes, indicators may arise suggesting that one should avoid them. Just as ʿAbd al-Jabbār upheld the primordial state of permissibility despite subsequent divine decrees, al-Baṣrī held that at a primordial point in creation benefits are presumed to be initially good. The empirically determinable benefit implicitly conveys the normative good inherent in it, as a function of God's creative will, without denying the possibility that God may later provide different indicators of His will to the contrary. The fact of the good is fused with a normative goodness stemming from God's purposeful will and as such justifies one's acting in a way that maximizes that benefit, unless subsequent evidence suggests a contrary divine intent.

As an example of natural reasoning, al-Baṣrī looked to eating. He said that proof of its permissibility lies in the fact that eating poses a benefit that has no trace of evil (*al-intifāʿ bihā manfaʿa laysa fīhi wajh min wujūh al-qubḥ*).[138] The key terms of art in his example are *intifāʿ* and *manfaʿa*. They denote a type of benefit that arises from eating. They are empirically determinable qualities; but because fact and value are fused, these same empirical facts about the good

[136] Abū al-Ḥusayn al-Baṣrī, *al-Muʿtamad*, 2:320.
[137] Abū al-Ḥusayn al-Baṣrī, *al-Muʿtamad*, 2:320.
[138] Abū al-Ḥusayn al-Baṣrī, *al-Muʿtamad*, 2:315.

transform into a normative basis for asserting the Sharīʿa value of the underlying act. The empirically beneficial quality becomes the normative foundation for asserting the good. Al-Baṣrī stated: 'the benefit (*manfaʿa*) beckons [one to do] the act (*tadʿū ilā al-fiʿl*) and permits it since [gaining the benefit] is one of the purposes (*gharaḍ*) [of the act].'[139] Because of the fusion of fact and value, the potential benefit of an act is the normative foundation for performing the act.

For al-Baṣrī, fact and value are fused in the natural bounties of creation as an initial presumption. Consequently we are free to pursue such benefits unless there is evidence to the contrary. For instance, according to al-Baṣrī, eating fruit poses an unambiguous natural benefit in those instances where eating poses no harm (*lā maḍarra fīhi*).[140] This is not to suggest that all acts of eating are necessarily good; some may actually pose harm. But if that were the case, al-Baṣrī stated that a just God would have provided us the necessary indicators to make that determination (*lau kāna fīhi mafsada, la dallanā Allāhu ʿalayhā*).[141] Without such indicators to guide us, we can presumptively rely on a rational assessment whose normative value stems from the naturalist foundation of al-Baṣrī's presumption of permissibility.

To illustrate his rational methodology, al-Baṣrī addressed the case where one must investigate the existence of a benefit, such as breathing air (*al-tanaffus fī al-hawāʾ*). He said that the investigator:

> presumes that the good of this activity is established by the absence of aspects of evil in it (*bi intifāʾ wujūh al-qubḥ ʿanhu*). He investigates [for] the absence of any corruption (*mafsada*) in its being (*kawn*) [on the presumption that] if there were corruption [in the act], our knowledge of its nature as corrupt would, as a general matter, necessarily exist. This view [therefore] negates the evil in [the act] in light of [also] knowing that it is [presumptively] good. [This determination may] differ due to the presentation of evidence (*huwa mukhālaf li mawḍūʿ al-dalāla*).[142]

The good, in other words, is established not only by the fact that one presumes nature to be a positive good but also by the fact that

[139] Abū al-Ḥusayn al-Baṣrī, *al-Muʿtamad*, 2:315.
[140] Abū al-Ḥusayn al-Baṣrī, *al-Muʿtamad*, 2:315.
[141] Abū al-Ḥusayn al-Baṣrī, *al-Muʿtamad*, 2:315.
[142] Abū al-Ḥusayn al-Baṣrī, *al-Muʿtamad*, 2:316.

through an epistemic inquiry one finds no evidence of evil. The permissibility of an act, and hence its goodness, are functions of both an ontological presumption about nature and reason, and an epistemic search for contrary evidence. Where there is no evidence of evil or corruption in an act, the act is deemed to be good on naturalistic grounds. If it were harmful or evil, and God wanted us to avoid it, then God would have made the necessary evidence of His will available to us. Otherwise, to require us to avoid a beneficial act without giving us a way of knowing it should be avoided would be unfair and unjust. Since God is only just, the combination of the presumption of permissibility and the absence of contrary evidence provides the necessary foundation for the ontological authority of reasoned deliberation about the good. As al-Baṣrī said: 'when God does not inform us that the act is corrupt, we are certain that it poses no corruption' (*matā lam yukhbirnā Allāh anna al-fiʿl mafsada, an naqṭaʿu ʿalā annahu laysa bi mafsada*).[143]

For example, al-Baṣrī said that reasonable people (*al-ʿuqalāʾ*) will castigate someone who refrains from an act because of the possibility of harm even though no indication (*bi lā imāra*) of any harm may exist. Yet they will excuse one who refrains from an act where there is such proof.

> Do you see them reprimanding one who stands by a wall that is not leaning over (*lā mayl fīhi*), because of the [mere] possibility it may fall ... but not faulting one [for doing so] when it actually does lean over? They do not reproach one who refrains from delicious food when an indicator (*imāra*) suggests it is poisoned. But they do censure him on rational grounds (*min jihat al-ʿaql*) when he refrains from it due to the mere possibility it may be poisoned.[144]

The point for al-Baṣrī is that notions like blame, good and bad are dependent on indicators of the good, the bad, and the harmful. Where there is no indicator, either God did not provide an indicator or He did but we cannot find it. If we adopt the latter conclusion, we potentially forgo a commitment to naturalistic reasoning and instead may be in a state of suspension about the law of God until we find

[143] Abū al-Ḥusayn al-Baṣrī, *al-Muʿtamad*, 2:316.
[144] Abū al-Ḥusayn al-Baṣrī, *al-Muʿtamad*, 2:317.

evidence.[145] If we accept the former, then we permit the naturalistic presumption to guide our behavior.

To emphasize further the link between his presumption and the authority of reason, al-Baṣrī challenged those who espoused a contrary presumption, namely the presumption of prohibition. This group, usually considered to be the Baghdād Muʿtazilites, argued that all of creation belongs to God. The benefits of creation, as well as one's efforts to take advantage of such benefits, involve utilizing the property of God. They argued that one is not allowed to utilize the property of another without the owner's permission (*taṣarrafa fī milk al-ghayr bi ghayr idhnihi*).[146] They extended this rule of property law to the case of naturalistic reasoning. Where God has not provided express permission to utilize the benefits of His property, one must refrain from doing so.[147] Al-Baṣrī responded that to analogize God's creation to human property relations is invalid. The *raison d'être* of property law is to ensure that the one most entitled to enjoy the benefits arising from a property claim can do so against all others absolutely (*annā aḥaqqu bi al-intifāʿ bihi min ghayrinā ʿalā al-iṭlāq*).[148] That is not the case with God. The significance of God being an 'owner' of things has to do with the fact that He has the power to bring things into being and to remove them from existence (*qādir ʿalā ījādihi wa ifnāʾihi*).[149] Furthermore, the prohibition against using someone else's property without his permission has less to do with the fact that someone else owns the property, and more to do with the fact that he may be injured by our use of his items. But God cannot be harmed by us:[150] 'Do you not notice that it is good for us to seek the shade under someone else's wall, or to look into his mirror... without his permission where that does not harm him?'[151] Likewise, since God suffers nothing from our use of the created world, we cannot consider all things to be presumptively prohibited. Instead, we look for

[145] Interestingly, the Voluntarist jurists addressed in the next chapter would suggest this very outcome.

[146] Abū al-Ḥusayn al-Baṣrī, *al-Muʿtamad*, 2:319.

[147] Abū al-Ḥusayn al-Baṣrī, *al-Muʿtamad*, 2:319.

[148] Abū al-Ḥusayn al-Baṣrī, *al-Muʿtamad*, 2:319.

[149] Abū al-Ḥusayn al-Baṣrī, *al-Muʿtamad*, 2:319.

[150] Abū al-Ḥusayn al-Baṣrī, *al-Muʿtamad*, 2:320.

[151] Abū al-Ḥusayn al-Baṣrī, *al-Muʿtamad*, 2:320.

evidence of prohibition. In the absence of such evidence, we rely on the presumption of permissibility to justify and legitimate our reasoned conclusions about the good to be pursued.

Al-Baṣrī's Paradigm of Naturalistic Reasoning

We may begin with a naturalistic presumption in legal analysis, but natural reason is not the only authority to consider. Rather, we may encounter evidence of a divine will that rebuts the presumption of permissibility. Al-Baṣrī's natural law theory brings together the authority of both reason and source-texts to develop a model of practical reasoning in which we move from a rationally based presumption of permissibility to a firm Sharīʿa obligation or prohibition. As a preliminary matter, before something can be a divine rule of law, it must be susceptible to being known, either through a rational or scripturally authorized proof. Not all matters can be known without reference to an authoritative scriptural proof. For example, al-Baṣrī acknowledged that we cannot know the requirement to fast the first day of Ramaḍān but not the days before that month begins without some explicit decree. 'If knowledge of [this] is not intuitive, then it is not possible for us to reach it except by a command that leads us to [such knowledge], whether through experience (*idrāk*), recurrent reports (*khabar mutawātir*), or an indicator (*dalīl*) that can be known.'[152] Consequently, al-Baṣrī readily recognized that naturalistic reasoning, while authoritative and legitimate, has its limits depending on the susceptibility of the underlying issue to reasoned deliberation.

According to al-Baṣrī, reason provides us with knowledge of the authenticity of scripture (*ṣiḥḥat al-sharʿ*), knowledge of God and His characteristics, and the fact that God does not perform evil acts (*lā yafʿalu al-qabīḥ*).[153]

We know the authority of scripture (*ṣiḥḥat al-sharʿ*) when we know the honesty of the prophets (*ṣidq al-anbiyāʾ*) ...We know their honesty by way of miracles when we know that it is not possible for God to place [miracles] in the hands of a liar (*ʿalā yadd kadhdhāb*). We know [God does not

[152] Abū al-Ḥusayn al-Baṣrī, *al-Muʿtamad*, 2:323.
[153] Abū al-Ḥusayn al-Baṣrī, *al-Muʿtamad*, 2:327.

> have liars perform miracles] when we know that having [liars] perform [miracles] is evil (*qabīḥ*) and that [God] does not do evil. We know that [God] does not perform evil when we know that God is aware of the corruptness of evil (*ʿālim bi qubḥ al-qabīḥ*) and that He is free from it. Knowledge of that is part of the knowledge [of God]. These first principles necessarily precede [one's acceptance of] the scripture. The nature of scripture does not provide a method to [arrive at] them.[154]

These presumptions operate as a starting point in al-Baṣrī's model of naturalistic reasoning, and therefore set the framework for the authority of both reason and source-texts as sources of Sharīʿa.

Certainly some Sharīʿa rules can be determined by either scripture or reason. Such matters include the knowledge that there is one God, the obligation to return another's deposit (*radd al-wadīʿa*), and that one can benefit from things that do not pose harm to anyone else.[155] But in other cases, scripture alone is a basis for certain kinds of rules. Examples of this category include all those acts by which we express our devotion to God in accordance with the Sharīʿa (*al-afʿāl allatī taʿabbadnā bi fiʿlihā aw tarkihā bi al-sharīʿa*), such as the obligatory prayers or avoiding the consumption of wine.[156] These sorts of obligations involve matters that reason has no capacity to address:

> If reason provided evidence of [them], then that evidence would be a rule rendering the matter obligatory (*ḥukm mūjib*), or a characteristic rendering it obligatory (*wajh mūjib*). A rule making something obligatory involves blame and praise (*al-dhamm wa al-madḥ*)...We do not know through reason whether one who delays fasting from the first day of Ramaḍān deserves blame as opposed to one who starts at [the beginning of the month]...It is also known that we do not know through reason whether these religious practices entail a benefit or ward off harm in the hereafter.[157]

For al-Baṣrī, natural reasoning about the good and the bad involves a series of principles and premises that contribute to a method of inquiry into the various indicators at one's disposal. At times, these indicators may be reason, where its authority is based on al-Baṣrī's fusion of fact and value in his presumption of permissibility. At

[154] Abū al-Ḥusayn al-Baṣrī, *al-Muʿtamad*, 2:327.
[155] Abū al-Ḥusayn al-Baṣrī, *al-Muʿtamad*, 2:327.
[156] Abū al-Ḥusayn al-Baṣrī, *al-Muʿtamad*, 2:328.
[157] Abū al-Ḥusayn al-Baṣrī, *al-Muʿtamad*, 2:328.

other times, the indicators are source-texts, whose authority is built upon a series of principled presumptions.

At the heart of al-Baṣrī's method of practical reasoning, though, is an inquiry into the mechanics of how one actually determines the Sharīʿa value of acts, utilizing naturalistic reasoning as a methodological starting point. To illustrate his method, al-Baṣrī wrote about the possibility that God might say to the Prophet or to scholars 'rule and whatever you decide is correct.' The question underlying this proposition is whether correctness is a function of the individual's voluntaristic and even radical choice (*ikhtiyār*) or something else. Some held that the Prophet Muḥammad was the only one who could exercise this type of authority. Others granted the possibility to both Muḥammad and the religious scholars (*ʿulamāʾ*). However, al-Baṣrī noted that most jurists deny both possibilities. People may not always choose the good, and instead may engage in an act of corruption (*qad yakhtāru al-fasād*).[158] Consequently, 'if God most high permitted one to rule by reference to his choice (*al-ḥukm bi mā yakhtāruhu*), [this would entail the possibility] of permitting a ruling that involves a corrupt matter.'[159] Even if God were to state that one's choice will always be right and correct (*al-ḥaqq wa al-ṣawāb*), that would not matter, according to al-Baṣrī. He argued that one cannot consistently select the good (*al-ṣalāḥ*) over the corrupt without knowing the essence of the good *and* the corrupt (*aʿyān al-ṣalāḥ wa al-fasād*).[160] These qualities are not subjective, but rather are objective aspects of reality that must be rationally understood to ensure a methodologically sound ruling is made. Furthermore, if one asserts that the scholars are correct by virtue of their choice, and not by virtue of some external methodological standard, one must also accept by extension that lay persons and not just jurists are correct in their opinions on Sharīʿa values. Al-Baṣrī argued that if rightness is a function of choice and not external standards of analysis, there is no reason to limit the delegation of legal authority only to the scholars.[161]

[158] Abū al-Ḥusayn al-Baṣrī, *al-Muʿtamad*, 2:329.
[159] Abū al-Ḥusayn al-Baṣrī, *al-Muʿtamad*, 2:329.
[160] Abū al-Ḥusayn al-Baṣrī, *al-Muʿtamad*, 2:330.
[161] Abū al-Ḥusayn al-Baṣrī, *al-Muʿtamad*, 2:330.

To establish an obligation, one must first know the good before acting upon it (*an yakūna al-mukallaf ʿālim bi ḥusn mā yaqdumu ʿalayhi min al-afʿāl qabla iqdāmihi*).[162] This knowledge of the good can only be known prior to any choice that the individual makes, thus rendering the method of knowing to be of paramount importance. The goodness of an act is not a consequence of choice, but rather is a *maṣlaḥa* or perceived good that is given effect through choice (*huwa maṣlaḥa fī nafsihi bi al-ikhtiyār*).[163] We determine the *maṣlaḥa* by reference to various indicators (*mā ẓanannāhu min al-imāra*), which speak to the overall goodness of an act.[164]

To investigate a matter and thereby make a decision about obligation and prohibition requires certain presumptions before one even begins to think about authoritative sources. According to al-Baṣrī, we must assume certain first principles to participate in his natural law model of legal analysis:[165]

> The character of the Obligor, by which one can investigate into the rules of obligation, consists of the fact that He is knowledgable of the badness of evil and the obligatoriness of obligation, that [God] knows He is free from engaging in any evil act or omitting any obligatory deed. When the investigator knows that, he knows that it is not possible that [God] would not inform us of our benefits and harms (*maṣāliḥanā wa mafāsidanā*).[166]

In other words, any inquiry proceeds on the presumption that the necessary evidence we need to establish an obligation exists for us to evaluate.

To make a determination of the rule of obligation, the jurist utilizes his naturalistic reasoning to determine what the proper rule is for the given situation. This is possible as a first step because of al-Baṣrī's naturalistic presumption: nature embodies the fusion of fact and value, given God's desire to benefit humanity through His creation. Subsequently, one inquires into whether the rationally based rule might change on the basis of scriptural proofs. 'If he does not find [in scripture] anything that changes [the rule] from the rationally based

[162] Abū al-Ḥusayn al-Baṣrī, *al-Muʿtamad*, 2:330.
[163] Abū al-Ḥusayn al-Baṣrī, *al-Muʿtamad*, 2:330.
[164] Abū al-Ḥusayn al-Baṣrī, *al-Muʿtamad*, 2:332–3.
[165] Abū al-Ḥusayn al-Baṣrī, *al-Muʿtamad*, 2:342
[166] Abū al-Ḥusayn al-Baṣrī, *al-Muʿtamad*, 2:343.

rule, then he decides in accordance with [the latter].'[167] But if he finds a source-text that rebuts or alters the rationally based rule, he must rule according to the source-text. 'Reason decides those rules on condition that a scriptural proof does not alter [our decision] on [them]' (*li anna al-ʿuqūl innamā dallat ʿalā tilka al-aḥkām bi sharṭ an lā yanqulunā ʿanhu dalīl sharʿī*).[168]

Naturalistic reason, therefore, is the initial mechanism by which Sharīʿa values are determined. It can justifiably be the basis for these rules because of the naturalistic presumption al-Baṣrī made about creation, reason and the benefit of an act. By fusing fact and value in the created world, al-Baṣrī articulated a theory of natural law that is tied to God's purposeful creation while restrained by the existence of source-texts.

Conclusion

The Mālikite-Ashʿarite jurist Shihāb al-Dīn al-Qarāfī (d. 684/1285) attacked the legacy of Muʿtazilite scholarship, which considered reason as a basis for establishing obligation. In doing so, however, he also criticized his Ashʿarite brethren for unfairly characterizing what we have called here Hard Natural Law. Many Ashʿarite authors, as will be seen below, believed that Hard Natural Law authorizes one to create Sharīʿa rules using only *ʿaql* (reason). For the Ashʿarites, it was as if the Hard Naturalists said that reason alone can establish obligation without any reference or regard to the divine will. But al-Qarāfī was quick to point out that this was not an accurate representation. The Hard Naturalists argued, according to al-Qarāfī, that God, through His clear wisdom, obligates people to avoid corruption and to achieve benefits. It is through reason that one knows what God obligates and prohibits; the Hard Naturalists did not simply state that one's reason alone obligates and prohibits. Rather the fundamental question is whether reason can make assessments of God's unexpressed will. According to al-Qarāfī, reason alone knows that God can obligate or prohibit, but this does not imply that one can assess

[167] Abū al-Ḥusayn al-Baṣrī, *al-Muʿtamad*, 2:343.
[168] Abū al-Ḥusayn al-Baṣrī, *al-Muʿtamad*, 2:343.

through reason that God has *in fact* established a specific obligation or prohibition despite the absence of any express indicator. According to al-Qarāfī, the Hard Naturalists argued that the ability to know the actual substance of God's obligations and prohibitions is of the same nature as knowing God to be knowledgeable, powerful, and perfect. In the same way that one rationally knows these latter characteristics of God, one also knows that God seeks the preservation of the good (*maṣlaḥa*). By investigating the good, the Hard Naturalists held that one can thereby associate rationally determined notions of the good and the bad with obligations and prohibitions stemming from the divine will. Consequently, the Hard Naturalists did not authorize radical choice or idiosyncratic reasoning to legislate Sharīʿa rules. They did not hold that reason alone can obligate without any connection to the divine.[169]

Al-Qarāfī's analysis illustrates his keen awareness of the Hard Naturalists' project. Hard Naturalists recognized that sometimes source-texts might not provide guidance on a certain matter. By rooting their inquiry into obligations in a theology of a just God and a concept of nature in which fact and value are fused, Hard Naturalists opened the door to reasoned deliberation in a way that philosophically limited the scope of one's subjectivity, and tied reasoned conclusions to the divine will. The Sharīʿa value of acts can be known through both source-texts and reason. But reason requires philosophical justification before it can be considered an authoritative source of law. To do this, the Hard Naturalists argued that all of creation was created by God for humanity's benefit, thereby uniting both fact and value in the created world. In other words, the empirical facts of nature and creation are the objects of analysis. They are the raw data to which reason is applied and by which reason is restrained. Because God is just, He creates nature to benefit humanity. Therefore to know God's will in cases where there is no source-text, we must take heed of the implications of the goodness of God's creation on how we should act and order our affairs. Nature becomes the objective basis for investigation and embodies a normative content that justifies the authority of reasoned deliberation in Sharīʿa.

[169] Al-Qarāfī, *Nafāʾis al-Uṣūl*, 1:140.

III

The Voluntarist Critique of Hard Natural Law

Those opposed to Hard Natural Law considered Sharīʿa values to be products of a Voluntarist divine will. These Voluntarist jurists, who we will learn generally adopted what we shall call Soft Natural Law, argued that without a scriptural basis (*sharʿ*) there can be no Sharīʿa valuation or divine obligation. For them, obligation implies punishment and reward, praise and blame—all of which are the products of God's express will. Certainly they admitted that human reason can make evaluative judgments, but such judgments are norms whose authority is limited by the contingencies and fallibilities of the jurist. To suggest such judgments reflect a divine intent is tantamount to holding God hostage to human reasoning, which would undermine the Voluntarists' theological commitment to God's omnipotence. To know whether an obligation arises from God's will, one must rely on express statements of the divine will to ensure that they are truly from God and not based on the idiosyncrasies of human reason.

The Voluntarists' argument against Hard Natural Law arose within a larger theological debate about the justice of God, the types of knowledge that exist, and the significance of the concepts *ḥusn* and *qubḥ* in a typology of knowledge. For many Voluntarists, *ḥusn* and *qubḥ* capture notions of good and bad that humans can determine by reference to reason. But the terms cannot connote divine obligations. Determining that a certain act is good or bad does not signify that one is thereby obligated to do that act or prohibited from doing it, with the consequence of divine sanction or praise. Voluntarist jurists thereby distinguished between moral norms and divine obligations, and held that the former did not lead to Sharīʿa legal values. It may be natural for humans to make moral inquiries and even order their affairs by their derived norms. But those moral norms are not tantamount to Sharīʿa obligations based on the authority of God's will.

Theologically, Voluntarists were unwilling to accept the Hard Naturalist theological principle that God only acts purposefully and only for the good. They viewed this principle as a fundamental restraint on God's omnipotence. As a philosophical implication of their theology, Voluntarist jurists refused to accept the fusion of fact and value in nature. Voluntarists argued that nature by itself is neither an objective nor a normative basis for a theory of obligation. Arguments from nature are not dispositive since we are not in a sufficiently strong epistemic position to know with certainty whether and how nature benefits humanity. In fact, it is possible that a certain act may cause harm and pose no benefit, thereby challenging the Hard Naturalist thesis altogether.

The Voluntarists' repudiation of Hard Natural Law, however, does not mean that they had no need to theorize about nature and its use as a foundation for juristic discretion. To the extent that they had to account for the authority of legal reasoning in cases where source-texts do not provide a resolution, we will see how they nonetheless resorted to a theory of nature to ground the authority of legal reasoning. As will be shown in the next chapter, Voluntarist jurists adopted their own version of natural law (Soft Natural Law) built upon a divine command theory. Ironically, they recognized the fusion of fact and value in nature. But for them, the fusion was *de facto*, being a result of God's grace (*faḍl, tafaḍḍul*), which is presumably subject to change if God chooses. By approaching the debate on *ḥusn* and *qubḥ* from the perspective of legal philosophy, this study both builds upon prior scholarship on voluntarism and ethical rationalism, and suggests that adopting the lens of legal philosophy can illustrate how such theological commitments lose some poignancy once we enter the realm of law.

Toward a Theory of Knowledge

To challenge the Hard Naturalist theory on nature and the authority of reason, Voluntarists first addressed (a) what constitutes knowledge, and (b) the capacity of unaided reason to assert true propositions of knowledge. The early Ashʿarite theologian Abū Bakr al-Bāqillānī (d. 403/1012) argued that there are two types of knowledge about Sharīʿa that concern authority and reason. The first is knowledge of the legal rules that designate acts as prohibited, permitted, obligated, or recommended.[1] The authority of the rules depends on the existing evidence of the divine will, and not on pure reason. Reason may play an epistemic role in sifting through evidence; but it offers no authoritative foundation for such rules. The second is innate knowledge that arises intuitively (for example through pure reason) in the individual (*ʿulūm al-ḍarūra al-mubtadiʾa fi al-nafs al-ʿilm*); but this knowledge has no authority to judge an act as obligatory or permissible. Such judgments are known only by reference to source-texts, but not by reason (*maʿlūm bi qaḍiyyat al-samʿ dūn al-ʿaql*).[2] At most, reason plays an epistemic role as a tool for understanding and evaluating authoritative source-texts. But by itself, pure reason is not an authoritative source for judging whether an act is obligatory or prohibited. Reference must be made to independent indicators of the divine will, such as scripture or other sources.

The Andalusian jurist Ibn Ḥazm (d. 456/1063) adopted a similar view. Despite being considered a staunch literalist, given his affiliation with the Ẓāhirī *madhhab*,[3] he recognized that reason can be an authoritative source for asserting propositions of knowledge. He denied that reasoned analysis is idiosyncratic or tantamount to mere taste or whimsy, which changes from day to day.[4] Certainly he conceded that reasoned conclusions are subject to change. But that does not detract from their normative authority. The point of any rational analysis is not to arrive at the undeniable truth. Rather reason allows us to participate in a process of analysis that is upright and methodologically systematic, moving from first principles (*awāʾil al-maʿārif*) to an authoritative legal ruling.[5]

[1] Abū Bakr Muḥammad b. al-Ṭayyib al-Bāqillānī, *al-Taqrīb wa al-Irshād al-Ṣaghīr*, ʿAbd al-Ḥamīd b. ʿAlī Abū Zunayd (ed) (Beirut: Muʾassasat al-Risāla, 1998) 1:171.

[2] Al-Bāqillānī, *al-Taqrīb wa al-Irshād*, 1:193.

[3] R Arnaldez, *EI2*, s.v. 'Ibn Ḥazm.'

[4] Abū Muḥammad ʿAlī Ibn Ḥazm, *al-Iḥkām fī Uṣūl al-Aḥkām* (Cairo: Dār al-Ḥadīth, 1984) 1:17.

[5] Ibn Ḥazm, *al-Iḥkām fī Uṣūl al-Aḥkām*, 1:17–18.

This is not to suggest, though, that Ibn Ḥazm upheld the authority of reason as a basis for Sharīʿa judgments on obligation and prohibition. For him, reason is an *epistemic tool* of investigation; it is not a foundation for obligation (*taklīf*). It can be used to describe reality in its empirical existence and assert first principles, but cannot justify specific obligations. Specifically, he stated:

> We have explained the reality of reason (*ḥaqīqat al-ʿaql*) as a [tool] of distinguishing (*tamyīz*) among things known by the senses and contemplation (*ḥawāss, fahm*), and for knowing the characteristics of things that, in accordance with those characteristics, arise . . . from the creation of the world, such as the fact that the creator is unitary and everlasting, that authority of prophecy lies with those who uphold the evidence of their prophecy, that [one is] obligated to obey [God] who promises hellfire upon disobedience, and that [one acts] by what reason considers correct [in light of the above] (*al-ʿamal bi mā ṣaḥḥahahu al-ʿaql min dhālik kullihi*) and all that is in the world beyond what is in the revealed laws (*sharāʾiʿ*). However, [reason] only concerns itself with describing all of that. As for reason establishing obligations such as pigs being prohibited or lawful, goats being prohibited or lawful, *ẓuhr* prayer being four [prostrations] and *maghrib* prayer being three [prostrations] . . . [these] are not matters for which reason can establish obligation or prohibition.[6]

For Ibn Ḥazm, reason is a tool of discernment, description, and understanding, but not a basis for making Sharīʿā judgments. It can empirically describe the genus of things, but it cannot impute to them a normative value on the authority of God. God commands and prohibits, and He does so as He wishes. Reason allows us to understand that fact, and to act in accordance with existing indicators that express God's will.[7] A Hard Naturalist such as al-Baṣrī,

[6] Ibn Ḥazm, *al-Iḥkām fī Uṣūl al-Aḥkām*, 1:31.

[7] Ibn Ḥazm, *al-Iḥkām fī Uṣūl al-Aḥkām*, 1:31. Ibn Ḥazm's contemporary, the Mālikī Abū al-Walīd al-Bājī (d. 474/1081), also argued that reason cannot obligate or prohibit. If reason could do so, then it would either be by necessity of reason (*ḍarūrat al-ʿaql*) or proof of reason (*dalīl al-ʿaql*). As there is no agreement on reason's ability to obligate, then the argument by necessity of reason fails. In other words, if it were necessarily so that reason could obligate, there would be no disagreement. As there is disagreement, the argument by necessity fails. Furthermore, if the argument rests on the proof value of reason, al-Bājī argued that Muʿtazilites present no rational proof for the obligation to thank the benefactor or the prohibition against oppression. Rather they claim these are known by necessity of reason, which al-Bājī has already shown does not exist. Abū al-Walīd al-Bājī, *Iḥkām al-Fuṣūl fī Aḥkām al-Uṣūl*, ʿAbd al-Majīd Turkī (ed) (2nd edn,

though, would agree with Ibn Ḥazm that reason cannot judge certain things as lawful or prohibited, such as the number of prostrations in the noon and sunset prayers. Consequently, we can criticize Ibn Ḥazm for using these extreme examples to make a principally polemical argument. Nonetheless his polemic reflects an important Voluntarist thesis, namely that reason operates epistemically as a tool of analysis, and cannot be an authoritative source for Sharīʿa.

The Shāfiʿite-Ashʿarite jurist Abū Ḥāmid al-Ghazālī (d. 505/1111) offered a more involved theory of knowledge in which pure reason is a source of certain forms of knowledge, but has no authority to assert Sharīʿa obligations. According to al-Ghazālī, there are three categories of knowledge. First are those things that are known by pure reason without reference to tradition or transmitted texts, such as mathematics and astronomy.[8] The second category refers to things known only by reference to transmitted source-texts. And lastly, are things known through a combined usage of both reason and scripture, such as legal doctrines (*fiqh*) and legal theory (*uṣūl al-fiqh*). According to al-Ghazālī, this third category is the most noble form of knowledge (*ashraf al-ʿulūm*).[9] In this last category, the truthfulness of Muḥammad's claim to prophecy is a rationally based assertion. But once this rational presumption is accepted, Sharīʿa-knowledge is based on Muḥammad's transmitted tradition, especially regarding those matters on which reason cannot actually provide guidance. Reason cannot independently provide insight into the nature of obedience (*kawn al-ṭāʿa*) as a cause (*sabab*) of success in the hereafter, or the nature of disobedience (*kawn al-maʿāṣī*) as a cause of misfortune.[10]

Beirut: Dār al-Gharb al-Islāmī, 1995) 2:687. Another jurist, the Ḥanafī-turned-Shāfiʿī Abū al-Muẓaffar al-Samʿānī (d. 489/1096), also held that reason cannot create obligations. Like Ibn Ḥazm, al-Samʿānī argued that, despite some Shāfiʿī jurists to the contrary, the Shāfiʿīs generally believed that reason is a tool of understanding (*ālat al-maʿārif*) and a mechanism by which one understands the reality of creation, but is not the means by which normative obligations are established. Abū al-Muẓaffar Manṣūr b. Muḥammad b. ʿAbd al-Jabbār al-Samʿānī, *Qawāṭiʿ al-Adilla fī al-Uṣūl*, Muḥammad Ḥasan Muḥammad Ḥasan Ismāʿīl al-Shāfiʿī (ed) (Beirut: Dār al-Kutub al-ʿIlmiyya, 1997) 1:22, 2:45–6.

[8] Abū Ḥāmid Muḥmmad b. Muḥammad al-Ghazālī, *al-Mustasfā min ʿIlm al-Uṣūl*, Ibrāhīm Muḥammad Ramaḍān (ed) (Beirut: Dār al-Arqam, n.d.) 1:11.

[9] Abū Ḥāmid al-Ghazālī, *al-Mustasfā*, 1:11–12.

[10] Abū Ḥāmid al-Ghazālī, *al-Mustasfā*, 1:19.

In other words, reason allows us to recognize the principle of Muḥammad's authority as a prophet, but it cannot determine the contours and details of what constitutes religious worship and commitment, such as prayer and fasting. In a sense, these three categories represent different epistemological modes of knowing things, whether as objects of inquiry or truth claims. But the fundamental question is whether and how one can know such things with certainty, and how the answer to that question will affect the nature of law.

For al-Ghazālī, an important mode for investigating truth claims is the syllogism. Made up of terms and premises, the *ʿilm* or truth of a syllogism will depend on whether we can trust the truth of the syllogism's component parts and the way in which they relate to each other.[11] For example, suppose someone says Zayd is a scholar. The terms 'Zayd' and 'scholar' must, as a preliminary matter, be known and understood before the truth of the proposition can be asserted. For al-Ghazālī, the preliminary understanding of the terms is called *maʿrifa*. *Taṣdīq* is his term that captures the process of judging or verifying the proposition as true, while *ʿilm* refers to the knowledge generated by a true proposition.[12] Put differently, the knowledge of *maʿrifa* constitutes the major and minor premises of a syllogism, the conclusion of which constitutes *ʿilm* through the medium of a rational, syllogistic proof, whose structure permits us carefully to verify the truth of the asserted conclusion.[13]

Importantly, by understanding the centrality of the syllogism to al-Ghazālī's theory of knowledge, we can better comprehend why he rejected reason as having any ontological authority as a source of Sharīʿa obligations. The certainty (*yaqīn*) that must inhere in the premises of a syllogism necessarily contributes to the ultimate truth value of the conclusion derived therefrom. The more we are confident that the premises reflect a certainty about the world, the more we can be confident of the truth value of any conclusions drawn therefrom. The questions this begs for al-Ghazālī concern the degree of confidence we must have in the truth of the premise to found a Sharīʿa judgment

[11] Abū Ḥāmid al-Ghazālī, *al-Mustasfā*, 1:31.
[12] Abū Ḥāmid al-Ghazālī, *al-Mustasfā*, 1:30–2.
[13] Abū Ḥāmid al-Ghazālī, *al-Mustasfā*, 1:33, 44–6.

authoritatively, and whether reasoned deliberation has the authority to offer substantive and justificatory content to the judgment.

For al-Ghazālī, the certainty of the premises depends on the nature of the knowledge underlying them. The following are al-Ghazālī's categories of knowledge and their implications for the certainty they can provide to premises:

- First principles (*al-awliyāt*), such as knowing the existence of a person, or the principle of non-contradiction.[14]
- Inner senses of the person (*al-mushāhidāt al-bāṭina*) that detect hunger, thirst, and fear.[15]
- Sensory perceptions (*al-maḥsūsāt al-ẓāhira*), or the kind of knowledge that arises from the five human senses of sight, hearing, taste, touch, and smell.[16]
- Experiential knowledge or *al-ʿādāt*, such as knowledge that fire burns and wine intoxicates.[17]
- Knowledge that is based on recurrent transmission and dissemination (*mutawātirāt*), such as the knowledge that there is a city called Mecca, or that there was a jurist named Muḥammad b. Idrīs al-Shāfiʿī (d. 204/820).[18]
- Knowledge that necessarily follows from a thing's existence. This category, called *al-wahmiyyāt*, refers to those things that are necessary consequences of knowledge based on sensory perceptions.[19]
- Popular knowledge (*al-mashhūrāt*) that we rely upon for reasons too innumerable to estimate. For instance, the evil of lying and ingratitude toward one's benefactor, as well as the goodness of thanking the benefactor are all things that are widely known through one's upbringing and education.[20]

This typology of premises provides al-Ghazālī with a basis for critiquing the premises that contribute to the production of knowledge.

[14] Abū Ḥāmid al-Ghazālī, *al-Mustasfā*, 1:107.
[15] Abū Ḥāmid al-Ghazālī, *al-Mustasfā*, 1:108.
[16] Abū Ḥāmid al-Ghazālī, *al-Mustasfā*, 1:109.
[17] Abū Ḥāmid al-Ghazālī, *al-Mustasfā*, 1:109.
[18] Abū Ḥāmid al-Ghazālī, *al-Mustasfā*, 1:112.
[19] Abū Ḥāmid al-Ghazālī, *al-Mustasfā*, 1:113.
[20] Abū Ḥāmid al-Ghazālī, *al-Mustasfā*, 1:116–18.

He is well aware that the authority of a syllogism's conclusion depends on the certainty of the major and minor premises. Consequently, the seven different sources of knowledge for the premises provide insights into the veracity of a premise and its capacity to contribute to a true proposition or *ʿilm*.

The last type of knowledge, popular knowledge or *al-mashhūrāt*, is most significant for the purpose of this study. The examples al-Ghazālī provided of this type of knowledge are the same ones that Hard Naturalists considered objectively determinable via reason as either good or bad, and hence capable of legitimating Sharīʿa obligations and prohibitions. Hard Naturalists used these specific examples to express and illustrate their model of natural law. But for al-Ghazālī, *mashhūrāt*-based knowledge is a problematic basis by which to make Sharīʿa judgments.[21]

According to al-Ghazālī, many theologians and jurists grant propositions based on *mashhūrāt* knowledge normative authority. In doing so, they contribute to the vast contradictions (*natāʾij mutanāqiḍa*) that exist in the law.[22] But for al-Ghazālī, such determinations of good and bad are psychologically driven by one's conditioning, and reflect nothing objectively true about the world. We cannot escape our socialization; and that socialization contributes to how we decide whether something is good or bad in the world.[23] Al-Ghazālī contended that this understanding of good and bad cannot necessarily lead to true knowledge in any absolute sense. Rather the truth of such conclusions is contingent on the context of the person asserting such truth claims. Unless we can investigate our social context and deconstruct it for its component parts, we will not be able to distinguish truth from falsehood in our beliefs. At most, such knowledge can contribute to probabilistic determinations (*al-fiqhiyyāt al-ẓanniyya*) and disputed rules of precedent (*al-aqīsa al-jadaliyya*), but not to certainty of any sort.[24] One cannot

[21] Abū Ḥāmid al-Ghazālī, *al-Mustasfā*, 1:116.
[22] Abū Ḥāmid al-Ghazālī, *al-Mustasfā*, 1:117.
[23] Abū Ḥāmid al-Ghazālī, *al-Mustasfā*, 1:116–18.
[24] Abū Ḥāmid al-Ghazālī, *al-Mustasfā*, 1:118. Al-Ghazālī seems to allow this type of knowledge to inform legal analysis. But as shown in Chapter IV, he does not require certitude of the truth of a matter in order to render a legal norm authoritative.

presume such conclusions are true because of the contingency of any claim about the good and the bad.

For al-Ghazālī, therefore, true knowledge (*ʿilm*) is a complex matter involving the construction of true and clear premises, and conclusive syllogistic proofs. Clearly reason and speculative inquiries have a role to play, but as can be seen in the above discussion, that role is defined in terms of the kind of certainty (or lack thereof) that inheres in our accepted premises. Importantly, al-Ghazālī considered *ḥusn* and *qubḥ* to reflect at most probabilistic or contextually conditioned truth claims.

The 5th–6th/11th–12th century Ḥanbalī jurist Ibn ʿAqīl (d. 513/1119) also addressed the nature of knowledge. Ibn ʿAqīl seemed to have certain intellectual battles that he was waging by writing his book on *uṣūl al-fiqh*. He was well versed in aspects of speculative theology, including Muʿtazilite views. His biography shows that he studied Muʿtazilite theology, even to the chagrin of and persecution by members of his own legal guild.[25] This is especially important when we consider that he wrote his work on *uṣūl al-fiqh* in light of other works of speculative theology and *uṣūl al-fiqh*, in particular Qāḍī ʿAbd al-Jabbār's *al-Mughnī*, discussed above. Framing Ibn ʿAqīl's legal theory in light of his complex intellectual journey is not meant to undermine his historic link to the Ḥanbalī school of law or his inclusion among Ashʿarite theologians. However, his biography illustrates a kind of intellectual depth and curiosity that suggests that, akin to al-Jaṣṣāṣ, his intellectual engagements may cross borders of thought and ideas that may be worthwhile to pursue from different perspectives, while remaining mindful of his affiliation to historical schools of thought.

Ibn ʿAqil constructed his theory of knowledge against the backdrop of Hard Natural Law.[26] For him, knowledge of the law (*ʿilm al-aḥkām al-sharʿiyya*) does not involve simply describing the world empirically.[27] Legal knowledge has a normative authority that lies

[25] For a biography of Ibn ʿAqīl, see George Makdisi, *Ibn ʿAqīl: Religion and Culture in Classical Islam* (Edinburgh: Edinburgh University Press, 1997).

[26] Makdisi, *Ibn ʿAqīl*, 77.

[27] Abū al-Wafāʾ ʿAlī b. ʿAqīl b. Muḥammad b. ʿAqīl al-Ḥanbalī, *al-Wāḍiḥ fī Uṣūl al-Fiqh*, George Makdisi (ed) (Beirut: Franz Steiner, 1996) 1:3.

outside the scope of what reasoned deliberation can offer. Reason is an epistemic tool used to investigate creation for its indicators of the divine will. Reason's function is purely epistemic.

Certainly investigating the empirical world may provide insights into the divine will. But reason does not provide the bridge to move from the empirical to the normative, from the 'is' to the 'ought'. We can know about the empirical world through our five senses and the process of investigative experiment, according to Ibn ʿAqīl.[28] These approaches lead to empirical knowledge concerning the existence of opposites: the sense of touch distinguishes between the soft and the coarse; the sense of taste differentiates between the sweet and the sour. The senses provide a type of experiential knowledge tied to the circumstances of a situation. The senses and investigation enable us to reach definitive truths about the world through inductive approaches of experimentation and analysis.[29]

But who or what provides normative authority for varying propositions of the empirical world? Although Ibn ʿAqīl granted that we could acquire knowledge of the world through various methods, he did not agree that any consequent normative authority is produced by or is a natural consequence of these methods (*ghayr mutawallada*).[30] In other words, he was unwilling to fuse fact and value. The normative value of any truth proposition arises purely out of the creative will of God. The methods of knowing the empirical world may involve the use of reason, but the normative content that arises therefrom is based on the authority of God's will.[31] In other words, while reason is an epistemic tool of investigation, any normative implication of its findings stems separately from God's will.

Ibn ʿAqīl's argument about knowledge was formulated in light of his critique of what he called the Ahl al-Ṭabʿ, or the People of Natural Dispositions. Adherents of this group argued that the individual is the fount of any normative authority associated with the knowledge he acquires.[32] For the Ahl al-Ṭabʿ, humans create

[28] Ibn ʿAqīl, *al-Wāḍiḥ fī Uṣūl al-Fiqh*, 1:8.
[29] Ibn ʿAqīl, *al-Wāḍīḥ fī Uṣūl al-Fiqh*, 1:8–9.
[30] Ibn ʿAqīl, *al-Wāḍīḥ fī Uṣūl al-Fiqh*, 1:9.
[31] Ibn ʿAqīl, *al-Wāḍīḥ fī Uṣūl al-Fiqh*, 1:9.
[32] Ibn ʿAqīl, *al-Wāḍīḥ fī Uṣūl al-Fiqh*, 1:9.

normative knowledge in light of their own natural dispositions.[33] For Ibn ʿAqīl, both reason and scripture deny the validity of this approach (*qāma bi fasādihi dalīlu al-ʿaql wa kadhdhabahu al-sharʿ*).[34] To adopt the view of the Ahl al-Ṭabʿ is tantamount to suggesting that someone other than God is a creative force in the world or is a partner with God in acts of creation and judgment.[35] Certainly people have experiential knowledge; but their experience has no ontological normative authority to order human affairs.[36]

Notably, Ibn ʿAqīl acknowledged that because of God's creative will, our experiences, conclusions, and reasoned deliberations have a type of authority. Indeed, he could not preclude the possibility that we would use our reason to order our affairs. As such, he acknowledged reason's authority while upholding God's omnipotence. To do so, he held that reason's authority emanates from God, and not from us in any way whatsoever. Reasoned deliberation embodies a normative authority; but it is a normative authority that is contingent on the fact that God created it. All of creation comes from God (*ḥāṣīla min Allāh fiʿl*); thereby, the knowledge that humanity acquires is the consequence of various epistemic methods (*ʿaqīb wujūd al-ṭurūq*) of investigation.[37] Humans have an epistemic ability to comprehend the world of experience, but they have no inherent ontological authority to create Sharīʿa norms of behavior. If reasoned deliberation is an authority, that is because it is actually based on God's creative will. In this sense, any authority we grant to conclusions of reasoned deliberation is derivative of God's authority over and in creation.

In some sense, Ibn ʿAqīl's approach to natural reason echoes Lisska's comment on Aquinas, namely that 'God as the "necessary being" accounts for why there is something rather than nothing. God provides the existence to the temporal essence whose structure

[33] Ibn ʿAqīl, *al-Wāḍīḥ fī Uṣūl al-Fiqh*, 1:9.
[34] Ibn ʿAqīl, *al-Wāḍīḥ fī Uṣūl al-Fiqh*, 1:9.
[35] Ibn ʿAqīl, *al-Wāḍīḥ fī Uṣūl al-Fiqh*, 1:9.
[36] Ibn ʿAqīl, *al-Wāḍīḥ fī Uṣūl al-Fiqh*, 1:9.
[37] Ibn ʿAqīl, *al-Wāḍīḥ fī Uṣūl al-Fiqh*, 1:9.

is contingent.'[38] In this fashion, Ibn ʿAqīl renders God's purposive power sufficiently distant from the actual act of natural reasoning so as to survive any theological implications that arise from granting natural reasoning ontological authority.

For all the authors noted above, their theories of knowledge were arguably used to understand the role of reason in reaching an understanding of the world and ascribing normative value to reasoned findings. All of them recognized and grappled with the inevitability of rational inquiry. Many of them relegated reason to the role of epistemological tool. Others like al-Ghazālī erected a complex system of knowledge where reason contributes to the values and ideals that one holds. Generally, though, Voluntarist jurists argued against the authority of reason to make Sharīʿa judgments. For many of them, reason operates within a structure of cultural and other normative imperatives. It is one thing to adhere to general norms of culture or morality, but quite another to use reason to assert the existence of obligations with the threat of divine sanction.

Ḥusn and *Qubḥ*: Moral Agency Amidst Fallibility

As noted earlier, Hard Naturalists argued that one can move from a descriptive evaluation of benefits and harms to Sharīʿa obligations and prohibitions, given the fusion of fact and value in nature. The resort to nature offers a degree of determinacy and objectivity by focusing one's inquiry on the empirical qualities of the natural order. By doing so, Hard Naturalists thereby distinguished rational naturalistic reasoning from purely idiosyncratic whimsy. Nature also provides a normative foundation given a theology of divine justice and purposeful creation. Voluntarists, on the other hand, rejected the theological premises of Hard Natural Law. They denied that acts have a naturalistically grounded objective determinacy that has a normative foundation in God's will.[39]

[38] Anthony J Lisska, *Aquinas's Theory of Natural Law: An Analytic Reconstruction* (Oxford: Clarendon Press, 1996) 130.

[39] See, eg, al-Bāqillānī (d. 403/1013), *al-Taqrīb wa al-Irshād*, 1:278; Abū Bakr Muḥammad b. Aḥmad b. Abī Sahl al-Sarakhsī, *al-Muḥarrar fī Uṣūl al-Fiqh*, Abū ʿAbd al-Raḥmān Ṣalāḥ b. Muḥammad b. ʿArīḍa (ed) (Beirut: Dār al-Kutub al-ʿIlmiyya, 1996)

The Voluntarist al-Bāqillānī argued that we can rationally know the good (*ḥusn al-fiʿl*) or the bad (*qubḥ*) of an act only in a general and abstract fashion. We can deem something bad, for example, on the basis of what our dispositions consider distasteful (*tanfuru ʿanhu al-nufūs*).[40] Or we can know without reference to scripture the goodness of the believer striking the unbeliever and the badness of the unbeliever striking the believer. But if we imply by *ḥusn* and *qubḥ* the existence of sanctions for a coercive legal order—such as praise (*madḥ*), blame (*dhamm*), reward (*thawāb*), or punishment (*ʿiqāb*)—reason cannot make such determinations.[41] Reason can identify moral content, but has no authority to transform general moral values into Sharīʿa obligations with the threat of divinely ordained sanctions in this world and the hereafter. Without reference to source-texts, one cannot assert obligations that are attributed to God and have the consequence of reward or punishment in the hereafter.[42]

1:42; al-Samʿānī (d. 489/1096), *Qawāṭiʿ al-Adilla fi al-Uṣūl*, 1:22; al-Ghazālī (d. 505/1111), *al-Mustasfā*, 1:23; Sayf al-Dīn Abū al-Ḥasan ʿAlī b. Abī ʿAlī b. Muḥammad al-Āmidī (d. 631/1233), *al-Iḥkām fī Uṣūl al-Aḥkām* (Beirut: Dār al-Fikr, 1997) 1:60–1; Shihāb al-Dīn Abū al-ʿAbbās Aḥmad b. Idrīs b. ʿAbd al-Raḥmān Al-Qarāfī, *Nafāʾis al-Uṣūl fī Sharḥ al-Maḥṣūl*, Muḥammad ʿAbd al-Qādir ʿAṭā (ed) (Beirut: Dār al-Kutub al-ʿIlmiyya, 2000) 1:141; Muḥammad Fayḍ al-Ḥasan al-Kankūhī, *ʿUmdat al-Ḥawāshī*, in the margins of *Uṣūl al-Shāshī*, by Abū ʿAlī al-Shāshī (Beirut: Dār al-Kitāb al-ʿArabī, 1982) 143. Ibn Rushd (Averroes) (d. 595/1198) noted that the *ahl al-sunna* argued that rules of law are dependent on scriptural discourses (*khiṭāb al-Sharʿ*), and not on the existence of some metaphysical *wasf* of an act's goodness or badness. This is contrary, he wrote, to the Muʿtazilites who did so hold. Abū al-Walīd Muḥammad b. Rushd al-Ḥafīd, *al-Ḍarūrā fī Uṣūl al-Fiqh aw Mukhtaṣar al-Mustasfā*, Jamāl al-Dīn al-ʿAlawī (ed) (Beirut: Dār al-Gharb al-Islāmī, 1994) 41. Ibn Taymiyya (d. 728/1328) argued that the Muʿtazilites and Sufis distinguished between the good and bad on the basis of their whims and not in terms of the book of God. Taqī al-Dīn Aḥmad b. Taymiyya, *al-Iḥtijāj bi al-Qadar* (Cairo: al-Maṭbaʿa al-Salafiyya, 1974) 25. Ibn Qayyim al-Jawziyya (d. 751/1350) argued that reason may establish an inherent character of an act, but that does not make it a basis for a rule of law. This, he said, is what the Muʿtazilites seem to ignore. Shams al-Dīn Abū ʿAbd Allāh Muḥammad b. Qayyim al-Jawziyya, *Miftāḥ Dār al-Saʿāda wa Manshūrāt Wilāyat al-ʿIlm wa al-Irāda*, Bashīr Muḥammad ʿUyūn (ed) (Damascus: Maktabat Dār al-Bayān, 1998) 2:3–15.

[40] Al-Bāqillānī, *al-Taqrīb wa al-Irshād*, 1:284.

[41] Al-Bāqillānī, *al-Taqrīb wa al-Irshād*, 1:284.

[42] A similar argument is made by Abū Isḥāq al-Shīrāzī (d. 476/1083) who wrote that in some instances, God may despise something deeply (*qad yakrahu al-shay' karāhata tanzīh*) such that one should avoid doing it. But such a determination does not imply that the matter is *qabīḥ*. For al-Shīrāzī in this context, *qabīḥ* implies a specified prohibition. He writes that something that is *qabīḥ* is like the prohibition against day-dreaming in prayer, and the prohibitions against fornication and theft. But just because

The later Ashʿarite-Shāfiʿite jurist Abū al-Maʿālī al-Juwaynī (d. 478/1085) knew clearly that at stake in the debate on *ḥusn* and *qubḥ* is the source of obligation. The question for him was whether obligation stems from God or can be a product of human rational investigation. While al-Juwaynī may seem to be a Voluntarist by suggesting that all obligations come from God, he actually adopted a more subtle approach to the notion of obligation which adds a degree of complexity to the image of Sharīʿa painted by al-Bāqillānī.

From the outset, al-Juwaynī argued that an act has no essential characteristics (*ṣifa*) that provide the kind of determinacy implied by the theory of nature adopted by Hard Natural Law jurists. Whether an act is required or prohibited depends not on some inherent characteristic of the act, but rather on a command or prohibition with the threat of sanction issued by a lawgiver. For example, drinking wine is prohibited in the Qur'ān[43] not because of some essential characteristic (*ṣifa dhātiyya*) of the act, but rather because of an express prohibition that entails a sanction. If drinking wine were unlawful because of a universal characteristic, then it would be prohibited in all situations, regardless of need or necessity. But as al-Juwaynī pointed out, drinking wine can be permitted in exigent circumstances.[44]

Al-Juwaynī did not deny that reason enables us to judge if something is dangerous (*ijtināb al-mahālik*) or offers certain benefits (*ibtidār al-manāfiʿ*). To deny this, he said, would be unreasonable (*khurūj ʿan al-maʿqūl*).[45] Such moral reasoning falls within the normal capacity of human activity, or what al-Juwaynī called the *ḥaqq al-ādamiyyīn*. But this is different from asking what is good or bad in terms of God's judgment (*ḥukm Allāh*).[46] For al-Juwaynī, God's

something is *qabīḥ*, in the sense of prohibition (*taḥrīm*), does not mean it takes greater moral priority over that which is simply despised. Rather what this shows is that only the express command can establish obligation. It does not suggest that one cannot make moral determinations; rather those moral determinations do not assume the position of obligations without resort to express commands and prohibitions. Abū Isḥāq Ibrāhīm b. ʿAlī b. Yūsuf al-Fayrūzābādī al-Shīrāzī, *al-Tabṣira fī Uṣūl al-Fiqh*, Muḥammad Ḥasan Haytū (ed) (Damascus: Dār al-Fikr, 1983) 30.

[43] Qur'ān, 2:219, 4:43, 5:90–1.

[44] Abū al-Maʿālī ʿAbd al-Mālik b. ʿAbd Allāh b. Yūsuf Al-Juwaynī, *al-Burhān fī Uṣūl al-Fiqh*, Ṣalāḥ b. Muḥammad b. ʿAwīḍa (ed) (Beirut: Dār al-Kutub al-ʿIlmiyya, 1997) 1:8. See also al-Juwaynī, *Kitāb al-Talkhīṣ fī Uṣūl al-Fiqh*, ʿAbd Allāh Julam al-Nībālī and Shabbīr Aḥmad al-ʿAmrī (eds) (Beirut: Dār al-Bashā'ir al-Islāmiyya, 1996) 1:155–6, 158.

[45] Al-Juwaynī, *al-Burhān*, 1:10.

[46] Al-Juwaynī, *al-Burhān*, 1:10.

determination of an act's Sharīʿa value has an authority that human reason cannot enjoy. In Sharīʿa, whether something is obligatory or prohibited depends on whether God has provided punishment or reward for the relevant acts (*wa mā kāna kadhālik fa mudraku qubḥihi wa ḥusnihi min ʿiqāb Allāh taʿālā iyāna wa iḥsānuhu ilaynā ʿina afʿālinā*).[47] Unless we have indicators from God, such matters are unknowable by humans (*wa dhālika ghayb*).[48] We cannot make Sharīʿa judgments based purely on a rational analysis into harms and benefits since any such conclusion offers no authority to justify divine sanction, whether in this life only or the Hereafter. This does not mean that we cannot make moral determinations of good and bad. Indeed, it is natural that we would do so. But we can do so only on issues not already addressed by God, and cannot claim divine authority for them since God has made no decision on them. As al-Juwaynī said, 'it is not prohibited to investigate these two characteristics [ie *ḥusn* and *qubḥ*] where harm may arise or where benefit is possible, on condition that [any determination] not be attributed to God, or obligate God to punish or reward.'[49]

For al-Juwaynī, obligation and prohibition in Sharīʿa imply reward and punishment in this life and the hereafter. Without divine punishment and reward there is no divine obligation. In fact, al-Juwaynī went so far as to say that if God deems certain acts to be obligatory, but does not provide a sanction for violation, it makes little sense to call the acts obligatory. While we can make rationally based determinations in areas not already addressed by God, our reasoned deliberations lack the necessary authority to render our rules and sanctions as tantamount to God's decree. They are rational determinations with a normative authority that cannot aspire to any more authority than our own human fallibility and contingency can offer.[50]

[47] Al-Juwaynī, *al-Burhān*, 1:10. [48] Al-Juwaynī, *al-Burhān*, 1:10.

[49] Al-Juwaynī, *al-Burhān*, 1:10. *lam yamtaniʿ ijrāʾ hādhayn al-waṣfayn fīnā idhā tanajjaza ḍarrarun aw amkana nafʿun bi sharṭ an lā yuʿzā ilā Allāh wa lā yūjibu ʿalayhi an yuʿāqibu aw yuthību*. As such a ruler can make laws in areas not addressed by God. But he cannot claim them to have the authority of Sharīʿa, as if they reflect the divine will.

[50] This kind of argument seems to animate al-Ghazālī's earlier discussed comment about the use of *mashhūrāt* knowledge as a source for *fiqh* rules.

To explain his approach, al-Juwaynī challenged arguments made by the Muʿtazilite Abū Hāshim al-Jubbā'ī (d. 321/933).[51] According to al-Juwaynī, Abū Hāshim argued that if someone is equally able to attain a desired result by being either honest or deceitful, he will opt for honesty as a matter of pure reason (*ʿaql*), thus proving that deceitfulness is bad in its essence.[52] Al-Juwaynī said, however, that this cannot be so since we know from authoritative scripture that the liar is considered blameworthy.[53] In other words, God has already decided this matter. But what if a group has not received authoritative scripture and can only rely on pure reason? For example, al-Juwaynī considered the case of the Brahmins, who were considered to have rejected all revealed scripture, yet still make determinations of the good and bad.[54] In such cases, remarked al-Juwaynī, where the two options of honesty and deceit are equally efficacious, pure reason cannot determine which to opt for.[55] This does not suggest that we will not decide to opt for one over the other. But any decision we reach bears no reflection on God's will. For al-Juwaynī, if the Brahmins consider their deliberations and decisions on obligation to stem from God they are fooling themselves. Rather what they deem good and bad is attributed to the realm of decision-making power that humans have (*fa innahum yaruddūna mā yuḥassinūna wa yuqabbiḥūna ilā ḥuqūqinā al-nājiza*).[56] Here the key word is *ḥuqūqinā*, invoking once again the

[51] For a biography of Abū Hāshim al-Jubbā'ī, see L Gardet, 'al- D̲Jubbā'ī, Abū ʿAlī Muḥammad b. ʿAbd al-Wahhāb' in P Bearman, T Bianquis, CE Bosworth, E van Donzel and WP Heinrichs (eds), *Encyclopaedia of Islam, Second Edition* (Leiden: Brill, 2009) [Brill Online. University of Toronto. http://www.brillonline.nl].

[52] Al-Juwaynī, *al-Burhān*, 1:11. [53] Al-Juwaynī, *al-Burhān*, 1:11.

[54] On the debates about the Barāhima as a literary device or historical reality, see Norman Calder, 'The Barahima: Literary Construct and Historical Reality' (1994) 57 *Bulletin of the School of Oriental and African Studies* 40.

[55] Al-Juwaynī, *al-Burhān*, 1:11.

[56] Al-Juwaynī, *al-Burhān*, 1:11. In his earlier work on *uṣūl al-fiqh*, al-Juwaynī considered the same argument but discussed it in a slightly different way. He wrote that if by *ḥusn* and *qubḥ* one means those things to which one's nature inclines (ie taste), then al-Juwaynī had no problem with the ability of reason to understand the value of such matters. But if by *ḥusn* and *qubḥ* one refers to matters of obligation (*taklīf*), then the Brahmins are not capable of assessing the good and the bad. And even if they fancy themselves as knowing the good and the bad, they do not have certainty as to the value of such matters (*wa in khuyyila la hum annahum ya'rifūnahu fa hum muqallidūn ghayr muqīnīn*). He analogized them to the general populace that does not rely on proof texts

idea of the *ḥaqq al-ādamiyyīn*, namely the capacity humans have to make value judgments that are limited in authority and not attributable to God.

Al-Juwaynī's student, Abū Ḥāmid al-Ghazālī (d. 505/1111), also argued that while one cannot rationally create Sharīʿa obligations, humans have the capacity to speculate morally, short of asserting divinely authorized obligations. As discussed above, al-Ghazālī articulated a theory of knowledge in which reason plays varying roles in determining whether a proposition is true. True knowledge (*ʿilm*) is established through a syllogistic approach in which major and minor premises lead to conclusions.[57] The quality of one's syllogistic conclusion depends on the quality of the premises used. For al-Ghazālī, as indicated above, there are different types of certainty. There is the certainty associated with pure rational principles (*al-ʿaqliyyāt al-maḥḍa*), as well as the certainty that arises from experience (*ʿādāt*).[58] One of the categories of knowledge that he addressed is comprised of those things that are well known (*al-mashhūrāt*).[59] As noted above, al-Ghazālī's examples of such well known premises include the evil of lying and ingratitude (*kufrān al-niʿam*), and the good of thankfulness (*shukr al-munʿim*).[60] For al-Ghazālī, these are things that are well known, but which in any specific case may be true or false. For instance, while lying is generally understood as bad, in some cases it might be good. Because these popular propositions may be false, one cannot garner certain

for their beliefs or engage in a critical analysis of such proofs. Such people cannot be fully aware of God's intent or decision in certain matters. Al-Juwaynī's point was that while one can inquire into God's determination of obligations, he cannot know for sure. It is one thing to engage in rational analyses of acts that have not been pre-empted by God. But it is another thing to assume that one can arrive at the same decision God has made solely by reason alone. He wrote: "For how many followers have considered themselves knowledgeable [of an affair], and yet the matter turned out to be contrary to what they decided?" Al-Juwaynī, *Kitāb al-Talkhīṣ*, 1:159. Again, al-Juwaynī's point seems to turn on the notion of God's express will. Humans can engage in rational analysis where God has not made a decision, and thereby make determinations of good and bad, but not obligation. But where God has decided the matter, its goodness or badness is a function of God's decision and not a matter of rational analysis.

[57] See Abū Ḥāmid al-Ghazālī, *al-Mustaṣfā*, 1:97–102, for the different types of syllogisms that constitute *burhān*.

[58] Abū Ḥāmid al-Ghazālī, *al-Mustaṣfā*, 1:107, 109.

[59] Abū Ḥāmid al-Ghazālī, *al-Mustaṣfā*, 1:116.

[60] Abū Ḥāmid al-Ghazālī, *al-Mustaṣfā*, 1:116.

knowledge from them through the syllogistic structure (*burhān*).[61] According to al-Ghazālī, these premises are not based on innate judgment (*fiṭra*) or first principles. Rather they are beliefs that we are conditioned to embrace from a young age. A person is socialized and nurtured through a variety of factors to believe that such things are good or bad (*innamā yangharisu qabūluhā fī al-nafs bi asbāb kathīra*).[62] Perhaps a person is raised with such a powerful sense of love and affection that he believes slaughtering animals is bad.[63] These beliefs might be true. But to rely on that truth with certainty would require such detailed investigation into the origins of such beliefs that al-Ghazālī considered the mind incapable of evaluating their truthfulness effectively.[64] Specifically, he stated:

> It is possible that extensive investigation (*al-istiqrāʾ al-kathīr*) may contribute to a sense of truth about [these determinations]. And perhaps they are true determinations (*al-qaḍiyya al-ṣādiqa*). But [they can only be validated] through such detailed [analysis] (*sharṭ daqīq*), which the mind is incapable of satisfying.[65]

For an example concerning legal theory, al-Ghazālī said that there are some who believe that we cannot reach true knowledge based on the grounds of *tawātur* where the underlying source-texts are actually *aḥādī* in nature. In other words, there are some source-texts (ie *ḥadīth*) that have been orally transmitted over generations with many narrators in each generation of a chain of transmission. Different schools require a certain number of narrators in each generation to create a presumption of certainty about the authenticity of the *ḥadīth*, and the truth of the matter asserted. Where that number is reached, the

[61] Abū Ḥāmid al-Ghazālī, *al-Mustaṣfā*, 1:116.

[62] Abū Ḥāmid al-Ghazālī, *al-Mustaṣfā*, 1:116.

[63] Abū Ḥāmid al-Ghazālī, *al-Mustaṣfā*, 1:116–18. This seems to have been a Muʿtazilite argument based on a rational inquiry into the context of killing and animal rights. Sherman Jackson, 'The Alchemy of Domination? Some Ashʿarite Responses to Muʿtazilite Ethics' (1999) 31 *International Journal of Middle East Studies* 185, 189.

[64] The Ḥanbalī jurist Ibn ʿAqīl (d. 513/1119) argued that, at most, reason could know the descriptive quality of an act, but not its evaluative content. In other words, one can, independently of scripture, describe an act as an objective phenomenon; but any determination of its normative value must rely on scripture. By itself, reason is an epistemological tool for inquiry, but does not form the basis for normative content. Ibn ʿAqīl, *al-Wāḍiḥ fī Uṣūl al-Fiqh*, 1:22–3, 44–5.

[65] Abū Ḥāmid al-Ghazālī, *al-Mustaṣfā*, 1:117.

tradition is considered *mutawātir*, or recurrent, and is presumptively deemed to constitute positive and true knowledge. Where the tradition does not have the requisite number of narrators in each generation, it is called singular or *aḥādī*, and only results in probable knowledge. In some cases, a body of *aḥādī* traditions may address the same topic but with different wording. Some argued that in such a case, the *aḥādī* traditions, in the aggregate, create certain knowledge concerning the matter asserted (*tawātur fī al-maʿnā*).[66] Al-Ghazālī seemed to share this opinion. But others argued that since the underlying traditions do not extend beyond the *aḥādī* level, they cannot collectively constitute a basis for true knowledge.[67] For al-Ghazālī, the truth of this latter position is something that is deeply rooted in the soul of such adherents (*yarsakhu fī nafsihi*).[68] However, he argued that despite this view being ingrained in his opponent's mind, it is nevertheless incorrect. A singular transmission by itself does not constitute a basis for knowledge, but for al-Ghazālī, a collection of singular transmissions on the same topic does in fact constitute a basis for the presumption of certainty.[69]

Of course, al-Ghazālī does not ask whether his own view is subject to the same critique. While we might imagine his opponents criticizing al-Ghazālī's view for the same reason, the point for al-Ghazālī in this passage is that one cannot think about such matters outside one's context. Context and upbringing provide the basis for beliefs on justice, goodness and evil. But because context is necessarily contingent, these beliefs can never result in universal, unambiguously true premises. For anyone to assert as a purely rational matter that justice is unquestionably and universally good and that

[66] For a discussion of *tawātur* and *aḥādī*, see Muḥammad ʿIjāj al-Khaṭīb, *al-Mukhtaṣar al-Wajīz fī ʿUlūm al-Ḥadīth* (Beirut: Mu'assasat al-Risāla, 1991) 125; Mohammad Hashim Kamali, *Principles of Islamic Jurisprudence* (3rd edn, Cambridge: Islamic Texts Society, 2003) 78–80.

[67] Abū Ḥāmid al-Ghazālī, *al-Mustasfā*, 1:116–18. For a discussion of those who held that *aḥādī ḥadīth* do not constitute *ʿilm*, see Abū al-Ḥusayn Al-Baṣrī, *al-Muʿtamad fī Uṣūl al-Fiqh* (Beirut: Dār al-Kutub al-ʿIlmiyya, n.d.) 2:92–6. Incidentally, al-Baṣrī argued that the singular transmission can be the basis for *ʿilm*, and not just *ẓann*.

[68] Abū Ḥāmid al-Ghazālī, *al-Mustasfā*, 1:117.

[69] Abū Ḥāmid al-Ghazālī, *al-Mustasfā*, 1:116–18. For the same view, see also al-Samʿānī, *Qawāṭiʿ al-Adilla*, 1:325.

lying is undeniably and universally bad, he would need to isolate himself from all people (*lam tuʿāshiru aḥadan wa lam tukhāliṭu ahl al-milla*), be ignorant of all related traditions, and not receive a good education.[70] For al-Ghazālī it is impossible to live outside one's context, thereby attacking the Hard Naturalist claims of objectivity. The fact that one upholds the view that lying is bad (*qabīḥ*) is a result of one's cultural experience (*ʿādāt*), ethical training (*akhlāq*), and acquaintance with the general welfare of humanity (*istiṣlāḥāt*).[71] At most, such matters can provide a basis for probabilistic rulings (*al-fiqhiyyāt al-ẓanniyya*) and for cases of disputed precedent (*al-aqīsa al-jadaliyya*), but cannot constitute the basis for clear and certain proofs.[72] In other words, one can hold such moral beliefs, and even derive rules of law of limited application. They may be used to establish mundane technical legal matters that require only a reasonable basis for their justification and are subject to dispute.[73] But it seems that they cannot be the basis for universal propositions along the lines that al-Jaṣṣāṣ asserted, for instance.

For the authors noted above, *ḥusn* and *qubḥ* are terms of art that connote the inevitability of human moral inquiry. They reflect values that are neither objective nor determinate. Instead, the values

[70] Abū Ḥāmid al-Ghazālī, *al-Mustaṣfā*, 1:118.

[71] Abū Ḥāmid al-Ghazālī, *al-Mustaṣfā*, 1:118.

[72] Abū Ḥāmid al-Ghazālī, *al-Mustaṣfā*, 1:118.

[73] The Mālikī judge and philosopher Ibn Rushd (Averroes) (d. 595/1198) also argued for a broad notion of moral inquiry, while distinguishing it from the nature of obligation. In his summary of al-Ghazālī's *al-Mustaṣfā*, he reviewed the basic positions of the Muʿtazilites and those he called the *ahl al-sunna*. The Muʿtazilites argued that acts have essential characteristics. Some of those characteristics are known by pure reason, such as the evil of lying; other characteristics are known by reference to scripture. Ibn Rushd, *al-Ḍarūra fī Uṣūl al-Fiqh*, 41. The *ahl al-sunna* countered that a rule of law arises from the discourse of scripture (*khiṭāb al-sharʿ*) and that the value of an act is not dependent on some essential characteristic of the act (*waṣf dhātī*). Ibn Rushd, *al-Ḍarūra fī Uṣūl al-Fiqh*, 41. They argued that the value of acts is purely contingent and not metaphysically objective. In other words, for them, the value one ascribes to an act depends either on whether the act coincides with his goals (*gharaḍ*), what the *sharʿ* renders as good or bad, or what is simply permissible (*mubāḥ*) for one to do. In these three circumstances, the goodness or badness of an act depends on some circumstantial factor (*iḍāfiyya*) that does not inhere in the act, but is external to the act itself. Ibn Rushd, *al-Ḍarūra fī Uṣūl al-Fiqh*, 41. Goals and scripture pose external factors rendering the act good or bad, while the permissibility of an act does not involve the quality of good or bad at all. This differs from some Muʿtazilites who consider permissibility a type of good (*ḥasan*). See discussion on al-Baṣrī above.

arising from such moral inquiry only attest to how we are immersed in a context in which we make determinations of the good and the bad all the time. Moral inquiry is part of the human condition. However, such moral inquiry cannot be presumed to lead to objective, determinate truths about the world or the divine. As such, the Hard Naturalist claims about an objective, determinate natural world in which fact and value are fused fails to account for the reality of human experience and the limits of moral inquiry. While we can make judgments, and even use them to order our world, we cannot presume they arise with any certainty from the divine will. Indeed, to presume this would further violate the fundamental Voluntarist commitment to God's omnipotence.

If we can reason to divine obligation and thereby determine sanctions for any violation thereof, we would be holding God obligated to adhere to our reasoned deliberations. This is the core of the difficulty the Voluntarists had with Hard Natural Law theory. To suggest that we could hold God obligated in any way goes against the Voluntarist theology of an omnipotent God. Consequently, for Voluntarists, while we can evaluate competing courses of conduct, no conduct can be deemed obligatory or prohibited as a matter of Sharīʿa without recourse to God's will. While Voluntarist jurists recognized and respected rational speculation, they emphasized that the ontological authority to assert Sharīʿa obligations is a separate affair. The question of authority in Sharīʿa is animated by principles of theology, authority, and sanction that render legal knowledge a special case that cannot so easily be opened to the operation of reason without raising concerns about human fallibility, the complexity of the human condition, and the omnipotence of God.

The Fallacy of Fusing Fact and Value

As indicated above, Hard Naturalists developed a theory of nature as both an objective basis for rational inquiry and a normative basis for asserting obligations. Voluntarist jurists argued that the Hard Naturalistic argument relied on a fallacy: nature can provide contradictory answers and therefore is neither an objective nor determinative basis for evaluation. Furthermore, they considered the Hard Naturalist fusion of fact and value in nature to be an imposition on God's omnipotence that fundamentally removes God's will from normative evaluation. If God is truly omnipotent, the theology that makes Hard Natural Law possible must fail. Consequently while Hard Naturalists fused fact and value in the presumption of permissibility,[74] the Voluntarists argued that acts not addressed by source-texts are in a state of suspended judgment (*tawaqquf*) for which there is no divine rule of obligation.[75] This position effectively rejects reason as an ontological authority for Sharīʿa rules of law.

The distinction between the two possibilities is important because there was a third group of jurists who argued on purely rational grounds that where there is no scripturally based proof on a matter, all acts are presumptively prohibited (*maḥẓūr*). Those who adopted this position, as noted above, included among others the Baghdad Muʿtazilites.[76] This group, often called the *ḥaẓariyya*,

[74] Not all Muʿtazilites adopted this view. The Baghdad school of Muʿtazilites took the opposite view, holding that all acts are presumptively prohibited (*maḥẓūr*) unless specified otherwise. See, eg, Abū Ḥāmid al-Ghazālī, *al-Mustaṣfā*, 1:151; al-Samʿānī, *Qawāṭiʿ al-Adilla*, 2:48; Abū Isḥāq Ibrāhīm b. ʿAlī b. Yūsuf al-Fayrūzābādī Al-Shīrāzī, *Sharḥ al-Lumʿa*, ʿAbd al-Majīd Turkī (ed) (Beirut: Dār al-Gharb al-Islāmī, 1988) 2:977. Furthermore, it is reported that even some Ashʿarites adopted this position. See Tāj al-Dīn ʿAbd al-Raḥmān b. Ibrāhīm Ibn al-Farikān, *Sharḥ al-Waraqāt*, Sārah Shāfī al-Hājirī (ed) (Beirut: Dār al-Bashā'ir al-Islāmiyya, 2001) 350. Abū al-Maʿālī al-Juwaynī indicated that this position was also adopted by the Ḥanafī school. Abū al-Maʿālī ʿAbd al-Mālik b. ʿAbd Allāh al-Juwaynī, *al-Ghiyāthī: Ghiyāth al-Umam fī Iltiyāth al-Ẓulam*, Khalīl al-Manṣūr (ed) (Beirut: Dār al-Kutub al-ʿIlmiyya, 1997) 225. On the other hand, al-Lāmishī wrote that the presumption of prohibition was adopted by the *aṣḥāb al-ḥadīth*. Maḥmūd b. Zayd al-Lāmishī, *Kitāb fī Uṣūl al-Fiqh*, ʿAbd al-Majīd Turkī (ed) (Beirut: Dār al-Gharb al-Islāmī, 1995) 105.

[75] Although, it seems that even some Muʿtazilīs held this view as well. For a list of names, see al-Samarqandī, *Mīzān al-Uṣūl*, 1:314.

[76] Others adopting this view include the *aṣḥāb al-ḥadīth*, and those from different legal schools, such as the Mālikis and Shāfiʿīs. Abū al-Ḥasan ʿAlī b. ʿUmar Ibn al-Qaṣṣār, *al-Muqaddima fī al-Uṣūl*, Muḥammad b. al-Ḥusayn al-Sulaymānī (ed) (Beirut: Dār al-Gharb al-Islāmī, 1996) 153–6, wrote that some Mālikīs held this view. Abū Isḥāq al-Shīrāzī, *Sharḥ al-Lumʿa*, 2:977, mentioned that this view was adopted by the Baghdad Muʿtazilites and the Shāfiʿī jurist Abū ʿAlī al-Ḥasan b. al-Ḥusayn b. Abī Hurayra (d. 345/956). Ibn Abī Hurayra was a Shāfiʿi faqīh who led the Shāfiʿī school in Iraq and died in Baghdad. Khayr al-Dīn Al-Ziriklī, *al- Aʿlām*, (12th edn, Beirut: Dār al-ʿIlm li al-Malayīn, 1997) 2:188. Al-Lāmishī, *Kitāb fī Uṣūl al-Fiqh*, 105, asserted that the *aṣḥāb al-ḥadīth* adopted this view. Fakhr al-Dīn al-Rāzī wrote that besides the Baghdad Muʿtazilites and Ibn Abī Hurayra, a group of Jaʿfarite Shiʿites held this view. Fakhr al-Dīn Muḥammad b. ʿUmar Al-Rāzī, *al-Maḥṣūl fī ʿIlm Uṣūl al-Fiqh*, Ṭāha Jābir Fayyāḍ al-ʿAlwāni (ed) (3rd edn, Beirut: Mu'assasat al-Risāla, 1997) 1:158.

argued on the basis of an analogy to property law that creation is entirely the property of God. Just as one cannot use the property of another (*milk al-ghayr*) without his prior permission (*idhn*), one cannot utilize the creation of God without His express permission. Consequently all acts, which involve human exertion, and hence the use of God's property, are presumptively prohibited unless otherwise specified by the divine owner.[77]

Voluntarist jurists generally argued that both Hard Naturalists and the *ḥaẓariyya* presumed too much about God. They held that both the presumption of permissibility and the presumption of prohibition implicitly grant ontological authority to reason to articulate Sharīʿa norms (permissibility and prohibition) without reference to any evidence with a divine provenance. Contrary to both positions, the Voluntarists cited Q 17:15, which states 'We do not punish until We send a messenger'[78] to prove that obligation and prohibition arise only after God has offered evidence of them.[79]

The Voluntarist argument against the *ḥaẓariyya* was relatively straightforward. Voluntarists argued that the analogy between human property relations and God's divine omnipotence over creation is a false one. We cannot use the property of another without his permission because of the harm that would thereby result to the owner from our unauthorized use. God, however, is free from such harm. Consequently, it is not surprising that in situations where a property owner is not actually harmed by our use

[77] For discussions of this argument, see al-Qaṣṣār, *al-Muqaddima fī al-Uṣūl*, 155; Abū al-Walīd al-Bājī, *Iḥkām al-Fuṣūl*, 1:691–2; Abū al-Ḥusayn al-Baṣrī, *al-Muʿtamad fī Uṣūl al-Fiqh*, 2:319–20; Ibn Ḥazm, *Iḥkām fī Uṣūl al-Aḥkām*, 1:52; Abū Ḥāmid al-Ghazālī, *al-Mustaṣfā*, 1:153; Abū Isḥāq al-Shīrāzī, *Sharḥ al-Lumʿa*, 2:980; Abū Bakr Aḥmad b. al-Khaṭīb al-Baghdādī, *Kitāb al-Faqīh wa al-Mutafaqqih* (n.p.: Maṭbaʿat al-Imtiyāz, 1977) 192–4; al-Samʿānī, *Qawāṭiʿ al-Adilla*, 2:49–51; Ibn al-Farikān, *Sharḥ al-Waraqāt, 350–2.*

[78] Qur'ān, 17:15.

[79] Ibn Qayyim al-Jawziyya, *Miftāḥ Dār al-Saʿāda*, 2:52–3, relied on this verse to argue against the determination of obligation or prohibition on a rational basis. See also al-Qarāfī, *Nafā'is al-Uṣūl*, 1:161–2. Al-Aṣfahānī (d. 653/1255) related how some rationalists held that the notion of 'messengers' left open the possibility that what is meant is human rational capacity. But he relied on this verse to argue against the Muʿtazilites who would otherwise allow for rational obligation and prohibition without a scriptural basis. Abū ʿAbd Allāh Muḥammad b. Maḥmūd b. ʿAbbād Al-Aṣfahānī, *al-Kāshif ʿan al-Maḥṣūl fī ʿIlm al-Uṣūl*, Ādil Aḥmad ʿAbd al-Mawjūd and ʿAlī Muḥammad Muʿawwaḍ (eds) (Beirut: Dār al-Kutub al-ʿIlmiyya, 1998) 1:357.

of his property, we are permitted to use the owner's property. For example, we can look into another's mirror without worrying about causing harm to its owner. Or we can walk in the shade of another's wall, despite the fact that we are 'using' or somehow benefiting from the property of another without his permission. Where there is no harm, permissibility follows. As God is always free of any such harm, the *ḥaẓariyya* argument must fail.[80]

But in most of the sources utilized for this study, the argument against the *ḥaẓariyya* did not seem to preoccupy Voluntarist jurists very much. They seemed more concerned with the Hard Naturalists who fused fact and value through the presumption of permissibility, and their related grant of ontological authority to reason as a source of Sharīʿa values. The Voluntarists argued that nature cannot provide a basis for establishing obligation since nature is neither determinate nor coincident with God's will. The Voluntarists acknowledged that reason can guide us to decide what

[80] Abū al-Walīd al-Bājī, *Iḥkām al-Fuṣūl*, 2:691–2; al-Khaṭīb al-Baghdādī, *Kitāb al-Faqīh wa al-Mutafaqqih*, 192–4; Abū Ḥāmid al-Ghazālī, *al-Mustaṣfā*, 1:153; al-Samʿānī, *Qawāṭiʿ al-Adilla*, 2:49–51; Ibn al-Farikān, *Sharḥ al-Waraqāt*, 350–2. See also the Muʿtazilite, Abū al-Ḥusayn al-Baṣrī, *al-Muʿtamad fī Uṣūl al-Fiqh*, 2:319–20. Ibn Ḥazm, *Iḥkām fī Uṣūl al-Aḥkām*, 1:52–3, held that the *ḥaẓariyya*'s reliance on the prohibition of using the property of another is not in fact a rational argument but one that is provided for in scripture. Ibn Ḥazm also wrote that there are instances, as in the case of providing support for a wife (*nafaqa*), where a person's property can be taken and utilized without his permission. Furthermore, this rational principle is premised on an analogy between God's reality and worldly reality (*ʿālam al-shāhid*), which is invalid. And lastly, he indicated that the rational presumption of prohibition creates inconsistencies. If humans are the property of God, then their act of procreation is a utilization of God's property. But if they do not procreate they diminish God's property. See also Abū Isḥāq al-Shīrāzī, *Sharḥ al-Lumʿa*, 2:980. Al-Samʿānī, *Qawāṭiʿ al-Adilla*, 2:56, argued that the *ḥaẓariyya* presumption is really a principle of prudence (*muntabih*), which cautions a distribution of goods pursuant to one's needs. Abū Ḥāmid al-Ghazālī argued that the example of looking into another's mirror does not constitute using one's property and so is an inappropriate basis for a prohibition. Abū Ḥāmid al-Ghazālī, *al-Mustaṣfā*, 1:154–5. Al-Samarqandī, *Mīzān al-Uṣūl*, 1:317–18, argued that the presumption of prohibition, like the presumption of permissibility, could be in conflict with scripture and as such cannot be the proper basis for obligation since both rational and scriptural proofs are from God. As there can be no conflict between them, nor internal contradiction within the scripture, al-Samarqandī argued that scripture is the proper basis for obligation. Abū al-Walīd al-Bājī, *Iḥkām al-Fuṣūl*, 2:687–8, relied on the notion that all of creation is God's property to assert that God must legislate in order to create obligations. However, he did not adopt the rational presumption of prohibition. Instead, he adopted the view of suspension (*waqf*) discussed below.

is beneficial, harmful, good (*maṣlaḥa*), and corrupt (*mafsada*); but these rational determinations do not have the authority to ground Sharīʿa obligations that would bind God in any way. For instance, Ibn Ḥazm wrote how those adopting the presumption of permissibility argued that it is impossible that God would create in us natural dispositions (*al-shahwāt al-muqtaḍiyya*), yet punish us for following them. Ibn Ḥazm retorted that this argument is 'plain pomposity' (*makābirat al-ʿiyān*).[81] He argued that God creates in us desires that often lead to misdeeds involving lewd behavior with beautiful women and handsome young men, the consumption of wine, abandoning the fight against unbelievers, and sleeping during prayers. Yet God expressly prohibits all of that. The point for Ibn Ḥazm is that we cannot make a Sharīʿa judgment based on our natural dispositions.[82]

Abū Ḥāmid al-Ghazālī (d. 505/1111) also argued against imputing normative content to empirical observations about the world. For example, just because God creates foods with sumptuous flavors does not mean that He wants us to benefit from such foods. Al-Ghazālī agreed that qualities such as taste and sumptuousness can be empirically verified. But by themselves, they say little about God's intent in creating them. Perhaps God created tasty foods not so that we would benefit from consuming them, but rather so that we could be rewarded for restraining our desirous self from them, just as we are rewarded for avoiding bad deeds that we might otherwise desire to do.[83] In other words, we cannot move from a description of the good to a normative claim that it must be pursued.

[81] Ibn Ḥazm, *Iḥkām fī Uṣūl al-Aḥkām*, 1:54.

[82] Abū al-Maʿālī al-Juwaynī, *al-Ghiyāthī*, 85, argued that the purpose of law and government is to keep people's desires (*hawā*) restrained. Consequently, such desires, for al-Juwaynī, cannot be the basis for determinations of obligation.

[83] Abū Ḥāmid al-Ghazālī, *al-Mustaṣfā*, 1:154–5. See also al-Khaṭīb al-Baghdādī, *Kitāb al-Faqīh wa al-Mutafaqqih*, 193–4; Abū Isḥāq al-Shīrāzī, *Sharḥ al-Lumʿa*, 2:984. Al-Samʿānī (d. 489/1096) countered those who argue for rational permissibility and obligation on the grounds of a benefit found to reside in the act (*manfaʿa*). He argued that the issue is not about whether there is benefit to an act, which thereby serves as the normative basis for the act's valuation. Rather what matters is whether there are indicators (*imāra*) that the act contains some evil (*qubḥ*). In other words, one does not make rational presumptions; rather one bases one's determination on the existence of actual evidence of harm and injury. Al-Samʿānī, *Qawāṭiʿ al-Adilla*, 2:49–50.

Abū Isḥāq al-Shīrāzī (d. 476/1083) provided various reasons why the argument from nature does not work. He disagreed that creation was made to benefit mankind, because this position assumes that God acts only with a reason in mind or with a rational basis (*muʿallila*).[84] According to al-Shirāzī, God does as He wishes and rules as He desires (*yafʿalu Allāh mā yashāʾ wa yaḥkumu mā yurīdu*).[85] Furthermore, he asked, if all of creation is for human benefit, how do Hard Naturalists explain the prohibition on wine and pork? Can we coherently maintain that all of creation is for mankind's benefit when in fact we find aspects of creation prohibited to humanity?[86] Perhaps, al-Shīrāzī argued, such things were created for a people who will come after us. But if that is so, we cannot thereby normatively posit that such things are presumptively permissible for us. Like al-Ghazālī, he wrote that it is possible that the natural world was created in order to test humanity. Perhaps the test is that one is rewarded for avoiding certain things and restraining one's desires. If these perspectives are all possible, the Hard Naturalistic arguments must fail.[87]

To further justify their opposition, some Voluntarists deconstructed the hypothetical of thanking the benefactor. For example, Fakhr al-Dīn al-Rāzī (d. 606/1209) said that rational determinations of benefit (*fāʾida*) do not offer sufficient authority to justify finding a Sharīʿa obligation to thank the benefactor. Al-Rāzī stated that Qurʾānic texts endorse the Voluntarist view that any Sharīʿa ruling must be based on an expression of the divine will. He referred, for instance, to the Qurʾānic verse noted above, namely: 'We do not punish until We send a messenger.'[88] Another verse reads: 'Messengers spreading the news and warning so that people will not have a claim against God after the messenger.'[89] Both of these verses show that judgment is dependent on God's indication of His will.

Furthermore, al-Rāzī argued that the mere fact that a benefit exists does not imply that one is thereby obligated to pursue that benefit. According to al-Rāzī, even if we accept the Hard

[84] Abū Isḥāq al-Shīrāzī, *Sharḥ al-Lumʿa*, 2:983–4.
[85] Abū Isḥāq al-Shīrāzī, *Sharḥ al-Lumʿa*, 2:983–4.
[86] Abū Isḥāq al-Shīrāzī, *Sharḥ al-Lumʿa*, 2:983–4.
[87] Abū Isḥāq al-Shīrāzī, *Sharḥ al-Lumʿa*, 2:983–4.
[88] Fakhr al-Dīn al-Rāzī, *al-Maḥṣūl*, 1:148, quoting Qurʾān 17:15.
[89] Fakhr al-Dīn al-Rāzī, *al-Maḥṣūl*, 1:148, quoting Qurʾān, 4:165.

Naturalists' premises about God's justice and the beneficial quality of creation for humanity, there is no reason to believe that seeking benefits is necessarily an obligation or in any way incumbent upon us. In other words, just because a benefit exists does not mean we must seek it. Indeed, it might be that thanking involves a harm to us, such as an expenditure of energy. But suppose the expenditure is necessary to gain a greater benefit. Even then, why should we suffer if we choose not to pursue the greater good?[90]

Voluntarists held that where there is no scripture to address the matter, the rule of obligation is in a state of suspended judgment (*waqf, tawaqquf*): where there is no source-text, there is no authoritative basis to assert a Sharīʿa rule.[91] Abū Walīd al-Bājī (d. 474/1081) argued that if it were true that one could create obligations on the basis of reason, such obligations would be based on either rational necessity (*ḍarūrat al-ʿaql*) or evidence from reasoned deliberation (*dalīl al-ʿaql*). If it were based on rational necessity, then there could be no

[90] Importantly, not all of al-Rāzī's commentators were of the same mind on this point. Both al-Qarāfī and al-Asfahānī challenged al-Rāzī's view that obtaining such a benefit is not obligatory. Indeed, al-Qarāfī argued that in some cases it may be obligatory where the benefit is necessary (*ḍarūrī*). Al-Qarāfī, *Nafāʾis al-Uṣūl*, 1:163; Abū ʿAbd Allāh al-Aṣfahānī, *al-Kāshif ʿan al-Maḥṣūl*, 1:359.

[91] Al-Khaṭīb al-Baghdādī, *Kitāb al-Faqīh wa al-Mutafaqqih*, 192–4; Ibn Ḥazm, *Iḥkām fī Uṣūl al-Aḥkām*, 1:52; al-Samʿānī, *Qawāṭiʿ al-Adilla*, 2:46–7, 52; Abū Isḥāq al-Shīrāzī, *Sharḥ al-Lumʿa*, 2:977; al-Qarāfī, *Nafāʾis al-Uṣūl*, 1:173; al-Samarqandī, *Mīzān al-Uṣūl*, 1:314. The Mālikī al-Qaṣṣār, *al-Muqaddima fī Uṣūl*, 153–5, wrote that some of his Mālikī companions adopted this view, arguing that one needs proof (*ḥujja*) to establish something as either permissible or prohibited. In other words, one cannot rely on reason to create obligations where there is no scripture. But for al-Qaṣṣār, there is no situation that is without a scriptural basis. The prophets after Adam have decided all matters of obligation, and as such there is nothing that has not been addressed. Al-Kankūhī, *ʿUmdat al-Ḥawāshī*, 143, said that where what is at stake is the question of reward and punishment, the Ashʿarites argued that such determinations can only come from scripture. Al Lāmishī, *Kitāb fī Uṣūl al-Fiqh*, 105, wrote that this position was held by the Māturīdites, the *aṣḥāb al-ḥadīth*, and some Muʿtazilites. For him, there is no room for reason to establish obligations (*lā ḥaẓẓ li [ʿaql] fī maʿrifa al-aḥkām al-sharʿiyya*). In matters not addressed by scripture, there is no rule of law. Ibn al-Farikān, *Sharḥ al-Waraqāt*, 347–50, wrote that this is the position adopted by the majority of Ashʿarites. Interestingly, Abū Ḥāmid al-Ghazālī said that a group of Muʿtazilites adopted this view as well, although their position of *waqf* was one that held that while there is no obligation without scripture, acts still have essential characteristics that reason can investigate. Abū Ḥāmid al-Ghazālī, *al-Mustaṣfā*, 1:151, 153. See also al-Samarqandī, *Mīzān al-Uṣūl*, 1:314, who listed Muʿtazilites who adopted the position of *tawaqquf*. He also mentioned that the *aṣḥāb al-ḥādīth* adopted this position as well.

disagreement on what is obligatory and what is prohibited. But as there is disagreement on such matters as thanking the benefactor, which is claimed to be rationally necessary, one cannot rely on arguments of rational necessity to justify obligations. Furthermore, he wrote that reasoned deliberation is an insufficient basis for Sharīʿa rules of law; rather, one must resort to source-texts. In his theory of law, obligation and prohibition require a legislative will to exist or, as he called it, an obligor (*mujīb*) and prohibitor (*ḥāẓir*). This legislative will comes from God. If reason were an authoritative basis for obligation, that would unacceptably diminish God's role as the obligor and prohibitor. Consequently, where God has not legislated, there is no authority to assert a Sharīʿa rule of obligation.[92]

Those who held the position of *tawaqquf* effectively seemed to allow a legal result that was tantamount to the Hard Naturalist presumption of permissibility. In fact, the Hard Naturalist al-Jaṣṣāṣ wrote that the only real difference between the position of suspended judgment and the presumption of permissibility is one of semantics. Both reach the same result, namely that there is no punishment or reward for committing or omitting an act. Whether one bases this on the presumption of permissibility or the suspension of judgment, the result is the same.[93]

Voluntarists countered this critique by saying that the position of *tawaqquf* is not an affirmative rational rule of Sharīʿa. It grants no ontological authority to reason, but rather limits reason to an epistemic function by which jurists determine whether or not a source-text exists that addresses the issue under consideration. The position of *tawaqquf* denies reason any ontological authority to establish any *Sharīʿa* rule of law. The rule of suspended judgment is not an affirmative rule of Sharīʿa, but rather is a negative epistemic method.[94]

[92] Abū Walīd al-Bājī, *Iḥkām al-Fuṣūl*, 2:687–8. See also Abū Isḥāq al-Shīrāzī, *Sharḥ al-Lumʿa*, 2:977–8, who wrote on the need for legislative will. Abū Ḥāmid al-Ghazālī, *al-Mustaṣfā*, 1:151, 155–6, said that for something to be permissible, a legislative will is necessary to deem it to be permissible. For al-Ghazālī, that legislative will is God's and is expressed through scripture.

[93] Al-Jaṣṣāṣ, *Uṣūl al-Jaṣṣāṣ*, 2:103.

[94] Abū Walīd al-Bājī, *Iḥkām al-Fuṣūl*, 2:689; Ibn Ḥazm, *al-Iḥkām fī Uṣūl al-Aḥkām*, 1:56; Abū Ḥāmid al-Ghazālī, *al-Mustaṣfā*, 1:133, 155–6; Fakhr al-Dīn al-Rāzī, *al-Maḥṣūl*, 1:159; al-Samarqandī, *Mīzān al-Uṣūl*, 1:315–16; al-Samʿānī, *Qawāṭiʿ al-Adilla*, 2:52; Abū Isḥāq al-Shīrāzī, *Sharḥ al-Lumʿa*, 2:979–80; al-Lāmishī, *Kitāb fī Uṣūl al-Fiqh*, 105; al-Qarāfī, *Nafāʾis al-Uṣūl*, 1:177; Jamāl al-Dīn ʿAbd al-Raḥīm b. al-Ḥasan

Voluntarists held that the position of suspended judgment properly embraces the epistemological weakness from which jurists necessarily suffer. For instance, in his commentary on Fakhr al-Dīn al-Rāzī's *al-Maḥṣūl*, al-Aṣfahānī related two apparently contradictory positions held by al-Rāzī. In the first instance, al-Rāzī asserted that before revelation, there is no scriptural discourse (*khiṭāb al-sharʿ*), and as such there is no rule of obligation in a given case. Nevertheless, al-Rāzī argued elsewhere that the divine discourse (*khiṭāb*), which contains the rules of obligation espoused by source-texts, is an eternal speech (*kalām al-nafs wa al-maʿnā al-qāʾim bi al-dhāt*).[95] The apparent contradiction lies in the fact that on the one hand the divine discourse on the existence of obligations is eternal, but on the other hand, the divine discourse is lacking in some cases. Al-Aṣfahānī argued that al-Rāzī had in mind two distinct claims, a metaphysical one and an epistemic one. For al-Rāzī, there is always a rule in a metaphysically objective sense for a given act. Such values and determinations exist in the 'mind of God.' But from an epistemological perspective, humans cannot know what that rule of obligation is when source-texts do not address the issue. Our knowledge of the Sharīʿa rule on a given issue depends on whether the divine discourse has come down to us in a given instance. We cannot know what those rules are without God's speech materializing in history. Without knowledge of those rules, we have no authority to assert a Sharīʿa obligation.[96]

The position of *tawaqquf* certainly provides a way to oppose the Hard Naturalistic fusion of fact and value, and its implication for the ontological authority of reason. *Tawaqquf* indicates that there is no evaluation on a given act. But does that mean one should avoid the act? What is the normative consequence of performing an act on which judgment has been suspended? The *tawaqquf* principle certainly challenges the Hard Naturalist fusion of fact and value. But from a law and order perspective, we are still left wondering how we

al-Asnawī, *Nihāyat al-Sūl fī Sharḥ Minhāj al-Wuṣūl ilā ʿIlm al-Uṣūl*, Shaʿbān Muḥammad Ismaʿīl (ed) (Beirut: Dār Ibn Ḥazm, 1999) 1:141.

[95] Abū ʿAbd Allāh al-Aṣfahānī, *al-Kāshif ʿan al-Maḥṣūl*, 1:370.

[96] Abū ʿAbd Allāh al-Aṣfahānī, *al-Kāshif ʿan al-Maḥṣūl*, 1:371. For a similar argument, see al-Samarqandī, *Mīzān al-Uṣūl*, 1:315–16, who said that there is always a rule of obligation that exists eternally (*al-ījāb al-azalī*) in the mind of God (*ʿinda Allāh*).

ought to act on a matter on which judgment is suspended, given the eschatological fact that God will still judge our behavior.

Voluntarist jurists who espoused the virtues of *tawaqquf* coupled it with an additional presumption to ensure that the position of suspended judgment did not leave us also wondering about the normative implications of acting one way or another. Voluntarists relied on a different presumption, namely the presumption of continuity (*istiṣḥāb al-ḥāl*) to offer some normative guidance on issues on which judgment is suspended. Under this presumption, where there is no source-text on an issue to determine the relevant obligation, we are presumptively free from any blame in what we choose to do (*al-aṣl barā'at al-dhimma*).[97] For instance Abū Walīd al-Bājī asked whether the *witr* prayer is obligatory or not. The *witr* prayer is a sixth prayer whose obligatory status was debated among different jurists. A Ḥanafī may ask the Mālikī about whether this prayer is obligatory. The Mālikī will say no.[98] When the Ḥanafī inquires about the Mālikī's basis for his determination, the Mālikī responds:

> The presumption is freedom from liability (*barā'at al-dhimma*) and the path to obligation is through scripture (*Sharʿ*). I have searched the scripture and did not find anything obligating [*witr* prayer]. If it were there, I would have found it with extensive research and investigation (*kathra al-baḥth wa al-naẓar*). So [the matter is decided] pursuant to the rule of the presumption of freedom from blame.[99]

For al-Bājī, the path to obligation is through scripture, and because of that he knows that Muslims are not punished if they fail to pray a sixth prayer, pay an additional alms tax (*zakāt*) or fast in a month outside of *Ramaḍān*.[100]

Abū Ḥāmid al-Ghazālī said that although reason cannot justify Sharīʿa obligations, reason can epistemically determine whether relevant evidence for an obligation exists or not. If not, the legal

[97] Abū Walīd al-Bājī, *Iḥkām al-Fuṣūl*, 2:700.

[98] Notably, the Ḥanafīs argued that *witr* prayer is obligatory and based their ruling on *ḥādīth* from the Prophet. But the Ḥanafīs did not consider those who rejected this obligation to be heretics. Abū al-Ḥasan ʿAlī b. Abī Bakr al-Farghānī al-Marghīnānī, *al-Hidāya: Sharḥ Bidāyat al-Mubtadi'*, Muḥammad Darwīsh (ed) (Beirut: Dār al-Arqam, n.d.) 1:80.

[99] Abū Walīd al-Bājī, *Iḥkām al-Fuṣūl*, 2:700.

[100] Abū Walīd al-Bājī, *Iḥkām al-Fuṣūl*, 2:700.

significance is that we incur no blame however we choose to act.[101] Therefore, while the principle of *istiṣḥāb al-ḥāl* is a rational presumption, it is not tantamount to the presumption of permissibility. The presumption of permissibility is an affirmative rational assertion about the goodness of an act based on the fusion of fact and value in nature. *Istiṣḥāb al-ḥāl*, like the notion of *tawaqquf*, is an epistemological rational proof based on the absence of scripture. The absence can be known epistemically by one's reason; where we find no source-text, there is no divine sanction. Where there is no sanction, there can be no obligation to act in one way or another. Hence the legal implication is that we are free from blame, no matter how we choose to act. While the outcome of *istiṣḥāb al-ḥāl* may be the same as the principle of permissibility, the role of reason (whether ontological or epistemological) in each presumption is quite different.[102]

Conclusion

Voluntarists argued against Hard Natural Law because they believed that only an express divine will can create Sharīʿa obligations with certitude. While reason and human dispositions may empower us to make decisions about the good and the bad, Voluntarists considered these conceptions as aesthetic, moral, or cultural considerations that have limited determinacy, and thereby limited authority on which to base Sharīʿa rules of law. It is one thing to make human determinations of the good, but it is another thing to ascribe such determinations to the will of God. Of course there will be situations not addressed by source-texts that we must confront. These novel situations are open to discussion and debate in light of the moral and cultural context of a given society. In such situations, the people of a given region may ascribe for themselves rules of conduct that assume the coercive force of law. But to suggest that these rules of

[101] Abū Ḥāmid al-Ghazālī, *al-Mustaṣfā*, 1:585.

[102] On the role of *istiṣḥāb al-ḥāl* for those who adopted the *tawaqquf* position of suspension, see al-Qaṣṣār, *al-Muqaddima fī al-Uṣūl*, 157; al-Khaṭīb al-Baghdādī, *Kitāb al-Faqīh wa al-Mutafaqqih*, 191–92; Abū Isḥāq al-Shīrāzī, *Sharḥ al-Lumʿa*, 2:986; al-Lāmishī, *Kitāb fī Uṣūl al-Fiqh*, 188; Ibn al-Farikān, *Sharḥ al-Waraqāt*, 352–4.

obligations and prohibitions are tantamount to God's law is inappropriate, according to the authors addressed in this chapter. One cannot speak on behalf of God unless there are indicators of the divine will. Although reason functions epistemically to allow us to investigate whether God has erected indicators of His will, the fallibility of human reason prevents us from attaining authoritative knowledge about the law of God, where no scriptural authority exists. Scripture, as both authoritative and determinate, provides the kind of clarity and authority that natural reasoning, plagued as it is by indeterminacy, can never provide.

The Voluntarist critique of Hard Naturalism was fundamentally premised on a theological principle about God's power and its scope. Voluntarists rejected legal philosophies that could be perceived as limiting the authority and omnipotence of God. Yet, for the purpose of developing their own legal philosophy about the authority of reason, Voluntarists could not ignore the fact that some aspects of lived experience are not governed by an express, authoritative source-text. This is not the same, though, as saying that the absence of an authoritative source precludes a Sharīʿa-based determination of right and wrong, obligatory and prohibited. Indeed, if they were to suggest as much, they would limit the scope of Sharīʿa's dominion, and thereby the scope of God's dominion, over human affairs. But to develop a Sharīʿa-based response to the world of lived experience where authoritative sources offer no guidance requires a legal philosophy that recognizes alternate bases of legal authority that are nonetheless linked to the will of God. As shown in the next chapter, Voluntarist jurists adopted what we shall call Islamic Soft Natural Law whereby they, like their Hard Natural Law opponents, fused fact and value in nature to render natural reason an ontologically authoritative source of law. They upheld their theological commitment to God's omnipotence by arguing, however, that God created the natural world to be good out of His grace (*tafaḍḍul*), and not because of any theological imperative that limits His scope of action. As a divine good created by God, the natural world reflects a fusion of fact and value. Natural reason, therefore, may be used to investigate the facts of lived experience, and proffer evaluations about those facts with a normative authority premised on God's creative will. Certainly, God can change His mind and make the world bad or evil. But so far He has not. Invoking the concept of grace allows the Voluntarists to develop a natural law jurisprudence without violating their theological tenets. The good of nature is something God chooses to create, but is not bound to do. He chooses, out of grace, to create the natural world as a good for humanity. Consequently, argued Voluntarist Soft Natural Law jurists, we can rely upon the findings of natural reason to know the good and the bad, and thereby develop Sharīʿa obligations and prohibitions. While Voluntarist Soft Natural Law jurists started from distinct and different theological principles than their Hard Natural Law opponents, their legal philosophy ironically fuses fact and value in a way that closely resembles the philosophy of law they so vehemently criticized.

IV

Soft Natural Law

Voluntarist jurists considered scriptural sources (such as the Qur'ān and *ḥadīth*)—and authoritative pronouncements derived therefrom—as authoritative sources of obligation. But they also recognized that such sources had their limits, leaving lacunae in the law that needed to be addressed. For many, the solution was to extend the scriptural law to analogous cases (ie *qiyās*), thereby continuing to rely on scriptural sources to extend the law. Jurists would extend rules by analogy where there is a sufficient nexus between the *ratio legis* or *ʿilla* of the precedent and the new rule under consideration, thereby avoiding the indeterminacy and idiosyncrasy that can come with legal analysis. The Ẓāhirīs were concerned even by this level of judicial discretion and opposed rule by *qiyās*.[1] But what we find in much pre-modern legal theory is that Voluntarist jurists who opposed Hard Naturalism nonetheless acknowledged that, in some cases, reliance on the presumption of continuity (*istiṣḥāb al-ḥāl*) and *qiyās* is not enough. Rather, at times they would need to construct a rule of Sharīʿa obligation with the consequence of sanctions *on the basis of reasoned deliberation*. As the Shāfiʿite-Ashʿarite jurist al-Juwaynī (d. 478/1085) remarked, even the Companions of Muḥammad could not rely on scriptural precedent to base all their rulings. The diversity of circumstances that arose in their time (*al-waqāʾiʿ*) exceeded the subject matter addressed by source-texts (*tuzīdu ʿalā al-manṣūṣāt*).[2] Consequently, some level of

[1] Mohammad Hashim Kamali, *Principles of Islamic Jurisprudence* (3rd edn, Cambridge: Islamic Texts Society, 2003) 265, 290–3; Ahmad Hasan, *Analogical Reasoning in Islamic Jurisprudence: A Study of the Juridical Principle of Qiyas* (Islamabad: Islamic Research Institute, 1986) 425–62.

[2] Abū al-Maʿālī Al-Juwaynī, *al-Burhān fī Uṣūl al-Fiqh*, Ṣalāḥ b. Muḥammad b. ʿAwīḍa (ed) (Beirut: Dār al-Kutub al-ʿIlmiyya, 1997) 2:13.

interpretive agency was required to make the law a workable system that could address situations as they arose. This chapter explores how Voluntarist jurists developed their own natural law theory (Soft Natural Law), and yet rejected Hard Natural Law. Again, the implication of their theory for the ontological authority of reason distinguishes this discussion from the debates on *ijtihād*.[3] Instead, the question this chapter addresses is how Voluntarists philosophically ascribed ontological authority to their reasoned deliberations about the Sharīʿa.

Specifically, this chapter inquires into what this study calls Soft Natural Law. As will be shown below, Voluntarists developed Soft Natural Law theories by which they fused fact and value in nature. In doing so, they had to justify extending the Sharīʿa on rational grounds while preserving their theological commitment to God's omnipotence. Soft Naturalists relied on arguments of divine grace (*tafaḍḍul*) and inferences from scriptural texts to fuse fact and value in nature. In Soft Natural Law, *maṣlaḥa*, as a technical term of art, captures the fusion of fact and value in nature in the same way that *ibāḥa* fuses them in the Hard Natural Law theories discussed earlier. The fundamental difference, though, is that Hard Natural Law infuses nature with a normativity that is unchanging and is merely corroborated by scriptural sources. Soft Natural Law theories rely on a theology of God's grace (*tafaḍḍul*, *faḍl*), and the authority of source-texts to justify fusing fact and value in nature, but contingently so. By fusing fact and value on the basis of divine grace (*faḍl*), Soft Natural Law jurists allowed for the possibility that God may change His mind. Divine grace in Soft Natural Law permits the fusion of fact and value in nature, while at the same time rendering nature contingent in a way that Hard Natural Law theorists did not allow. Because of the philosophical contingency in nature's goodness, this study calls this second natural law approach *soft*.

To illustrate approaches to Soft Natural Law, this chapter will focus on how particular jurists designed their theories using the

[3] The scholarly literature on that topic is well developed and illustrates that jurists throughout the centuries utilized *ijtihād*, despite contentions in the scholarly literature that the 'door of *ijtihād*' was closed. Wael B Hallaq, 'Was the Gate of Ijtihad Closed?' (1984) 16 *International Journal of Middle East Studies* 3; Shiasta P Ali-Karamali and Fiona Dunne, 'The Ijtihad Controversy' (1994) 9 *Arab Law Quarterly* 238.

terms *faḍl* and *tafaḍḍul, maqāṣid al-sharīʿa, maṣlaḥa*, and *munāsaba* to justify reason as a source of Sharīʿa, where no source-text exists for a given issue. Their conception of *maṣlaḥa* operates at two levels. At its most general level, *maṣlaḥa* speaks to the broad jurisprudential themes of rendering nature normatively foundational. *Maṣlaḥa* contributes to the philosophical debate about the fusion of fact and value, and the ontological authority of reason in the law. In more context-specific cases *maṣlaḥa* is aimed at limiting the scope of reasoned deliberation; in this context, it becomes part of an epistemic method of analysis. Certainly, Sunnī jurists of different schools seemed to suggest that the Mālikīs extensively relied on this latter device to extend the law.[4] In fact, some would say that the Mālikīs went too far in their resort to such rational speculations.[5] But as the Mālikī al-Qarāfī stated, all the Sunnī schools seem to rely on arguments from *maṣlaḥa* in some fashion (*bal al-madhāhib kulluhā mushtarika fīhā*).[6] In other words, for al-Qarāfī, whether one uses terms such as *maṣlaḥa, maṣlaḥa mursala* or *istiḥsān*, underlying these technical terms is a recognition of the authority of reason, despite considerable anxiety about limiting its scope.

Reason, Authority, and Scope

This chapter begins with a preliminary analysis of two Shāfiʿite jurists concerned with the authority to develop rules of Sharīʿa where source-texts are silent. This preliminary discussion offers a starting point for this chapter because Soft Natural Law jurists had to justify and to limit reason in a way that did not result in massive or radical indeterminacy. This initial discussion on the scope and authority of

[4] Sayf al-Dīn Abū al-Ḥasan ʿAlī b. Abī ʿAlī b. Muḥammad Al-Āmidī, *al-Iḥkām fī Uṣūl al-Aḥkām* (Beirut: Dār al-Fikr, 1997) 3–4:308; Fakhr al-Dīn Muḥammad b. ʿUmar Al-Rāzī, *al-Maḥṣūl fī ʿIlm Uṣūl al-Fiqh*, Ṭāha al-ʿAlwāni (ed) (3rd edn, Beirut: Mu'assasat al-Risāla, 1997) 6:165; Shihāb al-Dīn Abū al-ʿAbbās Aḥmad b. Idrīs b. ʿAbd al-Raḥmān Al-Qarāfī, *Nafā'is al-Uṣūl fī Sharḥ al-Maḥṣūl*, Muḥammad ʿAbd al-Qādir ʿAṭā (ed) (Beirut: Dār al-Kutub al-ʿIlmiyya, 2000) 4:701; ʿAlī b. ʿAbd al-Kāfī al-Subkī and Tāj al-Dīn ʿAbd al-Wahhāb b. ʿAlī al-Subkī, *al-Ibhāj fī Sharḥ al-Minhāj* (Beirut: Dār al-Kutub al-ʿIlmiyya, 1995) 3:178.

[5] Al-Juwaynī, *al-Burhān*, 2:161; al-Qarāfī, *Nafā'is al-Uṣūl*, 4:701.

[6] Al-Qarāfī, *Nafā'is al-Uṣūl*, 4:705.

reasoned deliberation illustrates the basic tensions Soft Natural Law jurists contended with when developing not only their theory of natural law, but also their respective models of practical reasoning.

The Shāfiʿite contemporaries al-Juwaynī (d. 478/1085) and Abū al-Muẓaffar al-Samʿānī (d. 489/1096)[7] asked what a jurist can do in situations where there is no direct precedent on point. For both, the answer lay in reasoning through the legal problems, or what they called *istidlāl*. Al-Juwaynī defined *istidlāl* as a mode of reasoning to law from principle. For him, *istidlāl* involves 'a principle that suggests a corresponding ruling on the basis of reasoned deliberation, without finding a source that is agreed upon' (*maʿnā mashʿar bi al-ḥukm munāsab lahu fīmā yaqtaḍayhi al-fikr al-ʿaqlī min ghayr wajdān aṣl muttafaq ʿalayhi*).[8] Al-Samʿānī conveyed the same definition word for word.[9]

Both recognized that the use of *istidlāl* was a contentious matter among the Sunnī legal schools. Al-Juwaynī and al-Samʿānī said that many jurists rejected its use and instead resorted to methods of analysis that rely on authoritative sources of Sharīʿa, such as the Qurʾān and *ḥadīth*. But they noted that Mālik b. Anas, the eponym of the Mālikī school, was an ardent proponent of *istidlāl*. In fact, al-Juwaynī suggested that Mālik went too far in utilizing this technique by relying on rationales that pose too loose a rational nexus (*baʿīda*) to those policies and rationales already well established in extant Sharīʿa doctrines.[10] The Shāfiʿites and the Ḥanafites, they both argued, relied on *istidlāl* to a more limited extent. According to al-Juwaynī, if they could not find an agreed-upon scriptural source, they would utilize *istidlāl* but without indulging in extremes (*al-ifrāṭ*) or relying on reasons that display a loose rational nexus to the established body of the Sharīʿa. Instead, Shāfiʿites and Ḥanafites argued on the basis of perceived goods that were similar to those

[7] Al-Samʿānī was originally a Ḥanafite, following his family in that regard. However biographical accounts state that he later abandoned the Ḥanafite *madhhab* and adopted the Shāfiʿite school as his *madhhab*. Tāj al-Dīn al-Subkī, *Ṭabaqāt al-Shāfiʿiyya al-Kubrā*, 3:278–82; Shams al-Dīn Muḥammad b. Aḥmad ʿUthmān Al-Dhahabī, *Siyar Aʿlām al-Nubalāʾ*, Shuʿayb al-Arnaʾūt and Akram al-Būshi (eds) (Beirut: Muʾassasat al-Risāla, 1986) 19:114.

[8] Al-Juwaynī, *al-Burhān*, 2:161.

[9] Abū al-Muẓaffar Al-Samʿānī, *Qawāṭiʿ al-Adilla fī al-Uṣūl*, Muḥammad Ḥasan Muḥammad Ḥasan Ismāʿīl al-Shāfiʿī (ed) (Beirut: Dār al-Kutub al-ʿIlmiyya, 1997) 2:259.

[10] Al-Samʿānī, *Qawāṭiʿ al-Adilla*, 2:259; al-Juwaynī, *al-Burhān*, 2:161.

already agreed upon or in scriptural sources.[11] For instance, when al-Samʿānī wrote about the Shāfiʿite use of *istidlāl*, he said that Shāfiʿite jurists would consider *istidlāl* as evidence for a rule where there is no specific source-text to rely upon, as long as there is a tight nexus (*qurb*) between the reason underlying the new rule and the totality of rationales underlying rules already agreed upon and established pursuant to authoritative sources.[12]

For both jurists, the fundamental challenge to the use of *istidlāl* was the threat of rampant indeterminacy, and consequently an illegitimacy stemming from the possibility of unchecked legal pluralism and juridical discretion. For instance, one might presume that any rationales contained in sources such as the Qurʾān, Sunna of the Prophet, and consensus (*ijmāʿ*) can be legitimately relied upon as the product of the divine will (*munḥaṣira fī ḍabṭ al-shāriʿ*).[13] But if one's analysis does not rely on such sources, they worried that the matter will become wide open, the law will be subject to idiosyncratic assertions, and the jurist will unduly assume the legislative authority of the prophets. Each person will do as he sees fit and the law will differ with every change in time and place in a way that will depart from the precedent of the first generations of Muslims.[14] 'Veritably this is a way of invalidating the splendor of the Sharīʿa' (*wa hādha dharīʿa fī al-ḥaqīqa ilā ibṭāl ubbahat al-sharīʿa*).[15] If one could rely on sources other than source-texts or consensus, the result would be massive indeterminacy. In such a case, 'the law of God today would be different from what it was yesterday, and the law for one person will differ from [the law] for his neighbor'.[16]

Despite this criticism, both jurists recognized the inevitability of reasoned deliberation in the Sharīʿa. For them, every situation requires a rule from God (*ḥukm Allāh*) and every contemporary situation (*ḥādith, wāqiʿa*) should be addressed in a matter consistent with the Sharīʿa. This is not to say that God has provided an express statement of the relevant ruling for every situation. Rather, this reflects an imperative to ensure order through the law, even where there is no express directive from an authoritative source-text.

[11] Al-Juwaynī, *al-Burhān*, 2:161.
[12] Al-Samʿānī, *Qawāṭiʿ al-Adilla*, 2:259.
[13] Al-Juwaynī, *al-Burhān*, 2:162.
[14] Al-Juwaynī, *al-Burhān*, 2:162.
[15] Al-Juwaynī, *al-Burhān*, 2:162. For the same language, see al-Samʿānī, *Qawāṭiʿ al-Adilla*, 2:259.
[16] Al-Samʿānī, *Qawāṭiʿ al-Adilla*, 2:260.

To otherwise refrain from judgment would lead to the implication that the Sharīʿa does not and cannot offer a system of legal ordering and governance. As al-Juwaynī and al-Samʿānī would have rejected such an implication, they held that through interpretation and analysis a jurist could arrive at a legal answer that is consistent and coherent with the established body of Sharīʿa, which checks against idiosyncrasy and indeterminacy in the law.[17]

Since both believed that *istidlāl* is a necessity, they had to justify it against charges of illegitimacy and indeterminacy. The legitimacy of *istidlāl*, they argued, is based on the actions of the Companions of Muḥammad, who looked beyond source-texts to determine rules of conduct for themselves as circumstances changed. Both al-Juwaynī and al-Samʿānī wrote that the companions utilized reason without turning to foundational sources of legal authority (*yakhūḍūna fī wujūh al-raʾy min ghayr iltifāt ilā al-uṣūl*),[18] thereby justifying the authority of reasoned deliberation in the form of *istidlāl*.

Furthermore and most interestingly, they argued that authoritative sources such as source-texts are not by themselves the justificatory foundation for Sharīʿa rules to begin with. Rather, the purpose of Sharīʿa is to effectuate the underlying principles that animate the rules found in such sources. Relying on the authority of al-Shāfiʿī himself, al-Juwaynī and al-Samʿānī said that when principles of law (*al-maʿānī*) have a basis in authoritative sources (*al-uṣūl*), relying on and adhering to them is permitted. Indeed, the principles underlying the scriptural proofs provide the foundational justification for the rules.[19] The principles are not evident by themselves of course: scriptural sources must be utilized to reveal what they are. But fundamentally, the justificatory basis for rules of law is the *maʿnā* or legal principle. The *naṣṣ* or authoritative textual source simply provides the epistemic medium by which jurists know what the principle is. Consequently, by reducing the role of source-texts to being epistemic instruments in legal interpretation,

[17] Al-Samʿānī, *Qawāṭiʿ al-Adilla*, 2:260; al-Juwaynī, *al-Burhān*, 2:162.

[18] Al-Juwaynī, *al-Burhān*, 2:163; al-Samʿānī, *Qawāṭiʿ al-Adilla*, 2:260. Notably, al-Samʿānī used the same language as al-Juwaynī.

[19] Al-Samʿānī, *Qawāṭiʿ al-Adilla*, 2:260. For similar language, see al-Juwaynī, *al-Burhān*, 2:163.

al-Juwaynī and al-Samʿānī focused attention on the content of the principle, rather than upon its provenance. By emphasizing the content of the principle, the jurists implicitly granted authority to reasoned deliberation to ascertain the implications of a given principle in legal analysis.

Having established the legitimacy of reason, both jurists still had to contend with the possibility of indeterminacy. To respond to this concern, both authors introduced the term *taqrīb* or 'rational nexus'. Al-Juwaynī, for instance, admitted that if we rely on every independent judgment without recourse to some nexus (*min ghayr qurb wa madānā*), the rational person is left to judge only by what he thinks is best. But this is not a position he favored.[20] Rather, if jurists tightly link (*yuqarribūna*) their rational assessment to the 'established principles of the Sharīʿa' (*al-qawāʿid al-thābita fī al-sharīʿa*), that would be sufficient, as long as there is no scriptural or consensual source that opposes the conclusion reached through *istidlāl*.[21] *Taqrīb* captures how the scope of reasoned deliberation is limited to the confines of the totality of principles and rationales already established in the Sharīʿa. Those scripturally based principles in the Sharīʿa are considered inviolable (*muʿtaṣamī*).[22] Any subsequent rational proofs based on *istidlāl* must pose a nexus to those principles. Specifically, al-Juwaynī said:

> I correlate the *istidlāl* proofs [with the well established rules] . . . such that the [former] become similar to the [latter] . . . When the rationale of a jurist and investigator poses a close nexus to the revealed law, and no source opposes it, it is an accepted form of *istidlāl*.[23]

As will be shown below, Soft Naturalists justified the ontological authority of reason by fusing fact and value. To do so they concentrated on the technical term *maṣlaḥa*. *Maṣlaḥa* means something that poses a good.[24] Through their use of *maṣlaḥa*, Soft Naturalists

[20] Al-Juwaynī, *al-Burhān*, 2:164. [21] Al-Juwaynī, *al-Burhān*, 2:164.

[22] Al-Juwaynī, *al-Burhān*, 2:165.

[23] Al-Juwaynī, *al-Burhān*, 2:164-165. For similar language, see, al-Samʿānī, *Qawāṭiʿ al-Adilla*, 2:261.

[24] Abū al-Faḍl Jamāl al-Dīn Muḥammad b. Makram Ibn Manẓūr, *Lisān al-ʿArab* (6th edn, Beirut: Dar al-Ṣadr, 1997) 2:517; Muḥibb al-Dīn Abū Fayḍ Muḥammad Murtaḍā al-Ḥusayni Al-Zabīḍdī, *Tāj al-ʿUrūs min Jawāhir al-Qāmūs*, ʿAlī Shīrī (ed) 20 vols (Beirut: Dār al-Fikr, 1994) 4:125–6.

fused the empiricism of nature with a normativity that could serve as the foundation for naturalistic reasoning about Sharīʿa obligations. Soft Naturalists recognized that at times one must formulate rules of Sharīʿa by reference to the natural order. Their resort to a naturalist account of the law arguably puts them in a similar position as Hard Naturalists, who also fused fact and value in nature. Our concern in this chapter, though, is how these Soft Naturalists justified their resort to reason while remaining distinct from the Hard Naturalists.

To justify their jurisprudential approach, they invoked Qurʾānic verses and *ḥadīth* accounts that command believers to look to nature and the created world for guidance on how to evaluate and at times even construct the law without reference to any specific source-text. Consequently, whereas the Hard Naturalists viewed these source-texts as merely corroborating what they already knew rationally, Soft Naturalist jurists relied on scripture as a necessary foundation for their resort to natural reasoning. Furthermore, Soft Naturalists relied on the concept of God's grace (*tafaḍḍul*) to avoid their theological concerns with Hard Naturalism. Certainly scripture tells people to look to nature for indicators of God's will. But it is God who created that nature out of His grace, which He can presumably change if and when He desires. By relying on the concept of divine grace and the authority of scripture, the Soft Naturalists could look to the natural world's bounties, which God created out of His grace. In doing so, they both preserved God's omnipotence and fused fact and value in nature to justify the authority of reason in Sharīʿa. The Soft Naturalists may have started from theological premises that counter those of Hard Naturalists. But ironically, their natural law jurisprudence resembles Hard Natural Law, with some differences that will be elaborated upon below.

One important development in Soft Natural Law theory is the framework of practical reasoning offered by many Soft Naturalist jurists. Soft Naturalists argued that the totality of Sharīʿa shows that the law is designed to uphold five basic goals or purposes, namely the preservation of life, lineage, property, mind, and religion. These aims, or *maqāṣid*, are what any legal system or community would uphold. These intuitively established basic aims provide the telos of Sharīʿa. But these aims alone cannot offer a method of analysis. Soft

Naturalist jurists erected a system of practical reasoning that allowed them to develop rules of Sharīʿa in narrowly defined areas in accordance with the aims of the Sharīʿa. In some areas of human behavior, the law must offer guidance if the purposes of Sharīʿa are to be met. Yet, for our Soft Naturalists, those areas must be narrowly tailored in order to limit the scope of reasoned deliberation and thereby ensure that the authority of Sharīʿa remains closely linked to the will of God.

Below are four analyses of Soft Natural Law theories. Starting with the Shāfiʿite Abū Ḥāmid al-Ghazālī (d. 505/1111), this chapter will illustrate how he fused fact and value, and show its importance to his model of practical reasoning. Subsequent authors such as the Shāfiʿite Fakhr al-Dīn al-Rāzī (d. 606/1209) and the Mālikite Shihāb al-Dīn al-Qarāfī (d. 684/1285) built upon al-Ghazālī's work while contributing their own philosophical insights and nuances to their Soft Natural Law. The Ḥanbalī Najm al-Dīn al-Ṭūfī (d. 8th/14th century) attempted to go beyond these authors by expanding the scope of application for his Soft Naturalism. Lastly the Mālikite al-Shāṭibī (d. 790/1388), familiar with al-Ghazālī, al-Rāzī and al-Qarāfi, provided the most conceptually involved natural law theory, which built on what came before him and extended the analysis considerably to account for how nature, through conventionalism, can be utilized as a basis for generating Sharīʿa obligations.

Abū Ḥāmid al-Ghazālī (d. 505/1111)

Al-Ghazālī wrote two works that addressed relevant topics for this discussion. The first is *Shifāʾ al-Ghalīl*, and the second is his monumental treatise, *al-Mustaṣfā min ʿIlm al-Uṣūl. Shifāʾ al-Ghalīl* seems to have preceded *al-Mustaṣfā*, while *al-Mustaṣfā* represents al-Ghazālī's mature ideas on the topic of legal philosophy.[25] In the discussion on *maṣlaḥa* and its related technical terms, the discussions in both works overlap, with some differences. This study will

[25] Abū Isḥāq b. Ibrāhīm b. Mūsā b. Muḥammad al-Shāṭibī, *al-Iʿtiṣām*, Salīm b. ʿĪd al-Halālī (ed) (Khobar: Dār Ibn ʿAffān, 1997) 2:608.

focus primarily on *al-Mustaṣfā*, while indicating where al-Ghazālī modified his earlier views by reference to relevant passages from *Shifāʾ al-Ghalīl*.

The Authority of *Maṣlaḥa*-Reasoning: al-Ghazālī's Natural Law Theory

Important to this discussion is how al-Ghazālī proffered his Soft Natural Law theory while also remaining distinct from Hard Natural Law. Al-Ghazālī used the term *maṣlaḥa* to fuse fact and value in nature, and thereby grant reason ontological authority in the Sharīʿa. But al-Ghazālī made it quite clear that although he fused fact and value in nature, his jurisprudence should not be confused with the Hard Naturalist approach, which presumes, in part, that God is obligated to do the good. He avoided entangling himself with Hard Natural Law by asserting that the fusion of fact and value is possible because of divine grace. In doing so, al-Ghazālī preserved God's voluntaristic omnipotence while fusing fact and value in nature, thereby enabling the necessary philosophical conditions to render reason authoritative.

Al-Ghazālī's fusion of fact and value is apparent where he addressed the authority of *maṣlaḥa*-based reasoning in relation to fulfilling the aims of the Sharīʿa. When writing about the nature of *maṣlaḥa*, al-Ghazālī said that fulfilling *maṣlaḥa* is the goal of the divine legislator (*maqṣūd al-shāriʿ*) and is required for the wellbeing and fulfillment (*ḍarūrat al-khalq*) of all God's creation. Importantly, he stated:

> Reason evaluates [the *maṣlaḥa*] and judges whether or not there is express law (*lau lā wurūd al-sharāʾiʿ*)[substantiating it]. No law can be without [*maṣlaḥa*], according to those who speak of the good and the bad as rational matters (*taḥsīn al-ʿaql wa taqbīḥihi*). We say: It is for God most high to do as He wishes with his servants; it is not obligatory on Him to uphold the good (*riʿāyat al-ṣalāḥ*). [But] we do not deny the power of rational capacities to indicate the beneficial and the corrupt (*al-maṣāliḥ wa al-mafāsid*), and their ability to warn against harm and to desire obtaining bounties and fulfillment. Nor do we deny that the prophets, on them be peace, were sent for the benefit of creation in matters of this world and religion (*li maṣāliḥ al-khalq fī al-dīn wa al-dunyā*) – as a mercy and grace

from God on creation (*raḥma, faḍl*), and not [because of] an imposition or obligation on Him. God most high said: 'We did not send you except as a mercy for the world' and so on, from verses that illustrate as much. Indeed we have explained [ourselves] to this extent in order that we not be associated with the beliefs of the Muʿtazila (*iʿtiqād al-iʿtizāl*).[26]

Al-Ghazālī argued that one's rational capacities can empirically investigate the good and the bad. We know from source-texts that God creates in order to benefit humanity. He is not required to do so. Rather He chooses to do so. The correlation between source-texts and our empirical observations about the world suggests that the good we discern in the world is indeed intended and desired by God. The correlation between the fact of the good in the world, and the fact that God has chosen to benefit humanity through His creative power, provides the basis for infusing our empirical findings with normative content.

The normative content that infuses any such empirical assessment, though, is based on a voluntaristic theory of divine creation that preserves God's omnipotence. God provides, out of His grace, various benefits to human beings through His act of creation. The created world becomes a normative foundation for reasoned deliberation because of God's voluntaristic grace and not because of any obligations upon God. Fact and value are fused through the jurisprudence of *maṣlaḥa* without indulging in any theological implications that undermine God's omnipotence. Under al-Ghazālī's version of nature, God is not bound to do the good, but He does so out of His choice and purposiveness. We as humans can both rely on the constancy that results from God's gracious creation of an affirmatively beneficial nature, and create Sharīʿa norms through reasoned deliberation about the world around us. But we are also aware that God can alter His grace if He chooses. Al-Ghazālī's Soft Natural Law preserves a commitment to divine omnipotence, repudiates Hard Natural Law, and renders reason ontologically authoritative in Sharīʿa matters.

[26] Abū Ḥāmid Muḥammad al-Ghazālī, *Shifāʾ al-Ghalīl fī Bayān al-Shabh wa al-Mukhīl wa Masālik al-Taʿlīl*, Muḥammad al-Kubaysī (ed) (Baghdad: Raʿāsa Dīwān al-Awqāf, 1971) 162–3.

Maṣlaḥa, *Maqāṣid*, and Practical Reasoning

Having fused fact and value in nature (and thereby in *maṣlaḥa*), al-Ghazālī illustrated how his naturalistic model contributes to a model of practical reasoning. In other words, assuming the fusion of fact and value above, al-Ghazālī moved from the more general task of philosophizing about nature and the ontological authority of reason to the more specific task of reasoning to a Sharīʿa ruling. To do so, he utilized the term *maṣlaḥa* in a second register, namely as a specific, more context-sensitive, principle of a good to be achieved. In this context, the term *maṣlaḥa* does not mean simply anything that allows one to obtain a benefit (*jalb manfaʿa*) or to repel a harm (*dafʿ maḍarra*).[27] Al-Ghazālī's use of the term has a more technical meaning than this general linguistic understanding. For al-Ghazālī *maṣlaḥa* as a technical Sharīʿa term of art refers to any interest that upholds and preserves the purpose of the divine law (*al-muḥāfiẓa ʿalā maqṣūd al-sharʿ*).[28] The purpose of the law consists of preserving religion (*dīn*), life (*nafs*), reason (*ʿaql*), lineage (*nasl*), and property (*māl*). 'Whatever involves the preservation of these five fundamental values is a *maṣlaḥa*. Whatever neglects these fundamental values is corrupt, and so repelling it is a *maṣlaḥa*.'[29] Al-Ghazālī illustrated these five values by referring to various scriptural examples. For instance, punishing an unbeliever who leads others astray upholds and protects the value of religion.[30] The value of life is upheld by the punishment of execution for murder or retribution for a physical injury (ie *qiṣāṣ*).[31] The punishment for consuming alcohol upholds the virtue of having a sound mind,[32] while the punishments for fornication and adultery protect the integrity of family and lineage.[33] Finally, the punishments for theft and usurpation maintain the basic aim of upholding property interests.[34]

[27] Abū Ḥāmid Muḥammad b. Muḥammad al-Ghazālī, *al-Mustasfā min ʿIlm al-Uṣūl*, Ibrāhīm Muḥammad Ramaḍān (ed) (Beirut: Dār al-Arqam, n.d.) 1:636. Ibn Manẓūr, *Lisān al-ʿArab*, 2:517, defined the term as the good or *ṣalāḥ*. For the same definition, see al-Zabīdī, *Tāj al-ʿUrūs*, 4:125–6.

[28] Al-Ghazālī, *al-Mustasfā*, 1:636.

[29] Al-Ghazālī, *al-Mustasfā*, 1:636.

[30] Al-Ghazālī, *al-Mustasfā*, 1:637.

[31] Al-Ghazālī, *al-Mustasfā*, 1:637.

[32] Al-Ghazālī, *al-Mustasfā*, 1:637.

[33] Al-Ghazālī, *al-Mustasfā*, 1:637.

[34] Al-Ghazālī, *al-Mustasfā*, 1:637.

Importantly, the basic aims of the Sharīʿa are not derived from scriptural source-texts. Source-texts, at most, confirm and corroborate them. For al-Ghazālī, these values are *intuitively* known. They are the kinds of values that any society or legal tradition would uphold if it values the preservation and flourishing of society. He stated: 'It is impossible that any society (*milla min al-milal*) or any legal system (*sharīʿa min al-sharāʾiʿ*), which aims for the benefit of creation (*iṣlāḥ al-khalq*) would not include prohibitions against neglect of and restraint from these five values.'[35] These five aims provide the telos to which any *maṣlaḥa* must pose a nexus before it can contribute to the development of a Sharīʿa rule.

Not every *maṣlaḥa* can enjoy such authority, though. Al-Ghazālī judged the authority of a *maṣlaḥa* by reference to its nexus to the totality of source-texts, and its nexus to the five basic values. With respect to the first nexus, al-Ghazālī offered three categories of *maṣlaḥa*. As will be illustrated, the *maṣlaḥa* that matters the most for Soft Natural Law is the one on which scriptural sources are silent. For instance, a *maṣlaḥa* might be positively affirmed by scripture; al-Ghazālī called this type of *maṣlaḥa* '*muʿtabar*'. An example of this kind of *maṣlaḥa* would be the prohibition of any intoxicant. The Qurʾān condemns the consumption of wine.[36] One can use this source-text reference to wine as a basis for creating other prohibitions against any and all intoxicating substances on the ground that such prohibitions protect the integrity of the mind. Although the scriptural provision specifies wine, nonetheless, a rule by prior precedent (*qiyās*) can extend the ban on wine to include a ban on all intoxicants.[37] Importantly, though, this example is not technically a rule based on *maṣlaḥa*. Rather this is a rule by reference to a precedent (*qiyās*), according to al-Ghazālī, and consequently is not central to an inquiry into al-Ghazālī's theory of naturalistic practical reasoning.

On the other hand, a *maṣlaḥa* might be expressly repudiated in source-texts. Al-Ghazālī mentioned as an example the case of the king who has sex during the day in the month of Ramaḍān, when

[35] Al-Ghazālī, *al-Mustasfā*, 1:637. [36] Qurʾān, 2:219, 4:43, 5:90–1.
[37] Al-Ghazālī, *al-Mustasfā*, 1:634–5.

Muslims are required, during daylight hours, to abstain from food, drink, and sex. Jurists debated how he should expiate the sin of deliberately breaking his fast in this fashion. The Qurʾān stipulates as expiation that one should free a slave. But if one cannot do so, one should fast for two consecutive months. If that is not possible, one should feed sixty indigent people.[38] Some jurists argued that a king should fast two consecutive months and not free a slave, despite the latter being mentioned first in the Qurʾānic verse, and presumably taking priority over the other options for expiation. They argued that since the king has such great wealth, freeing a slave does not pose a significant deterrent to him. To deter him from breaking his fast, he should be required to fast two consecutive months instead. But for al-Ghazālī, this view is invalid despite being based on a reasonable *maṣlaḥa*. He believed that this rationale contradicts the text of the Qurʾān, which provides a clear indication of the order of priority by which the expiations should be applied to the wrongdoer. To open the door to this kind of *maṣlaḥa*, argued al-Ghazālī, would lead to a change in all the limits of the law (*ḥudūd al-sharāʾiʿ*) because of changes in circumstance or context.[39] Such interpretations would undermine determinacy in the law and diminish the integrity of jurists among the people.[40] Again, however, this particular type of *maṣlaḥa* is not central to al-Ghazālī's Soft Natural Law. He may very well sympathize with the rationale underlying it. But to give it legal effect would have negative effects on other important issues that pertain to the legal system as a whole, rather than to the specific issue of the wealthy ruler. For our purposes, though, al-Ghazālī's characterization of this *maṣlaḥa* illustrates the ongoing importance and centrality of source-texts in al-Ghazālī's legal method. It is arguably offered to circumscribe the extent to which reasoned deliberation about *maṣlaḥa* values can operate in the law.

The last category of *maṣlaḥa* is the one on which scripture is completely silent: there is no express adoption or rejection of

[38] Qurʾān, 58:3–4. This verse actually addresses the expiation for illegitimately rejecting one's wife and marital union through the mechanisms of *ẓihār*. However, as jurists such as al-Marghīnānī wrote, the expiation for violating the fast was the same as for engaging in *ẓihār*. Al-Marghīnānī, *al-Hidāya*, 1–2:150.

[39] Al-Ghazālī, *al-Mustasfā*, 1:635.

[40] Al-Ghazālī, *al-Mustasfā*, 1:635.

this *maṣlaḥa* by any specific textual indicator (*naṣṣ muʿayyan*).[41] This type of *maṣlaḥa* is the one that can be the basis for generating *de novo* rules of law and is central to al-Ghazālī's theory of practical reasoning. It represents the limited sphere in which a jurist can exercise reason, since the other types of *maṣlaḥa* are either accepted or rejected by scripture.

The second nexus that al-Ghazālī addressed involves the relationship between the silent *maṣlaḥa* and the five values of the legal system. A silent *maṣlaḥa* can pose a nexus to these values of the Sharīʿa in three different ways. First it may present a necessary interest (*ḍarūrāt*), in which case the *maṣlaḥa* is of the highest order. Alternatively, it can pose only a basic need (*ḥājāt*), where the *maṣlaḥa* is deemed important, but does not rise to the highest order. And lastly, a silent *maṣlaḥa* can present an edificatory interest (*tazyīnāt, taḥsīnāt*), which occupies the lowest priority of interests for the purposes of practical reasoning.[42] The silent *maṣlaḥa* is divided into these three subcategories to emphasize the strength (*quwwa*) of the nexus to the five basic aims of Sharīʿa, and therefore to the wellbeing of society.[43] Examples of necessary interests include punishments for consumption of alcohol, murder, and adultery. Of course, those punishments are based on scriptural texts and are not derived from a silent *maṣlaḥa*; however they illustrate for al-Ghazālī the kind of nexus to the basic values that he had in mind when addressing the silent *maṣlaḥa* that pose necessary interests. An example of a *maṣlaḥa* that poses only a need might be the rule empowering a guardian (*taslīṭ al-walī*) over a minor in matters of marriage. This is not a necessary interest since the marriage of minors is not significant for furthering social wellbeing. It is a rule that upholds the underlying *maṣlaḥa* of ensuring that the minor marries someone who is suitable. 'But this is not like empowering the *walī* over upbringing (*tarbiyatihi*), nursing (*irḍāʿihi*), and buying clothing and food.'[44] These latter responsibilities pose necessary interests with a tight nexus to the basic aims of the law. In fact, they are so central to society that no disagreement about them can be imagined, according to

[41] Al-Ghazālī, *al-Mustaṣfā*, 1:635–6. [42] Al-Ghazālī, *al-Mustaṣfā*, 1:636.
[43] Al-Ghazālī, *al-Mustaṣfā*, 1:635–6. Underlying each of these categories of interests are subsidiary interests that supplement or perfect the primary rules of these categories (*takmila, tatimma*). [44] Al-Ghazālī, *al-Mustaṣfā*, 1:638.

al-Ghazālī.[45] Marriage of a minor does not pose such a necessity. According to al-Ghazālī, the longings of desire do not overtake children (*fa lā yarhaqu ilayhi tawaqān shahwa*), nor the need to procreate. Instead such marriages are intended to link clans (*ishtibāk al-ʿashāʾir*).[46] The nexus between this *maṣlaḥa* and the basic values is too weak to rise to the level of a necessity.

The weakest nexus that a silent *maṣlaḥa* can pose to the basic values is one that is neither necessary nor needed, but rather raises a society's level of excellence (*mazāya*) and perfection by upholding the best courses of conduct in how we deal with each other (*raʿāyat aḥsan al-manāhij fī al-ʿādāt wa al-muʿāmalāt*).[47] As an example, al-Ghazālī referred to the rule denying the slave any capacity to give testimony in court (*salb al-ʿabd ahliyya al-shahāda*).[48] The rationale for this rule is that slaves occupy a low social rank due to their subordinated status, and their deference to their masters. 'It is not appropriate to [the slave's] status that he issue testimony.'[49] Where issuing testimony in court holds a certain social meaning concerning social status, slaves are thereby denied any participation in this activity. However, the rule denying them this capacity poses the lowest level of a rational nexus to the basic values, thus indicating its peripherality to the law. In contrast to this, the rule denying slaves the capacity to be a guardian over a minor is of greater significance and appeals to a general need (*ḥāja*). It involves a public interest of greater importance than denying the slave the capacity to testify in court. The slave is denied the capacity to be a guardian because, according to al-Ghazālī, guardianship over a minor requires significant time and commitment; however the slave is already burdened with service to his master. Consequently, 'delegating the matters of children to him would cause an injury to the children'.[50]

Al-Ghazālī presented the two nexuses to source-texts and to the basic aims to make a significant and central point for his model of practical reasoning: a silent *maṣlaḥa* that only poses a need (*ḥāja*) or vindicates an edificatory interest (*taḥsīn/tazyīn*) cannot be the basis for creating new Sharīʿa rules.[51] In other words, the two lowest

[45] Al-Ghazālī, *al-Mustaṣfā*, 1:638.
[46] Al-Ghazālī, *al-Mustaṣfā*, 1:638.
[47] Al-Ghazālī, *al-Mustaṣfā*, 1:639.
[48] Al-Ghazālī, *al-Mustaṣfā*, 1:639.
[49] Al-Ghazālī, *al-Mustaṣfā*, 1:639.
[50] Al-Ghazālī, *al-Mustaṣfā*, 1:639.
[51] Al-Ghazālī, *al-Mustaṣfā*, 1:640.

categories, which pose the weakest nexus to the basic values of the legal system, cannot provide a basis for any rule of law by themselves. Rather, only the silent *maṣlaḥa* that poses the strongest nexus to the basic values, namely the necessities (*ḍarūrāt*), has sufficient authority to justify a Sharīʿa ruling. As al-Ghazālī stated, 'it is not farfetched that the interpretation of a jurist would lead to such a [*ḍarūra*-based] rule although no specific source of law exists as evidence for it' (*fa lā buʿd fī an yuʾdī ilayhi ijtihād mujtahid wa in lam yashhad lahu aṣl muʿayyan*).[52]

To illustrate how his notion of a necessary silent *maṣlaḥa* can provide a basis for generating a rule of law, al-Ghazālī presented a series of examples. Importantly, as will be discussed later, subsequent jurists utilized these hypotheticals in their own discussions on the use of *maṣlaḥa* as a basis for Sharīʿa analysis. Al-Ghazālī's examples illustrate that before any *maṣlaḥa* can constitute an authoritative basis for a rule of law, it must satisfy four conditions. First, it must be a silent *maṣlaḥa*. Secondly, the silent *maṣlaḥa* must pose a necessary interest (*ḍarūra*) that presents a tight nexus to the aims of the legal system. Thirdly, there must be certainty (*qaṭʿiyya*) that the interest at stake in a given situation can be satisfied by the proposed course of conduct. Lastly, the interest served must be for the benefit and perfection of society at large (*kulliyya*) and not for a defined group of people or special interest group, majoritarian or otherwise.

Al-Ghazālī's first example involves a hypothetical where unbelievers waging war against a Muslim army use Muslim civilians as human shields to protect their front line. Al-Ghazālī asked whether in this situation the Muslim army can fire upon the unbelievers, knowing that in doing so the Muslim army will kill the Muslim civilians used as shields. The answer to this question involves a context-sensitive inquiry into the nature of the interest involved. He wrote:

If we refrain from [the unbelievers] they will charge into us and conquer the land of Islam and kill the rest of the Muslims. But if we strike at the

[52] Al-Ghazālī, *al-Mustaṣfā*, 1:640–1. Notably, in his earlier work, *Shifāʾ al-Ghalīl*, al-Ghazālī stated that one could rely on both the *ḥāja* and the *ḍarūra* for independent analysis, as long as they inductively pose a nexus to the body of Sharīʿa (*kāna mulāʾim li taṣarrufāt al-sharʿ*). However, the third weakest category could not be used for such analysis. Al-Ghazālī, *Shifāʾ al-Ghalīl*, 208–9. On the notion of inductive suitability (*mulāʾim*), see below.

shield, we shall kill a Muslim who is innocent and who has committed no infraction. There is no knowledge of this [issue] in the *sharʿ*. If we refrain, the unbelievers will take power over all the Muslims and will kill them, and then will kill the prisoners [used as a shield]. So it is possible that one could say: 'This prisoner will be killed in any case. Protecting all the Muslims poses a tighter nexus (*aqrab*) to the aim of the law because we know with certainty that the aim of the law is to reduce killing, just as it aims to terminate killing entirely where possible. If we are not able to terminate [killing] we can reduce it. This involves a resort to a *maṣlaḥa* whose nature as a goal of the law is known by necessity, not by one piece of evidence or a specific scriptural source, but by evidence beyond estimation (*bi adilla khārija ʿan al-ḥaṣr*).[53]

If instead the enemy were fortified in a castle and still used Muslims as human shields, the analysis would change according to al-Ghazālī. In this case, the Muslims cannot be certain that they can conquer the enemy in the castle given its fortifications. Furthermore, conquering the castle does not pose a necessary interest as the non-Muslims penned up inside do not pose a risk to neighboring Muslim lands.[54]

This is not to suggest that al-Ghazālī relied on a stark utilitarian calculus concerning the good of the many. His approach to *maṣlaḥa* is not about maximizing the good while a minority bears the burden of the expense. Rather, his approach involves a conception of the good that contributes to the perfection of society. For instance, al-Ghazālī's second example concerns the passengers of a sinking boat. Suppose the passengers come to the conclusion that if they choose one person by lottery and throw him over board the boat will not sink and the rest of the passengers will be saved. Despite the one death, the value of life will be upheld by preserving the lives of those that remain. But even if the passengers have utter certitude about their survival if they adopt the lottery, al-Ghazālī held that the condition of scope is missing. The interest served is not *kullī* because those affected by the sinking boat are limited in number. Their reasoning reflects a utilitarian decision that violates the integrity of the individual. The injury the passengers would suffer is not tantamount to the massive destruction that could be imposed on Muslim society at large if, as in the earlier hypotheticals, the

[53] Al-Ghazālī, *al-Mustasfā*, 1:641–2. [54] Al-Ghazālī, *al-Mustasfā*, 1:642.

enemy makes advances in battle and conquers swathes of Muslim land.[55] The condition that a *maṣlaḥa* must pose a universal value for all of society suggests that al-Ghazālī's model of practical reasoning is not framed as a utilitarian principle of maximizing happiness for the greatest number of people. Surely the passengers may still hold a lottery and throw one person overboard. But they cannot justify their actions on Sharīʿa grounds. Any lottery in this case would fall outside the scope of what can be incorporated within the Sharīʿa. Instead, Sharīʿa embodies an aim and goal for society at large, in which individuals are themselves fulfilled by being respected and treated with integrity

Another example involves beating someone suspected of having stolen property. Certainly, to beat him and obtain a confession poses a positive public interest. Al-Ghazālī even noted that Mālik b. Anas allowed this practice.[56] But al-Ghazālī rejected its use. He admitted that torture can aid the resolution of criminal cases. But it conflicts with another public interest, namely protecting the alleged thief. 'Perhaps [the alleged thief] is innocent of the infraction. Omitting physical injury on a guilty person is less important (*ahwan*) than hitting the innocent. In hitting is an open door to deterring theft, but in hitting is an opening to punishing the innocent.'[57] While torture may present some benefit to law enforcement officials as they seek to convict criminals, it conflicts with a competing *maṣlaḥa* that has greater weight.[58] The greater weight of the defendant's right is represented by al-Ghazālī's use of the term *ahwan*, which is an evaluative term about the relative weight of the two *maṣlaḥa* interests involved here. How he strikes this balance is left unexplained. Perhaps, like his basic goods, he relies on intuition.

Suppose someone causes corruption in the land to achieve social discord (*fitna*). Is it lawful to kill this person? Certainly there is a

[55] Al-Ghazālī, *al-Mustasfā*, 1:642. [56] Al-Ghazālī, *al-Mustasfā*, 1:643.

[57] Al-Ghazālī, *al-Mustasfā*, 1:642–3.

[58] Noel Coulson argues contrary to this view, suggesting that Muslim jurists allowed rulers to use special measures such as threats and corporal punishment to extort confessions from alleged criminals. 'The State and the Individual in Islamic Law' (1957) 6 *International and Comparative Law Quarterly* 49, 52. However Coulson relies solely on the Mālikī jurist Ibn Farḥūn and his text *Tabṣirat al-Ḥukkām* for his assertion. See Coulson, 'The State,' 52 n 10, which significantly limits the scope of his conclusions.

public interest in doing so. But does it rise to the level of a *maṣlaḥa* on which we can base a Sharīʿa rule of law? Al-Ghazālī answered that the resolution to this question depends on the circumstances. If the individual has not engaged in any criminal activity requiring his execution, the authorities should only imprison him. Life imprisonment (*takhlīd al-ḥabs ʿalayhi*) is sufficient to counter the evil that this person inflicts on society.[59] There is no need to kill him because 'this *maṣlaḥa* is not *ḍarūra*'.[60] In other words, al-Ghazālī weighed the need to protect human life and limit government uses of violence with the need to ensure public order by using *maṣlaḥa* to decide how best to resolve this situation in a way that poses the best and most suitable nexus to the overall goals of the legal system.

But suppose that this agitator lives in an era of extreme social discord when the existing government may be toppled any day and cannot guarantee that it can keep the agitator imprisoned for life. Further, suppose that imprisoning the agitator for life will only increase his anger and hatred, thus rendering him even more dangerous. In this case, is it permissible to kill the agitator? For al-Ghazālī, these circumstances raise important questions but at the same time are purely speculative. There is no way to determine what will happen in advance, and one cannot thereby operate on what is tantamount to mere conjecture and speculation (*rajm bi al-ẓann wa ḥukm bi al-wahm*).[61]

This last hypothetical takes al-Ghazālī back to his first one concerning the enemy who uses Muslims as human shields. Suppose the Muslim commander is not certain that non-Muslims will overrun Muslim lands if the shields are left intact, but only knows that is likely to happen (*bi ghalabat al-ẓann*). Is this a sufficient standard of proof to authorize the Muslim army to fire on the Muslim shields? For al-Ghazālī, firing on the human shields is permitted if one can reach certainty that it is necessary, or at least a degree of likelihood that approximates certainty (*al-qaṭʿ aw ẓann qarīb min al-qaṭʿ*).[62] But even then, this type of near certainty can only be relied upon in those circumstances where the interest is of such universal scope and grave significance (*ṣāra kulliyyan*

[59] Al-Ghazālī, *al-Mustaṣfā*, 1:644.
[60] Al-Ghazālī, *al-Mustaṣfā*, 1:643–4.
[61] Al-Ghazālī, *al-Mustaṣfā*, 1:644.
[62] Al-Ghazālī, *al-Mustaṣfā*, 1:644–5.

wa ʿaẓuma al-khaṭar fīhi) that all people are concerned by the situation.[63] In other words, between certainty and mere speculation is a middle ground where something less than certainty may suffice to support a *maṣlaḥa*-based rule of Sharīʿa in a case where no specific source-text exists, but which poses a gravely significant matter that has society-wide ramifications.

Of course this hypothetical runs into a conflict with Qurʾānic verses that prohibit killing a believer intentionally or killing one without a right against him.[64] Is it possible to justify killing Muslim human shields on the basis of a *maṣlaḥa* where that *maṣlaḥa* seems to contradict scriptural prohibitions quite starkly? Al-Ghazālī was keen to suggest that he is not advocating a type of utilitarian inquiry into what benefits the many over the few. This, he suggested, was evident in his hypothetical about the sinking boat. Rather in this case one must first investigate the totality of the law. 'We know that the law prefers the universal scope (*al-kullī*), over the particular or narrow scope (*al-juzʾī*).'[65] Protecting the people of Islamic lands from their enemies is 'more important for the aims of the law (*ahamm fī maqṣūd al-sharʿ*) than protecting the life of a single Muslim'.[66] And importantly, for al-Ghazālī's intuitively based practical reasoning, this knowledge of the law's purpose is so certain and clear that it does not need any specific scriptural evidence to say so: 'Its certainty is not in need of any evidence' (*wa al-maqṭūʿ bihi lā yaḥtāju ilā shahādat aṣl*).[67] Juxtaposing the purpose with the scriptural prohibition on murder, al-Ghazālī is able to reason his way to a rule of law without violating his commitment to source-texts or his method of analysis. Indeed, legislating by resort to *maṣlaḥa* involves upholding the purposes of the law (*ḥafẓ maqāṣid al-sharʿ*) as articulated in the Qurʾān, Sunna and *ijmāʿ*.[68] Whether one looks to the totality of these sources (*taṣarrufāt al-sharʿ*) to justify a *maṣlaḥa* inductively or to corroborate basic values and goods, al-Ghazālī held that a *maṣlaḥa* analysis implicitly relies on these sources to authorize the investigation and infuse it with normative value.[69]

[63] Al-Ghazālī, *al-Mustasfā*, 1:644–5.
[64] See Qurʾān, 4:92–3, 5:32, 17:33.
[65] Al-Ghazālī, *al-Mustasfā*, 1:647.
[66] Al-Ghazālī, *al-Mustasfā*, 1:647.
[67] Al-Ghazālī, *al-Mustasfā*, 1:647.
[68] Al-Ghazālī, *al-Mustasfā*, 1:652.
[69] Al-Ghazālī, *al-Mustasfā*, 1:652–3.

While al-Ghazālī utilized other examples to illustrate his point about the use of *maṣlaḥa*, the above examples show how he created a system of practical reasoning that presumes the ontological authority of reason. His resort to intuition about the basic goods of society provides him with universal values that constitute the telos of his interpretive system. The *maṣlaḥa* that he identified poses public policy questions that address no specific party in interest. Rather the public policy questions concern society as a whole and its pursuit of perfection both at the individual and communal level. Ruling by *maṣlaḥa* is intended to fulfill and satisfy a basic aim of the law that is known not by a single piece of evidence but by an inestimable amount of evidence from the Qur'ān, Sunna, the context of situations, and various distinct indices (*bi adilla kathīra lā ḥaṣr lahā min al-kitāb wa al-sunna wa qarā'in al-aḥwāl wa tafārīq al-imārāt*).[70] Consequently, the basic purposes of the law are not solely captured by some inductive analysis of scriptural text. The totality of circumstances, whether textual or contextual, plays into the determination of the basic goods of society and the law. They are known intuitively, and as such a silent *maṣlaḥa* that poses the necessary nexus to those goods can be the basis for a rule of law.

From *Maṣlaḥa* to the *Ratio Legis* of a Rule

To bring the process of practical reasoning to its conclusion, al-Ghazālī required the silent *maṣlaḥa* to pose a third nexus, namely to the specific rule (*ḥukm*) to be created. The *maṣlaḥa* mediates between the basic values of the legal system (*maqāṣid*) and a particular rule of law (*ḥukm*). Al-Ghazālī referred to the nexus between the *maṣlaḥa* and a particular rule using the term *munāsaba*. The *munāsaba* is a rationale that so persuasively links the *maṣlaḥa* to the proffered rule of law that anyone who rejects it is simply obstinate (*ʿinād*).[71] The *munāsaba* puts forward the *ratio legis* that best ensures the rule upholds the basic aims of the Sharīʿa.

For example, al-Ghazālī wrote about the prohibition on wine consumption and asked whether wine's intoxicating quality provides the rationale for the prohibition. Intoxicants other than wine

[70] Al-Ghazālī, *al-Mustaṣfā*, 1:652–4. [71] Al-Ghazālī, *Shifā' al-Ghalīl*, 142.

are not specified in the Qurʾānic condemnation. Nonetheless, al-Ghazālī inferred from the prohibition that the *munāsaba* or rational principle underlying the prohibition has to do with wine's intoxicating effect. The characteristic of intoxication is reasonably related to the purpose of the original ban, namely to protect the integrity of the mind.[72] The *munāsaba* helps identify the *ratio legis* (*ʿilla*) of the rule in light of the purpose the rule is designed to achieve.[73]

According to al-Ghazālī, the legitimacy of a *munāsaba* depends on whether it is consistent with both the totality of scripture and the *maṣlaḥa* animating the given rule (*yujānisu taṣarrufātahu fī mulāḥiẓa al-maʿānī*).[74] First, if a *munāsaba* corresponds with the totality of the law, the *munāsaba* is *mulāʾim* or sufficiently related to the body of Sharīʿa rules. In this case, the *munāsaba* has the requisite nexus to legitimate a rule. Admittedly, this nexus is more a matter of degree than a bright line demarcation.[75] But it ensures that any rule of law does not depart from the already extant tradition of Sharīʿa.

Secondly, the *munāsaba* links the underlying *ratio legis* of a rule to a *maṣlaḥa* that upholds the basic values of the law.[76] In doing so, the *munāsaba* ensures that any rule contributes to the purpose of the Sharīʿa, namely to uphold the five basic values of the law. Specifically, al-Ghazālī wrote that the *munāsaba* 'indicates aspects of *maṣāliḥ* and is a sign of them' (*mā tushīru ilā wujūh al-maṣāliḥ wa imārātihā*).[77] With these two nexuses, the *munāsaba* both enables and limits the role of reason in al-Ghazālī's model of practical reasoning.

* * * * *

Al-Ghazālī's Soft Natural Law offers more than a counter-argument to Hard Natural Law. It becomes a foundation for his theory of practical reasoning. To use reason as a source for the Sharīʿa requires a legal philosophy that renders reason an authoritative basis of the law. Yet for those, such as al-Ghazālī, who were anxious about

[72] Al-Ghazālī, *Shifāʾ al-Ghalīl*, 146. [73] Al-Ghazālī, *Shifāʾ al-Ghalīl*, 145.

[74] Al-Ghazālī, *Shifāʾ al-Ghalīl*, 148.

[75] Al-Ghazālī, *Shifāʾ al-Ghalīl*, 148–9; Al-Ghazālī, *al-Mustaṣfā*, 2:386–7, 388–9.

[76] Al-Ghazālī, *Shifāʾ al-Ghalīl*, 160–1.

[77] Al-Ghazālī, *Shifāʾ al-Ghalīl*, 159. See also Al-Ghazālī, *al-Mustaṣfā*, 2:384, where he said that the *munāsaba* is what conveys and designates the *maṣāliḥ*, (*huwa ʿalā minhāj al-maṣāliḥ*).

trampling on the domain of God, no theory of reason could violate theological commitments to God's omnipotence and voluntaristic will. Hence, al-Ghazālī's natural law theory relies on a concept of divine grace, as opposed to divine justice, to fuse fact and value in nature. The fusion is possible because God, out of His grace, chose to create the world to benefit humanity. That does not mean God has to benefit humanity or is bound to continue to benefit humanity with every creative act. Rather, it means that to the extent God has already created the world, we can reasonably know that it is designed to benefit humanity. For that reason, al-Ghazālī could fuse fact and value in a manner that thereby renders natural reason an ontologically authoritative source of Sharīʿa.

To render natural reason an authoritative source of law, however, is not meant to give jurists a general license to develop the law as they please. The anxiety of unchecked reason seems to animate al-Ghazālī's theory of practical reasoning, which severely limits the scope of reasoned deliberation in the law. Only where certain goods are deemed necessary and are neither affirmed nor repudiated by source-texts, can we rely on reason as a source of law in a given instance. Despite his rejection of Hard Natural Law, al-Ghazālī's model of practical reasoning relies on reason as an ontological source of legal authority for the ongoing development of Sharīʿa. Yet, the nexuses that al-Ghazālī described are designed to limit the scope of reasoned deliberation.

Fakhr al-Dīn al-Rāzī (d. 606/1209) and Shihāb al-Dīn al-Qarāfī (d. 684/1285)

Fakhr al-Dīn al-Rāzī lived nearly a century after al-Ghazālī. Both were Shāfiʿi jurists, and both wrote in the field of legal theory (*uṣūl al-fiqh*).[78] Al-Rāzī's *al-Maḥṣūl* is a major work of legal theory that draws upon the earlier work of the Hard Naturalist Abū al-Ḥusayn al-Baṣrī, discussed above. Subsequent jurists devoted considerable

[78] Abū al-Falāḥ ʿAbd al-Ḥayy Ibn al-ʿImād, *Shadharāt al-Dhahab fī Akhbār man Dhahab* (Beirut: Dār al-Kutub al-ʿIlmiyya, n.d.) 5:21–2; Tāj al-Dīn al-Subkī, *Ṭabaqāt al-Shāfiʿiyya al-Kubrā*, 4:283–92.

attention to al-Rāzī's work, writing extensive commentaries on it.[79] Shihāb al-Dīn al-Qarāfī, a famous Mālikī jurist in Egypt, wrote two commentaries on al-Rāzī's *al-Maḥṣūl*.[80] Al-Qarāfī's shorter treatise, *Sharḥ Tanqīḥ al-Fuṣūl*, is a handbook that covers in brief the themes that al-Rāzī addressed in his treatise. However, in his *Nafā'is al-Uṣūl*, al-Qarāfī delved into the details of al-Rāzī's work, providing cogent explanatory points and criticisms of al-Rāzī's arguments.

The Authority of *Maṣlaḥa*—Reasoning: al-Rāzī's Natural Law Theory

Al-Rāzī's justification of reasoned deliberation where Sharīʿa is silent turns on his fusion of fact and value in his use of *maṣlaḥa*. Al-Rāzī argued that God legislates rules for the benefit or *maṣlaḥa* of the people. When we know a specific rule satisfies a *maṣlaḥa* or a good, we can reasonably assert that God legislates that rule to achieve the underlying *maṣlaḥa*. Specifically, al-Rāzī stated: 'God most high legislates rules to achieve the interests of people (*li maṣlaḥa al-ʿibād*). When [these rules satisfy] a *maṣlaḥa*, it is reasonable (*yaḥṣulu ẓann*) that God legislated [the rule] for this *maṣlaḥa* (*sharaʿahu li ḥādhahi al-maṣlaḥa*).'[81]

To prove that God legislates to achieve the *maṣlaḥa* of the people, al-Rāzī offered four arguments. First, he argued on theological grounds that God created nature to benefit humanity. He posited that God legislates a specific rule (*al-ḥukm muʿayyan*) for a specific situation (*al-wāqiʿa al-muʿayyana*) either because of some prevailing rationale (*murajjiḥ*) or none at all.[82] Al-Rāzī rejected the possibility that there is no animating rationale to a rule since such a possibility would undermine any notion of meaningful determinacy in the law. Also, if no rationality underlies the law, there is no point to rational deliberation at all, and certainly no authority for reason in the law. Consequently there must be some rationale that animates divine

[79] See, eg, Abū ʿAbd Allāh Muḥammad b. Maḥmūd b. ʿAbbād Al-Aṣfahānī, *al-Kāshif ʿan al-Maḥṣūl fī ʿIlm al-Uṣūl*, ʿĀdil Aḥmad ʿAbd al-Mawjūd and ʿAlī Muḥammad Muʿawwaḍ (eds) (Beirut: Dār al-Kutub al-ʿIlmiyya, 1998).

[80] For a history of al-Qarāfī's life, see Sherman Jackson, *Islamic Law and the State: The Constitutional Jurisprudence of Shihāb al-Dīn al-Qarāfī* (Leiden: EJ Brill, 1996).

[81] Al-Rāzī, *al-Maḥṣūl*, 5:172. [82] Al-Rāzī, *al-Maḥṣūl*, 5:172.

legislation, which either has to do with God and His needs, or with the needs of humanity. The consensus of Muslims, said al-Rāzī, rejects any notion that God has needs.[83] Therefore, the rationale must have something to do with humanity. Either this rationale involves something that benefits humanity (*an yakūna maṣlaḥa al-ʿabd*), harms humanity, or has no effect either way.[84] According to al-Rāzī, the second and third options are void (*bāṭil*) by consensus. Consequently al-Rāzī concluded that God 'indeed legislates rules for the benefit of people'.[85]

Secondly, al-Rāzī asserted that since God is wise (*ḥakīm*), He must act purposefully when using His creative power.[86] The very essence of wisdom, he argued, requires one to act to promote a good (*wa al-ḥakīm lā yafʿalu illā li maṣlaḥa*).[87] If one does not act pursuant to a *maṣlaḥa*, he is an *ʿābith* or foolhardy person. But since God cannot be foolhardy, given al-Rāzī's theology of God, He must act with a beneficial purpose in mind.

Al-Qarāfī also agreed that God is wise. But he disagreed with al-Rāzī's two arguments above out of concern that al-Rāzī opened the door to the Hard Naturalist presumption that God only acts justly. Al-Qarāfī wrote that when Hard Naturalists said that God is *ḥakīm*, they meant that God upholds the good (*yurāʿī al-maṣāliḥ*).[88] However al-Qarāfī rejected that theology of God.[89] God acts voluntaristically, pursuant to His will (*irāda*). He needs no rationale to animate or direct His actions.[90] While the Hard Naturalists would critique al-Qarāfī for implicitly suggesting that God may act with futility, al-Qarāfī retorted that the very idea of divine futility only makes sense to those who believe God only acts with justice and purpose. For Voluntarist Soft Naturalists, God simply wills and legislates, which by definition results in beneficial consequences, or a *maṣlaḥa*.

Al-Rāzī's third argument emphasizes that God created human beings as honorable and noble (*musharraf mukarram*).[91] In fact, the

[83] Al-Rāzī, *al-Maḥṣūl*, 5:172–3.
[84] Al-Rāzī, *al-Maḥṣūl*, 5:173.
[85] Al-Rāzī, *al-Maḥṣūl*, 5:173.
[86] Al-Rāzī, *al-Maḥṣūl*, 5:173.
[87] Al-Rāzī, *al-Maḥṣūl*, 5:173.
[88] Al-Qarāfī, *Nafāʾis al-Uṣūl*, 4:201–2.
[89] Indeed al-Qarāfī said, approvingly, that the *ahl al-sunna* reject such a theological position. Al-Qarāfī, *Nafāʾis al-Uṣūl*, 4:201–2.
[90] Al-Qarāfī, *Nafāʾis al-Uṣūl*, 4:201–2.
[91] Al-Rāzī, *al-Maḥṣūl*, 5:174.

Qur'ān states: 'Verily we honored humanity' (*laqad karramnā banī Ādam*).[92] According to al-Rāzī, where A creates B honored and dignified, and B pursues his aims and goals, B's efforts to do so are good and naturally reasonable.[93] Consequently, the view that individuals are noble leads to the presumption that they are predisposed to seek the noble and the good.[94]

Al-Qarāfī disagreed with al-Rāzī on this point. Al-Rāzī seemed to come dangerously close to fusing fact and value in a way that led to Hard Naturalism. By presuming humanity to be noble, al-Rāzī fused fact and value in human dispositions, and thereby threatened to shift the epistemic inquiry away from God's will to the telos of human dispositions. Al-Qarāfī argued that human nature is not, and cannot be, dispositive of the law in this fashion. We cannot assume that human beings necessarily act in noble ways that lead to the good. Al-Qarāfī could not adopt al-Rāzī's position given the undeniable fact of sinfulness and disbelief in the world. Hence human nature cannot be dispositive of the good.[95]

In his last argument, al-Rāzī noted that the Qur'ān asserts that God upholds the good and legislates for humanity's benefit. For instance, Q 45:13 reads: '[God] has made subservient to you all that is in the heavens and earth.'[96] Interestingly, he also cited Q 2:29: '[God] created for you all that is in the earth' (*khalaqa lakum mā fī al-arḍ jamīʿ*).[97] This latter verse is the same one that Hard Naturalists used as scriptural corroboration for their natural law theory. And lastly, al-Rāzī cited Q 2:185: 'God wants for you ease and does not want for you hardship.'[98] In response, al-Qarāfī argued that al-Rāzī misunderstood the import of Q 2:185. He said this verse means that 'God *wills* for you the easy and did not *will* for you hardship.'[99] In other words, al-Qarāfī was keen on preserving God's voluntarist will.

[92] Al-Rāzī, *al-Maḥṣūl*, 5:174, quoting Qur'ān, 17:70.
[93] Al-Rāzī, *al-Maḥṣūl*, 5:174 [94] Al-Rāzī, *al-Maḥṣūl*, 5:174.
[95] Al-Qarāfī, *Nafā'is al-Uṣūl*, 4:202.
[96] Al-Rāzī, *al-Maḥṣūl*, 5:175, quoting Qur'ān, 45:13.
[97] Al-Rāzī, *al-Maḥṣūl*, 5:175, quoting Qur'ān, 2:29.
[98] Al-Rāzī, *al-Maḥṣūl*, 5:175, quoting Qur'ān, 2:185.
[99] Al-Qarāfī, *Nafā'is al-Uṣūl*, 4:203 (emphasis added).

Al-Rāzī presented these four arguments in order to show that God legislates in order to uphold the *maṣlaḥa* or the good for people. But as happened in al-Ghazālī's analysis, one challenge for Soft Naturalist jurists like al-Rāzī was to avoid the theological implications of Hard Naturalism. This concern is central to al-Qarāfī's critiques of al-Rāzī. Al-Rāzī was not unmindful of this dilemma though. He wrote that his reliance on *maṣlaḥa* need not invoke the theological position that God is bound and obligated to uphold the good. In noting the considerable disagreement on this point, he wrote that Muʿtazilites infer from God's commitment to *maṣlaḥa* that it would be evil for God to do a bad or futile act, and that God's acts must be full of *maṣlaḥa* and purposefulness (*gharaḍ*).[100] The Voluntarists, on the other hand, declare that God legislates X rule for Y reason and policy, while rejecting the idea that God legislates pursuant to a purpose (*gharaḍ*) despite the fact that their approach implicitly invokes such a teleological view. However, al-Rāzī provided what shall become the typical Soft Naturalist response: 'although it is not obligatory on God to satisfy the *maṣāliḥ*, nevertheless [God] most high does not act except in light of what poses a *maṣlaḥa* for His servants, *out of a sense of grace and beneficence, but not obligation*' (*tafaḍḍul minhu wa iḥsān lā wujūb*).[101] The reference to grace and beneficence (*tafaḍḍul, iḥsān*) is, once again, key to understanding al-Rāzī's Soft Naturalism. God upholds the good out of grace, which He can presumably change if He so wishes. He is not obligated to uphold the good, but He does so in any case. For that reason, Voluntarists could hold that God legislates X rule for Y reason, and thereby invoke a corresponding teleology in the law, without at the same time imposing that teleology on God as a limit on His omnipotence. The resort to grace has both theological and jurisprudential implications. First, it preserves al-Rāzī's theological commitment to God's omnipotence. Second, it permits al-Rāzī to fuse fact and value in nature and thereby endow natural reason with ontological authority as a source of Sharīʿa. Al-Rāzī's Soft Natural Law theory fuses fact and

[100] Al-Rāzī, *al-Maḥṣūl*, 5:176.

[101] Al-Rāzī, *al-Maḥṣūl*, 5:176, emphasis added.

value in nature due to God's ever present grace, which of course He can choose to change at any time.[102]

As al-Qarāfī suggested, while God's acts certainly are not futile, it is not necessary to base God's acts on some rational or purposeful grounds. God can legislate pursuant to a *maṣlaḥa* in light of His wisdom, effective will, and power. Certainly it is true, said al-Qarāfī, that God 'did not send laws except as bounties (*maṣāliḥ*), but they are the product of grace (*ʿalā sabīl al-tafaḍḍul*).'[103] Consequently, while al-Qarāfī agreed that his view and the Hard Naturalist view relied on a sense of divine wisdom in nature and its bounties, the Hard Naturalists 'interpret [wisdom to mean that God] must uphold public interests (*marāʿāt al-maṣāliḥ wujūban*), whereas we reject [that meaning].'[104] Both groups agreed that God legislates with a *ḥikma* or wisdom; but they disagreed about what that wisdom implies about God and the fusion of fact and value in God's created world.

Authority and the Limits of Reason

Al-Qarāfī's critiques of al-Rāzī suggest a tension between al-Rāzī's theological commitments and his legal philosophy. Al-Rāzī was keen to render reason an authoritative source of law, but remained mindful of the implication his philosophy of law might have on Voluntarist theological propositions. He resolved this tension by further reflecting on the authority of reason amidst the limits of human knowledge. In doing so, he built into his Soft Natural Law theory an approach to reason whose ontological authority accounts for the variability of lived experience, the limits of human knowledge, and the unavoidable imperative of practical reasoning.

[102] Al-Rāzī, *al-Maḥṣūl*, 5:176. Al-Rāzī showed that every legal rule poses a *maṣlaḥa* in fact. This is predominantly an empirical inquiry that focuses on the significant characteristics (*waṣf*) of the act underlying the rule, and how those characteristics are rationally related to a *maṣlaḥa*. Notably, al-Rāzī did not provide much commentary on this point. Nonetheless, its significance is to illustrate that the *maṣlaḥa* is the mechanism by which the empiricism of a benefit is fused with value to create a naturalistic foundation for obligation.

[103] Al-Qarāfī, *Nafāʾis al-Uṣūl*, 4:642.

[104] Al-Qarāfī, *Nafāʾis al-Uṣūl*, 4:642.

Al-Rāzī asked whether having a reasonable belief (*ẓann*), as opposed to certitude, that a particular rule of law satisfies a particular *maṣlaḥa* is epistemically sufficient to assert authoritatively that 'this *maṣlaḥa* is what suggested to God to legislate that rule' (*anna al-dāʿī lahu taʿālā ilā sharʿ dhālika al-ḥukm hādhihi al-maṣlaḥa*).[105] In other words, given the limits of reason, how can any reasoned conclusion be authoritative if it necessarily suffers from humanity's epistemic weakness. Al-Rāzī's response to this question illustrates how strongly committed he was to the authority of reason as a source of Sharīʿa norms.

He began his argument with a familiar theological first principle: it is reasonable to believe that the divine legislator is wise (*ḥakīm*). When we know that a specific rule contains a certain rationality and wisdom (*hādha al-ḥukm fīhi hādhihi al-jiha min al-ḥikma*), we know the wise legislator decreed that matter in order to achieve the underlying good.[106] The reasonability of this assessment is based on what al-Rāzī considered empirical reality and experience (*fī al-shāhid*).[107] In other words, in the world of human experience we find this kind of rational nexus between legislators and legislation, between acts and consequences. For instance, if we assume a king only acts wisely, then if we see the king giving property to a poor person, we can reasonably conclude, without knowing with certainty, that the latter's poverty is rationally related to the king's act of giving. We reach a 'reasonable likelihood that [the king] gave the property because of [the recipient's] poverty'.[108] Al-Rāzī used this example to analogize from the world of existence (*al-shāhid*) to the world of God and divine intentionality.[109]

However, to assume that a king (and God) acts with wisdom comes dangerously close to the Hard Naturalist theology that God acts only with a *maṣlaḥa* in mind. To avoid this position, al-Rāzī argued that the rational link between a rule and its animating *maṣlaḥa* is not tantamount to a theological proof that God only acts justly or for human benefit. The rational link exists as a matter of human experience, but does not have a necessary theological

[105] Al-Rāzī, *al-Maḥṣūl*, 5:176.
[106] Al-Rāzī, *al-Maḥṣūl*, 5:177.
[107] Al-Rāzī, *al-Maḥṣūl*, 5:177.
[108] Al-Rāzī, *al-Maḥṣūl*, 5:177.
[109] Al-Rāzī, *al-Maḥṣūl*, 5:178

significance. In other words, the rational link illustrates only a correlation, but makes no claim about causation. The rational link, which he calls a *munāsib*, is merely a sign of the probable likelihood that a certain rule of law is designed to achieve a certain *maṣlaḥa*. The nexus does not impart clear or certain knowledge. It is merely a rational relation that we can rely upon as a matter of law, but which has no implications on the theology of God's omnipotence.[110] For al-Rāzī, the legal efficacy of the *munāsib* requires only probability (*ẓann*) as a sufficient standard of proof to justify the implementation and coercive power of a rule of law. Since the standard of proof is not truth or certitude, it can apply to the law without having theological implications. In this sense, by using *munāsab* to articulate a standard of proof sufficient for the law, al-Rāzī separated the ontological authority of reason in the Sharīʿa from issues of theology, and thereby insulated the legal authority of reason from theological attack. The *munāsib* allows al-Rāzī to marginalize the question of the provenance of the law, whether divine or human, and to emphasize the nature of analytical legal inquiry. He stated:

> It is not necessary (*ghayr wājib*) that the rotation of celestial bodies and the rising and setting of stars continue in perpetuity... Rather given that God most high manifests His habits (*ʿādatahu*) by preserving them in such a uniform fashion, certainly it is reasonably likely that they will remain as such tomorrow and thereafter in accordance with these characteristics. Likewise the falling of rain from damp clouds, the satiety arising from eating, the quenching of thirst from drinking, and the burning from touching fire are not necessary (*ghayr wājib*). Rather when the custom (*al-ʿādat*) is continuous in that fashion, reasonability approaching certainty arises that [the custom] will remain in that fashion.[111]

For al-Rāzī, God has a habit or style of doing things that generally remains constant. Certainly God can change things if He wants, thereby preserving God's purposive voluntarism. But the constancy that characterizes the observed natural world is a virtual given that human beings can rely upon, assess, and analyze. Relying on this constancy for the purpose of natural reasoning, though, does not impede or limit God's omnipotence, especially since the constancy we perceive is still vulnerable to the fallibility of human perception.

[110] Al-Rāzī, *al-Maḥṣūl*, 5:179.

[111] Al-Rāzī, *al-Maḥṣūl*, 5:179.

The indeterminacy arising from human fallibility, though, does not undermine the authority of law derived from our reasoned deliberation about the natural order.

Al-Rāzī attributed the natural world's goodness to God's grace; but once we accept *theologically* that God put this particular version of creation into being to benefit humanity, we can jurisprudentially rely on the presumptive goodness of the world for the purpose of interpreting the law, even though we are theologically aware that God may change the world. Al-Rāzī suggested that if we assume nature as generally constant, and investigate various legal systems, we find a correlation between rules of law and underlying goods (*maṣāliḥ*). This need not suggest that God legislates such laws only for these goods. God is not bound to certain goals or aims. However, God uses His grace to create the good. Given the way God creates nature and the patterns we can rationally comprehend, we can use our reason to assert Sharīʿa norms.

Munāsib, Maqāṣid and Practical Reasoning

Al-Rāzī used the term *maṣlaḥa* to theorize about the ontological authority of natural reason. In doing so, he created an initial point of departure for his model of practical reasoning. *Maṣlaḥa* contributes both an empirical and normative ground for identifying and justifying the *ratio legis* (*ʿilla*) of a rule of law. Among the various ways to identify the *ʿilla* for a given rule, the one most central to al-Rāzī's natural law account was one that involved the use of the *munāsib* to link the *ratio legis* of a rule to the basic aim of the law to uphold benefit and repel harm.[112] In his commentary, al-Qarāfī stated that the *munāsab* involves a rational nexus between the attending circumstances (*waṣf*) constituting a *ratio legis* and the fulfillment of perceived goods (*fī naẓar riʿāyat al-maṣāliḥ*).[113] The circumstances and the telos of the good contribute the factual and normative content for a rule, which aims to ensure people live their lives to the fullest.[114] The *munāsib* for al-Rāzī (and al-Qarāfī)

[112] Al-Rāzī, *al-Maḥṣūl*, 5:157. [113] Al-Qarāfī, *Nafāʾis al-Uṣūl*, 4:170–1.
[114] Al-Qarāfī, *Nafāʾis al-Uṣūl*, 4:170–1.

provides the link between the operative cause (*ʿilla*) for a rule of law and the purpose the rule is meant to achieve.

According to al-Rāzī, a *munāsib* can either be concrete (*ḥaqīqī*), or merely persuasive (*iqnāʿī*).[115] The concrete *munāsib* is the one to which al-Rāzī devoted considerable attention in his discussion of practical reasoning. Concerning matters of this world (*al-dunyā*), the *munāsib* is the rational nexus between a given rule under consideration and the five basic goals or aims of the law, namely the preservation of life (*nafs*), property (*māl*), lineage or family (*nasab*), religion (*dīn*), and the mind (*ʿaql*).[116] These five values are the same ones that al-Ghazālī noted earlier. Importantly, al-Qarāfī argued that the value of dignity or honor (*ʿirḍ*) could substitute itself for the value of religion, or alternatively should be considered a sixth value.[117] Although al-Rāzī did not indicate how he reached these values, al-Qarāfī provided an explanation: no society or legal system exists that does not uphold these values.[118] Again we find an argument of intuitivism, as was the case with al-Ghazālī above. For al-Qarāfī, these values are basic to society and satisfy the needs of reasonable people. For instance, he wrote:

> The prohibition of killing is rationally related to what the reasonable person does voluntarily (*mulāʾim li al-afʿāl al-marḍiyya li al-ʿuqalāʾ*). The obligation to save the drowning person is rationally related to the action of reasonable people (*li fiʿl al-ʿūqalāʾ*), as opposed to the [action] of unreasonable people (*ghayr al-ʿuqalāʾ*) who are corrupt.[119]

The *munāsib* therefore links (1) the attending circumstances (*waṣf ẓāhir munḍabaṭ*) of a rule of law (2) to specific goods (*maṣāliḥ*) (3) in order to vindicate the basic aim of the law.[120] Like al-Ghazālī before him, al-Rāzī tied the *munāsib*, which legitimated specific rules of law, to the *maṣlaḥa*, which in turn linked the rule of law to the basic purpose of the law.

[115] Al-Rāzī, *al-Maḥṣūl*, 5:162. The latter is one that at first seems compelling, but after further investigation turns out to present a false nexus.

[116] Al-Rāzī, *al-Maḥṣūl*, 5:160.

[117] Al-Qarāfī, *Nafāʾis al-Uṣul*, 4:170; Shihāb al-Dīn Al-Qarāfī, *Sharḥ Tanqīḥ al-Fuṣūl fī Ikhtiṣār al-Maḥṣūl fī al-Uṣūl*, ʿAbd al-Raʾūf Saʿīd (ed) (Cairo: Dār al-Fikr, 1973) 391, 392.

[118] Al-Qarāfī, *Nafāʾis al-Uṣūl*, 4:173; Al-Qarāfī, *Sharḥ Tanqīḥ al-Fuṣūl*, 392.

[119] Al-Qarāfī, *Nafāʾis al-Uṣūl*, 4:172.

[120] Al-Qarāfī, *Nafāʾis al-Uṣūl*, 4:172.

Furthermore, like al-Ghazālī, al-Rāzī did not consider every *maṣlaḥa* to be a basis for a Sharīʿa rule. The strength of a nexus between the *maṣlaḥa* and basic aim of the law determines whether a *maṣlaḥa* can be an authoritative basis for the law. The nexus between a *maṣlaḥa* and the basic goods may reflect either a necessary interest (*ḍarūra*), a need (*ḥāja*), or a perfectionist value (*taḥṣīnāt*).[121] These categories, referred to by both al-Rāzī and al-Qarāfi, were the ones utilized by al-Ghazālī to limit the extent to which a given *maṣlaḥa* could be the basis for a rule of law.

For example, to illustrate what he called *al-maṣāliḥ al-ḍarūriyya*, or the necessary goods, al-Rāzī provided the following examples.

- Life is preserved by the implementation of *lex talionis* or *qiṣāṣ*.[122] In fact, Q 2:179 states: 'For you in *qiṣāṣ* is life.'[123]
- Property is protected by the legal requirements of compensatory liability for damages suffered (*al-ḍamanāt*) and the *ḥudūd* penalties for theft.[124]
- The rules against fornication and adultery uphold the values of family and lineage.
- The basic aim of religion is satisfied by rules deterring apostasy and commanding one to fight the unbelievers.
- The values of mind and reason are upheld by the prohibition against intoxicants.[125]

Needs or *ḥāja* interests are a step below *ḍarūra* interests. Again we find as an example illustrating this category the same one used by al-Ghazālī, namely the rule requiring a guardian over a minor in matters of marriage.[126] Al-Rāzī said that marriages of this type do not present necessary interests but only 'needs', which at the very least ensure a suitable match between children.[127]

Lastly, perfectionist interests or the *taḥṣīnāt* are edificatory in nature and advance the moral fiber of people (*taqrīr al-nās ʿalā makārim al-akhlāq*),[128] such as denying slaves the capacity to testify

[121] Al-Rāzī, *al-Maḥṣūl*, 6:163. Al-Qarāfī uses the term *tatimma* to designate the third category. Al-Qarāfī, *Nafāʾis al-Uṣūl*, 4:171.
[122] Al-Rāzī, *al-Maḥṣūl*, 5:166.
[123] Al-Rāzī, *al-Maḥṣūl*, 5:160, quoting Qurʾān, 2:179.
[124] Al-Rāzī, *al-Maḥṣūl*, 5:160.
[125] Al-Rāzī, *al-Maḥṣūl*, 5:160.
[126] Al-Rāzī, *al-Maḥṣūl*, 5:160; al-Qarāfī, *Sharḥ Tanqīḥ al-Fuṣūl*, 391.
[127] Al-Rāzī, *al-Maḥṣūl*, 5:160.
[128] Al-Rāzī, *al-Maḥṣūl*, 5:160–1.

in court (*salb ahliyya al-shahāda ʿan al-raqīq*).[129] For al-Rāzī, the privilege to give testimony implies that one has a noble status (*manṣab sharīf*). Since the slave occupies a diminished social status, to allow him to testify would be inappropriate (*ghayr mutalāʾim*) to the nature of testifying in court.[130]

Importantly, referring to al-Ghazālī, al-Rāzī stated that one cannot base a rule on *maṣlaḥa* interests that pose either a need or edificatory relationship to the basic aims of the law.[131] Rather, one can only use necessary interests as a basis for creating and extending the law.[132]

This nexus requires a jurist to ensure that yet another nexus exists, namely that the necessary interest under consideration poses a sufficient rational nexus to the overall spirit of the legal tradition.[133] The goods that are *ḍarūra* in nature are valid bases for rules of law only so long as they are not addressed by any specific source-text but still pose a nexus to the totality of the Sharīʿa tradition. Al-Rāzī wrote:

> We find a situation . . . and there is nothing found in the law that addresses it in light of its general characteristics in a way that poses a tight nexus [to scripture]. But it is the case that the [body of] scripture addresses its general characteristics in a way that poses a looser nexus in light of its nature as a pure benefit or harm, or a predominant benefit or harm.[134]

Likewise, al-Qarāfī said that a *maṣlaḥa* can inform the law because of its general relation to the demands of scripture (*li mūjib al-khiṭāb*).[135]

For instance, paralleling the work of al-Ghazālī, al-Rāzī said that in relation to scriptural traditions, goods or *maṣālīḥ* are divided into three categories: those recognized by scripture, those rejected by scripture, and those on which scripture is silent.[136] The first type of

[129] Al-Rāzī, *al-Maḥṣūl*, 5:161.
[130] Al-Rāzī, *al-Maḥṣūl*, 5:161. At this point, al-Rāzī also addressed the nature of interests that involve acts related to the hereafter. Such acts are those that involve people engaging in acts that improve their character, whereby any benefit from them is directed to achieving eternal happiness. Al-Rāzī, *al-Maḥṣūl*, 5:161.
[131] Al-Rāzī, *al-Maḥṣūl*, 6:163.
[132] Al-Rāzī, *al-Maḥṣūl*, 6:163. See also al-Qarāfī, *Sharḥ Tanqīḥ al-Fuṣūl*, 446.
[133] Al-Rāzī, *al-Maḥṣūl*, 5:163.
[134] Al-Rāzī, *al-Maḥṣūl*, 6:166.
[135] Al-Qarāfī, *Nafāʾis al-Uṣūl*, 4:700–1.
[136] Al-Rāzī, *al-Maḥṣūl*, 6:162–3.

maṣlaḥa can be used to extend rules on the grounds of *qiyās* or rule by analogy with a precedent.[137] This nexus is expressly identified in source-texts, thereby implying that the divine or prophetic legislator intended to give it force (ie *anna al-shāriʿ iʿtabarahu*).[138] The second type of *maṣlaḥa* is entirely rejected by source-texts, and cannot be used as a basis for rules of law.[139] Notably, neither of these *maṣlaḥa* inquiries relies on a Soft Naturalist theory to legitimate any rule therefrom. They are based on the authority of scripture, and so lie outside the realm of a Soft Naturalist ambit. The third type is the one where no specific evidentiary basis exists (*naṣṣ muʿayyan*), but which violates no source-text. This type of *maṣlaḥa* is a suitable starting point for any act of practical reasoning.[140] For the purpose of this study, these silent, necessary *maṣlaḥa* are of special interest because the authority of a rule that rests on such interests will depend on the ontological authority of reason.[141]

To illustrate his model of practical reasoning, al-Rāzī followed al-Ghazālī and held that to rely on a silent, necessary *maṣlaḥa* for a Sharīʿa rule of law, the *maṣlaḥa* must involve an interest that affects society at large (*kulliyya*) and will be satisfied with certainty (*qaṭʿiyya*) by the proposed rule.[142] Invoking al-Ghazālī's hypotheticals, al-Rāzī considered the case of non-Muslims fighting a Muslim army, and using Muslim civilians as human shields. If the Muslim commander is unsure whether the enemy will overtake Muslim lands if the Muslims do not fire on the human shields, the Muslim army cannot fire upon the human shields. Similarly, if the enemy is held up in a castle and utilizes the human shields as a defense tactic, the Muslim army cannot fire upon the human shields as there is no real danger to Muslim society as a whole, since the enemy is penned up in a castle.[143] Finally, if a group of people are in a sinking boat and can be saved by throwing one person overboard, they cannot do so on Sharīʿa grounds because the benefit of sacrificing one person for the remaining few is not of a sufficient

[137] Al-Rāzī, *al-Maḥṣūl*, 6:162.
[138] Al-Rāzī, *al-Maḥṣūl*, 5:163.
[139] Al-Rāzī, *al-Maḥṣūl*, 6:162.
[140] Al-Rāzī, *al-Maḥṣūl*, 6:163.
[141] Al-Rāzī, *al-Maḥṣūl*, 5:163–6.
[142] Al-Rāzī, *al-Maḥṣūl*, 6:164. See also al-Qarāfī, *Sharḥ Tanqīḥ al-Fuṣūl*, 446.
[143] Al-Rāzī, *al-Maḥṣūl*, 6:164.

scope. Sheer utilitarianism is not sufficient to justify a Sharīʿa rule of general application.[144]

What is evident from the above analysis is that al-Rāzī and al-Qarāfī fused fact and value in nature using the term *maṣlaḥa*, but struggled to justify it on grounds that did not fall foul of their critique of Hard Naturalism. Both suggested that the fundamental flaw of the Hard Naturalist account is that it assumes a certain consistency and permanent quality of the natural order that effectively obligates God to do the good in a way that undermines His omnipotence. Neither al-Rāzī nor al-Qarāfī wished to embrace this theological implication. Both adopted a Soft Naturalism by relying on God's grace to grant ontological authority to natural reasoning. God certainly created nature, and His grace (*tafaḍḍul*) provides the foundation for fusing fact and value in nature. For al-Rāzī, after that initial creative moment, we can reasonably rely, for jurisprudential purposes, on the regularity of nature and the benefits it presents, even though we are theologically aware it may change due to God's voluntaristic will. But any indeterminacy that may arise from the theological possibility that God may change His mind about the natural world, according to al-Rāzī, does not undermine the jurisprudential legitimacy and authority of naturalistically reasoned Sharīʿa rules of law.

Najm al-Dīn al-Ṭūfī (d. 716/1316)

The Ḥanbalite jurist Najm al-Dīn al-Ṭūfī is recognized by many to have embraced a radical use of *maṣlaḥa* as a basis for legislating the law.[145] Because of his importance in *maṣlaḥa* studies, a discussion of his theory seems appropriate. As will be seen below, despite the view that his approach to *maṣlaḥa* seems novel and unprecedented, his theory relies on a Soft Naturalism that

[144] Al-Rāzī, *al-Maḥṣūl*, 6:164.

[145] See, eg, Muṣṭafā Zayd, *al-Maṣlaḥa fī al-Tashrīʿ al-Islāmī wa Najm al-Dīn al-Ṭūfī* (2nd edn, n.p.: Dār al-Fikr al-ʿArabī, 1964); Ihsan Abdul Bagby, 'Utility in Classical Islamic Law: The Concept of "Maslahah" in "Usul al-Fiqh"' (PhD dissertation, University of Michigan, 1986) 166–72.

parallels the views of al-Ghazālī and al-Rāzī. Al-Ṭūfī's Soft Naturalism can be found in his well known discussion of *maṣlaḥa* in his commentary on al-Nawawī's collection of forty *ḥadīth, Kitāb al-Arbaʿīn.*[146] In that book, al-Nawawī related a *ḥadīth* that al-Ṭūfī considered central to his theory of *maṣlaḥa*. The *ḥadīth* states: 'There is no harm and no injury' (*lā ḍarar wa lā ḍirār*).[147] The *ḥadīth* is included in the collections of Ibn Mājah, Mālik b. Anas, and al-Dār Quṭnī.[148] An extended version of the *ḥadīth*, as related by al-Ḥākim al-Nīsābūrī, reads: 'There is no harm or injury. Whoever causes harm, God will harm him, and whoever causes distress, God will distress him.'[149] According to al-Ṭūfī, this *ḥadīth* fundamentally means that no harm befalls someone *as a matter of law* unless a specific indicator requires it (*lā luḥūq ḍarar sharʿan illa bi mūjib khāṣṣ mukhaṣṣaṣ*).[150] This is not to suggest in absolute terms that the law does not permit harm. In fact, pain and harm are sometimes legally required, such as in the case of criminal punishments. But for al-Ṭūfī, the presumptive state of things is that, as a matter of law, pain and harm are to be avoided, unless evidence to the contrary exists.

Like Soft Naturalists before him, al-Ṭūfī relied on the ontological authority of scripture to assert that the Sharīʿa upholds benefit and

[146] Muḥyī al-Dīn Yaḥyā b. Sharaf al-Dīn al-Nawawī, *Kitāb al-Arbaʿīn al-Nawawiyya* (n.p.: Dār Ḥarāʾ li al-Kitāb, 1987).

[147] Najm al-Dīn al-Ṭūfī, '*al-Ḥadīth al-Thānī wa al-Thalāthūn*' in Muṣṭafā Zayd, *al-Maṣlaḥa fī al-Tashrīʿ al-Islāmī wa Najm al-Dīn al-Ṭūfī* (2nd edn, n.p.: Dār al-Fikr al-ʿArabī, 1964) 205–240, 206. See also al-Nawawī, *Kitāb al-Arbaʿīn*, 67, for the tradition.

[148] The version in Ibn Mājah's work is narrated by Ibn ʿAbbās. Ibn Mājah, *al-Sunan*, Muḥammad Nāṣir al-Dīn al-Albānī and ʿAlī b. Ḥasan b. ʿAlī b. ʿAbd al-Ḥamīd al-ʿḤalabī al-Atharī (eds) (Riyadh: Maktabat al-Maʿārif li al-Nashr wa al-Tawzīʿ, 1998) 2:534–5. The version of the *ḥadīth* in Mālik b. Anas' work is narrated by the father of ʿAmrū b. Yaḥyā al-Māzanī. Mālik b. Anas, *al-Muwaṭṭaʾ(as narrated by al-Laythī)*, Bashshār ʿAwād Maʿrūf (ed) (Beirut: Dār al-Gharb al-Islāmī, 1997) 2: 290. The version in al-Dār Quṭnī's collection is narrated by Muḥammad's wife ʿĀʾisha. ʿAlī b. ʿUmar al-Dār Quṭnī, *Sunan al-Dār Quṭnī*, Majdī b. Manṣūl b. Sayyid al-Shūra (ed) (Beirut: Dār al-Kutub al-ʿIlmiyya, 1996) 4:145–6.

[149] Abū ʿAbd Allāh Muḥammad b. ʿAbd Allāh al-Ḥākim al-Nīsābūrī, *al-Mustadrak ʿalā al-Ṣaḥīḥayn* (Beirut: Dār al-Maʿrifa, 1998) 2:369, who related the tradition as narrated by Abū Saʿīd al-Khudrī.

[150] Al-Ṭūfī, '*al-Ḥadīth al-Thānī wa al-Thalāthūn*,' 207.

repels harm. Scriptural precedents show that God desires the good for people:[151]

- Qur'ān 5:6: 'God does not want to place hardship upon you, but rather desires to purify you and perfect His bounties for you, so that you may show gratitude.'
- Qur'ān 22:78: 'Strive in the way of God, as He deserves. He has chosen you and has imposed upon you in religious matters no hardship.'

For al-Ṭūfī, '[i]f harm and injury were not rejected as a matter of law, then conflict would arise' over the meaning of these Qur'ānic verses.[152]

However al-Ṭūfī had to contend with the fact that there are rules in scriptural texts that occasion harm and injury in the form of punishments. For al-Ṭūfī, though, these texts do not reflect the presumptive state of affairs; rather they are exceptional. Al-Ṭūfī stated that the repudiation of harm and corruption (*nafy al-ḍarar wa al-mafāsid*) is a generally applicable rebuttable presumption.[153] If specific sources (*ḍalīl*) counter the presumption, the specific sources prevail.[154] For al-Ṭūfī, this means that the above *ḥadīth* reflects the presumptive position of the law, namely to reject all harm. This presumption is a first principle, thereby defining the telos of the law such that any evidence to the contrary can be characterized as exceptional. Specifically, he stated: 'This establishes the priority (*taqdīm*) of this *ḥadīth* over all legal proofs (*jamīʿ adilla al-sharʿ*), and the qualification of them all in light of the rejection of harm and the pursuit of good (*maṣlaḥa*).'[155] For al-Ṭūfī, without such a prioritization scheme, we would confront two conflicting proof-texts, and be forced to pick one while ignoring the other. His approach allows us to harmonize apparently conflicting precedents, which he considered to be the virtue of his approach: '[h]armonization (*al-jamʿ*) of scriptural texts... is better than disregarding some of them (*taʿṭīl*).'[156]

[151] Al-Ṭūfī, '*al-Ḥadīth al-Thānī wa al-Thalāthūn*,' 207–8, quoting Qur'ān, 2:185, 4:38, 5:6, 22:78.
[152] Al-Ṭūfī, '*al-Ḥadīth al-Thānī wa al-Thalāthūn*,' 208.
[153] Al-Ṭūfī, '*al-Ḥadīth al-Thānī wa al-Thalāthūn*,' 208.
[154] Al-Ṭūfī, '*al-Ḥadīth al-Thānī wa al-Thalāthūn*,' 208.
[155] Al-Ṭūfī, '*al-Ḥadīth al-Thānī wa al-Thalāthūn*,' 208.
[156] Al-Ṭūfī, '*al-Ḥadīth al-Thānī wa al-Thalāthūn*,' 208.

Al-Ṭūfī recognized that the two most ontologically authoritative sources of Sharīʿa are source-texts (ie *naṣṣ*) and rules by consensus (*ijmāʿ*).[157] Either the rules derived from these sources uphold the good or they do not. If they do not uphold the good, al-Ṭūfī suggested that they would need to be reinterpreted, given the presumptive first principle. For al-Ṭūfī, source-texts must be interpreted in such a way that they do not contravene the presumption of pursuing the good as a matter of Sharīʿa.[158]

To explain his theory of *maṣlaḥa*-reasoning, he noted that when we read a source-text, which requires imposing some sort of harm, we can read it either as defining the presumptive state of affairs, or providing an exception to a different presumptive state of affairs. If we read it as exceptional, we can still uphold the presumption to pursue the good (*maṣlaḥa*), and apply the source-text as a specific exception to the presumption. Consequently, we can uphold both the presumption and the authority of the source-texts in the Sharīʿa.[159] But if we read the source-text as defining the presumptive state of affairs, we will encounter conflict with the *ḥadīth* that prescribes the pursuit of the good as the default position of the law. To avoid this conflict, the source-texts requiring harm must be framed as exceptional in order to preserve the telos of the law. In some cases, the harm upheld by the source-texts can be limited, such as narrowly limiting the application of punitive measures to the crimes for which they are specifically designated. Criminal activity is something that the sources universally castigate without exception. But such acts are so narrowly delineated that what may appear like a general statement of punishment that contravenes the *maṣlaḥa*, is in fact quite narrowly applied. Hence, punishment is allowed but is considered an exception to the general presumption of upholding the good and avoiding harm.[160]

While keen to expand the scope of *maṣlaḥa* reasoning, al-Ṭūfī was mindful that not all issues could or should be susceptible to such reasoned deliberation. As a term of art, *maṣlaḥa* is a good that

[157] Al-Ṭūfī, '*al-Ḥadīth al-Thānī wa al-Thalāthūn*,' 208–9.
[158] Al-Ṭūfī, '*al-Ḥadīth al-Thānī wa al-Thalāthūn*,' 209.
[159] Al-Ṭūfī, '*al-Ḥadīth al-Thānī wa al-Thalāthūn*,' 209.
[160] Al-Ṭūfī, '*al-Ḥadīth al-Thānī wa al-Thalāthūn*,' 209–10.

upholds the goals of the lawgiver (*maqṣūd al-shāriʿ*) in matters of *both* worship *and* worldly affairs (*ʿibāda, ʿāda*). Some goods concern devotional requirements, such as ritual worship practices. Others are designed to benefit people as they live their lives.[161] Devotional acts must be distinguished from the latter because they reflect a divine will that can only be known by reference to scriptural proofs or consensus.[162] *Maṣlaḥa*-reasoning cannot contribute to this subject area of the law. In matters that involve general areas of human behavior and activity (*ʿādāt, muʿāmalāt*), the law must be developed in light of the general principle of avoiding harm. In these latter cases, *maṣlaḥa*-reasoning provides content to the law, such that source-text-based rules and consensus-based rules are interpreted so as to conform with the presumption of upholding the good.[163]

This last point about the scope of *maṣlaḥa*-based reasoning led al-Ṭūfī to discuss the theological question that has been so prominent among Soft Naturalists thus far, namely whether God acts with a rationale that upholds the good for people. Al-Ṭūfī held, like other Soft Naturalists, that God acts in a manner that benefits humanity. Indeed, without a rational basis, God's acts would be futile (*ʿabath*) according to al-Ṭūfī.[164] But al-Ṭūfī did not hold that all of God's acts must have a perceptible rational basis. For al-Ṭūfī, the presumption that God acts with a rational basis is not a universal claim concerning all of God's acts (*al-kulliyya*). Instead, it applies only to those matters that affect the created world (*fī ḥaqq al-makhlūqīn*).[165] In other words, al-Ṭūfī excluded rules of worship from his Soft Naturalism.[166] Hence in mundane worldly matters, God's laws are rationally based on an aim (*ghāya*) 'that benefits and perfects people, and does not benefit God'.[167]

Importantly, al-Ṭūfī considered his view to be distinct from Hard Natural Law because he did not believe that God is bound or

[161] Al-Ṭūfī, '*al-Ḥadīth al-Thānī wa al-Thalāthūn*,' 211.
[162] Al-Ṭūfī, '*al-Ḥadīth al-Thānī wa al-Thalāthūn*,' 213.
[163] Al-Ṭūfī, '*al-Ḥadīth al-Thānī wa al-Thalāthūn*,' 212–13.
[164] Al-Ṭūfī, '*al-Ḥadīth al-Thānī wa al-Thalāthūn*,' 213.
[165] Al-Ṭūfī, '*al-Ḥadīth al-Thānī wa al-Thalāthūn*,' 213.
[166] Al-Ṭūfī, '*al-Ḥadīth al-Thānī wa al-Thalāthūn*,' 211, where al-Ṭūfī says that rules of ritual worship involve the rights of God (*ḥaqqihi*).
[167] Al-Ṭūfī, '*al-Ḥadīth al-Thānī wa al-Thalāthūn*,' 213.

obligated to uphold the *maṣlaḥa* or good, despite the rational relation of some rules to the good. Just as we saw in the cases of al-Ghazālī, al-Rāzī, and al-Qarāfī, who adopted a theory of God's creative grace and beneficence, so too do we find al-Ṭūfī adopting this characteristically Soft Naturalistic approach to preserve God's omnipotence, while also fusing fact and value. Al-Ṭūfī wrote: 'upholding the good is a *grace* from God... (*riʿāyat al-maṣāliḥ tafaḍḍūl min Allāh*) upon His creation according to the *ahl al-sunna*, but obligatory upon Him according to the Muʿtazilites.'[168] Again we find the same key term of art, namely grace (*tafaḍḍul*), as the concept by which Soft Naturalists fused fact and value, preserved God's omnipotence, and distinguished their naturalism from Hard Naturalism. For al-Ṭūfī, *maṣlaḥa* must be upheld since it is an intended consequence of God's grace. But God is under no obligation to do the good. Upholding human interests certainly follows naturally from God's grace but is not an obligation upon God's self (*wājib minhu lā ʿalayhi*).[169] As a natural consequence of God's grace, the good can thereby be posited as the presumptive *telos* of the law, unless evidence exists to prove otherwise.

Al-Ṭūfī's theory of *maṣlaḥa* reflects a theoretical pattern that we have already seen in authors like al-Ghazālī, al-Rāzī, and al-Qarāfī. However, while those authors limited the use of *maṣlaḥa*-based reason in their discussion of practical reasoning, al-Ṭūfī argued that his *maṣlaḥa*-based practical reasoning has a broader scope of application. Certainly he recognized the centrality of Mālik b. Anas in developing a thick mechanism of *maṣlaḥa*-based practical reasoning, although he also acknowledged that others adopted the use of *maṣlaḥa* in legal interpretation.[170] However, al-Ṭūfī distinguished his approach from Mālik's through his reliance on the *ḥadīth* noted above as a basis for his theory. By relying on a scriptural text to justify his resort to *maṣlaḥa*, al-Ṭūfī claimed that his theory has a stronger ontological foundation than Mālik's *maṣlaḥa mursala*, and thereby has greater scope of application (*ablagh min dhālik*).[171]

[168] Al-Ṭūfī, '*al-Ḥadīth al-Thānī wa al-Thalāthūn*,' 213 (emphasis added).
[169] Al-Ṭūfī, '*al-Ḥadīth al-Thānī wa al-Thalāthūn*,' 214.
[170] Al-Ṭūfī, '*al-Ḥadīth al-Thānī wa al-Thalāthūn*,' 215.
[171] Al-Ṭūfī, '*al-Ḥadīth al-Thānī wa al-Thalāthūn*,' 235.

Although al-Ṭūfī removed matters of worship from the scope of his practical reasoning, he considered his resort to *maṣlaḥa* reasoning in matters of human interaction to exceed the scope of other models of practical reasoning which, as we have seen above, were often designed to limit the scope of reasoning.[172] Al-Ṭūfī's claim about scope and authority may have more to do with how he links the ontological authority for his *maṣlaḥa* jurisprudence directly to a scriptural text. For our purposes, though, the ontological authority of *maṣlaḥa*-reasoning relies on a Soft Natural Law theory that relies on a theology of God's grace to fuse fact and value in nature.

Abū Isḥāq Al-Shāṭibī (d. 790/1388)

The Mālikī jurist al-Shāṭibī wrote his book *al-Muwāfaqāt* with the express purpose of bridging the theoretical gaps separating the Mālikite and Ḥanafite schools.[173] Consequently, the book discusses conceptual issues that both Ḥanafites and Mālikites can agree upon, according to al-Ṣhāṭibī. In his treatise, al-Shāṭibī offered a jurisprudential theory that addresses the ontological authority of natural reason and offers a model of practical reasoning. Like the other Soft Naturalists addressed above, he relied on key conceptual terms such as *maṣlaḥa* and *maqāṣid*, both to justify resort to naturalistic reasoning, and to control concerns about indeterminacy that arise when considering the authority of reason in Sharīʿa.

A Work of General Jurisprudence

Al-Shāṭibī's treatise does not focus on specific rules of law, although such rules lie in the background of his work.[174] Rather, his paramount interest was to philosophize about the authority of reason as a source of Sharīʿa, and to develop a mode of practical reasoning in Sharīʿa. His philosophy of law rests on general principles that reflect the totality of the Sharīʿa (*kulliyyāt al-sharīʿa*).[175] Such principles

[172] Al-Ṭūfī, '*al-Ḥadīth al-Thānī wa al-Thalāthūn*,' 235.
[173] Abū Isḥāq al-Shāṭibī, *al-Muwāfaqāt fī Uṣul al-Sharīʿa*, ʿAbd Allāh Darāz et al (eds), 2 vols (Beirut: Dār al-Kutub al-ʿIlmiyya, n.d.) 1:17.
[174] Al-Shāṭibī, *al-Muwāfaqāt*, 1:19–20. [175] Al-Shāṭibī, *al-Muwāfaqāt*, 1:19.

are known with universal certitude because they are based either on rational proofs that admit no doubt, or on scriptural proofs that are determinative.[176] Any principle that poses indeterminacy cannot contribute to the foundation for his jurisprudence. Indeterminate principles may aid in the derivation of specific legal injunctions, but are not part of the core values that animate the legal system or legitimate reasoned deliberation.

For instance, one universal principle holds that the Sharīʿa has certain purposes that animate all of its extant laws and guide any act of practical reasoning. He wrote that all communities agree that law is imposed to uphold five necessary values of society, namely the protection of religion (*dīn*), life (*nafs*), family and lineage (*nasl*), property (*māl*), and reason or mind (*ʿaql*).[177] 'Knowledge of them in the community is tantamount to [rationally] necessary knowledge. [They are] not known to us by a specific piece of evidence, and no specific authoritative source attests [to them] for us . . . rather their suitability to the Sharīʿa is known by all evidence that is beyond calculation.'[178] The purposes of the law are known inductively, if not intuitively. We can extrapolate the purposes from scripture, although no specific scriptural source-text defines the value alone. Consequently, the five general aims of the legal system are scripturally based, rationally derived legal purposes that collectively represent the telos to which all reasoned deliberation in the law must aim.

Another principle classifies acts pursuant to whether they involve necessities, needs, or perfectionist interests (*al-ḍarūriyyāt, al-ḥājiyyāt, al-taḥsīniyyāt*), in light of the basic values of the legal system.[179] Whether a given act involves necessities, needs, or perfectionist interests is a different question entirely, and is subject to debate. Nevertheless, al-Shāṭibī asserted that it is universally accepted that we can classify acts into the above categories in relation to their nexus to the overarching purposes of the law.[180]

For al-Shāṭibī, the authority of reason is derived from the authority of source-texts, which reflect the divine will. This framing

[176] Al-Shāṭibī, *al-Muwāfaqāt*, 1:19–20.
[177] Al-Shāṭibī, *al-Muwāfaqāt*, 1:26.
[178] Al-Shāṭibī, *al-Muwāfaqāt*, 1:26.
[179] Al-Shāṭibī, *al-Muwāfaqāt*, 1:20.
[180] Al-Shāṭibī, *al-Muwāfaqāt*, 1:19–20.

of reason's authority is fundamentally tied to al-Shāṭibī's voluntarist theology. Al-Shāṭibī was keen to state that reason is not a legislative agent (*al-ʿaql laysa bi shāriʿ*).[181] Further, 'reason cannot determine the good or the bad' (*anna al-ʿaql lā yuḥassinu wa lā yuqabbiḥu*), with the consequent implication that it alone can render Sharīʿa obligations authoritative.[182] Reason is authoritative only to the extent source-texts provide. As he stated: 'Reason does not operate in a case of investigation except to the extent that transmitted proofs (*al-naql*) allow.'[183] Hence the authority of reason is justified by recourse to source-texts, and its scope is limited by reference to source-texts. For al-Shāṭibī, 'the essence of the Sharīʿa is that it defines for people the bounds of their acts, statements and beliefs... If it were possible that reason could exceed one boundary [established by scripturally-based proofs], it could exceed all such boundaries.'[184] For al-Shāṭibī, the authority of natural reason is, like the basic aims, founded upon the totality of scriptural sources. By relying on the authority of source-texts to develop his legal philosophy, al-Shāṭibī preserved the voluntarist theology of God while still reserving space for reason as an authoritative source of law.

Al-Shāṭibī limited the authority of reason in order to emphasize the will of God as central to the Sharīʿa. But in doing so, he created a philosophical opening to shift registers from his voluntaristic theology of God to a philosophy of natural law and practical reasoning. Al-Shāṭibī argued that by investigating scriptural sources, we find that God acts with the purpose of upholding the interests of humanity (*riʿāyat maṣāliḥ al-ʿibād*).[185] For instance, the Qurʾān states that God sent prophets as 'warners so that people would not have a claim against God after [the dispatch] of prophets.'[186] When the Qurʾān speaks of the Prophet Muḥammad, it states: 'We did not send you except as a mercy for the world.'[187] When the Qurʾān tells of God's creation, it states, '[God] did not create *jinn* and people

[181] Al-Shāṭibī, *al-Muwāfaqāt*, 1:24.
[182] Al-Shāṭibī, *al-Muwāfaqāt*, 1:61.
[183] Al-Shāṭibī, *al-Muwāfaqāt*, 1:61.
[184] Al-Shāṭibī, *al-Muwāfaqāt*, 1:61.
[185] Al-Shāṭibī, *al-Muwāfaqāt*, 2:4.
[186] Al-Shāṭibī, *al-Muwāfaqāt*, 2:4, quoting Qurʾān, 4:165.
[187] Al-Shāṭibī, *al-Muwāfaqāt*, 2:4, quoting Qurʾān, 21:107.

except so that they would worship.'[188] Relying on the descriptive force of scripture, al-Shāṭibī argued that God acts with a purpose.

To prove his point, and thereby lay the groundwork for his theory of natural reasoning, al-Shāṭibī addressed four questions:

- What is God's purpose for the Sharīʿa?
- Can we know what the Sharīʿa requires with any determinacy?
- What is the nature and purpose of obligation on humanity?
- How do conventions contribute to a theory of natural law and practical reasoning?

Together these four inquiries provide the bases by which he theorized about nature and reason in the Sharīʿa.

The Purpose of Sharīʿa

Why would God want to create the Sharīʿa at all? To answer this question, al-Shāṭibī looked to what the Sharīʿa does. According to al-Shāṭibī, we know from a review of the totality of scripture that the Sharīʿa upholds the good (*maṣlaḥa*) of people. The good reflects the basic aims or *maqāṣid* of the legal system in the created world. The good thereby contributes content to the different rules of law, which themselves are permeated by the *maqāṣid* or basic aims of the Sharīʿa. The *maqāṣid* are the purposes or aims of the law, and are designed to protect and preserve life, lineage, mind, religion and property. Al-Shāṭibī posited these five values intuitively, arguing that each society upholds them through its laws by imposing obligations or prohibitions.[189]

Al-Shāṭibī also listed three familiar degrees of nexus between the *maṣlaḥa* and the *maqāṣid*, namely 'necessities', 'needs', and 'perfectionist interests'.[190] Necessary interests are those which are required for upholding worldly and otherworldly interests (*qiyām maṣāliḥ al-dīn wa al-dunyā*), such that if they were absent, 'worldly interests

[188] Al-Shāṭibī, *al-Muwāfaqāt*, 2:4, quoting Qur'ān, 51:56.

[189] Al-Shāṭibī, *al-Muwāfaqāt*, 2:7–8.

[190] Al-Shāṭibī, *al-Muwāfaqāt*, 2:7. The three types of *maṣlaḥa-maqāṣid* nexuses are further supplemented by subsidiary rules that complement (*al-takmila, al-tatimma*) the substantive rules that speak directly to the different values of the legal system. Al-Shāṭibī, *al-Muwāfaqāt*, 2:10.

would not be upheld, but rather would be corrupted... and as to otherworldly interests, salvation and blessings would be lost.'[191] These interests are absolutely necessary to satisfy in order to uphold the Sharīʿa's five basic aims.

'Needs' pose a weaker nexus to the basic values of the legal system and are called in Arabic the *ḥājiyyāt*. 'Needs' lead to ease and the removal of hardship. According to al-Shāṭibī, if these interests are ignored, people will suffer difficulty and hardship (*al-ḥaraj wa al-mashaqqa*); but such hardship does not rise to the level of violating a general necessary interest.[192] Examples of this sort of interest would involve easing the ritual requirements of praying and fasting for those who are ill or traveling.[193]

Lastly, perfectionist interests present the weakest nexus to the basic values of the legal system. These acts, called the *taḥsīniyyāt*, attempt to perfect individuals in their manners, habits, and customs, thereby contributing to the development of good manners (*maḥāsin al-ʿādāt*) and ethical behavior (*makārim al-akhlāq*).[194] Examples include the ritual requirements to remove impurities and cover one's genitals and other private areas of the body. Other rules of a more worldly nature include prohibitions on the sale of impure substances, rules invalidating a slave's capacity to testify in court, and regulations that forbid a woman from marrying herself to her husband without the assistance of a guardian or agent.[195]

By offering this descriptive account of a hierarchy of interests reflected in the totality of Sharīʿa rules, al-Shāṭibī showed how the Sharīʿa *in toto* is designed to uphold the interests of humanity. Al-Shāṭibī adopts an inductive model of reasoning to illustrate, from the body of Sharīʿa values and traditions, that the Sharīʿā is designed to uphold certain basic aims that contribute to human flourishing. This is not meant to suggest that God therefore upholds the interests of humanity in a manner that limits His omnipotence. Rather the argument is one of correlation, at most. The fact of a correlation is separate and distinct from the theological question about God's omnipotence. Al-Shāṭibī's approach to addressing the

[191] Al-Shāṭibī, *al-Muwāfaqāt*, 2:7.
[192] Al-Shāṭibī, *al-Muwāfaqāt*, 2:9.
[193] Al-Shāṭibī, *al-Muwāfaqāt*, 2:9.
[194] Al-Shāṭibī, *al-Muwāfaqāt*, 2:9.
[195] Al-Shāṭibī, *al-Muwāfaqāt*, 2:9–10.

purpose of Sharīʿa illustrates the initial move he made to distance his legal philosophy from his theology. As illustrated below, the distance he created enabled him to philosophize about the authority of reason as a source of Sharīʿa, without running afoul of his theological commitments.

Determinacy in the Sharīʿa: *Maṣlaḥa* and the Limits of Knowledge

Thus far, al-Shāṭibī has provided a descriptive account of *maṣlaḥa* and *maqāṣid* in order to show the correlation between what source-texts require and how their requirements uphold the good. But how do we know when something is good and when it is not, particularly when source-texts are silent? To answer this question, al-Shāṭibī first had to address both the empirical and normative nature of *maṣlaḥa*, and its relation to the Sharīʿa in general. As critics of Hard Natural Law maintained, nature is not sufficiently determinate to provide a reliable empirical basis for investigation. Furthermore, only God's legislative will can be the basis for enduring norms. Al-Shāṭibī was no different. First, he dealt with the issue of nature's indeterminacy, and then addressed the fusion of fact and value in nature.

To address indeterminacy in nature, al-Shāṭibī first addressed what it means to have a determinate good and a determinate harm. He wrote that a pure good is something that leads to the fulfillment, ease, and perfection of human life (*qiyām ḥayāt al-insān wa tamām ʿayshihi*).[196] However, al-Shāṭibī held that the idea of a pure good is illusory. As a matter of fact, worldly goods (*al-maṣāliḥ al-dunyawiyya*) are never purely good. Instead, all goods include hardships as well.[197] Consequently, with regard to eating, drinking, finding a residence, and marriage, each poses a good, and involves effort and energy to obtain (ie *taʿb*).[198] Likewise, worldly harms are not purely harmful either. 'There is no harm that arises as a matter of prevailing custom, except that associated with it, or as a precondition or consequence of it, is much gentleness, bounty, and the attainment of

[196] Al-Shāṭibī, *al-Muwāfaqāt*, 2:20.
[197] Al-Shāṭibī, *al-Muwāfaqāt*, 2:20.
[198] Al-Shāṭibī, *al-Muwāfaqāt*, 2:20.

bliss.'[199] The fundamental point for al-Shāṭibī is that all matters in this world involve a mixture of both the good and the bad. 'Whoever hopes to extract one aspect alone from the world does not have the power to do that.'[200]

The mixed nature of goods and evils (*maṣāliḥ, mafāsid*), though, allowed al-Shāṭibī to accept the indeterminacy of the good as an inescapable matter of fact. But that factual indeterminacy need not result in legal indeterminacy. Rather, the interests that we must seek out as a matter of law are those in which the good is *predominant, as a matter of fact*. While a particular act may pose some evil or harm, we might nonetheless agree that the same act, *for the most part*, poses a good. For example, eating imposes the hardship of chewing, but as a matter of customary belief, eating is principally considered a general good. Al-Shāṭibī said:

> Good and corrupt acts in the world are understood in terms of the [aspect] that is predominant (*ghalaba*). If the predominant aspect (*al-ghālib*) is the aspect of the good, then it is good as a matter of custom (*ʿurf*). If the other aspect predominates, it is harmful as a matter of custom. Consequently the act has both qualities [as a matter of fact] but is identified, [as a matter of law], with the aspect that is dominant.[201]

The benefits and harms that are recognized by the law are presumptively understood to be pure goods and pure harms. Something that is predominantly good or bad *as a matter of fact* will be presumed to be purely good or bad *as a matter of law* (*fī al-ḥaqīqa al-sharʿiyya*), thereby discounting charges of indeterminacy in the use of *maṣlaḥa* in legal analysis.[202] By relying on the normative thrust of custom to get around issues of factual indeterminacy, al-Shāṭibī developed a theory of nature that counters charges of indeterminacy.

For al-Shāṭibī, when the predominant aspect of an act is good—in light of habit and custom—it is sought after *as a matter of law* in no uncertain terms (*fa hiyya al-maqṣūda sharʿ*).[203] In this sense, he fused fact and value in nature. To justify the normative imperative to pursue the predominant good, he fused the predominantly

[199] Al-Shāṭibī, *al-Muwāfaqāt*, 2:20.
[200] Al-Shāṭibī, *al-Muwāfaqāt*, 2:20.
[201] Al-Shāṭibī, *al-Muwāfaqāt*, 2:20.
[202] Al-Shāṭibī, *al-Muwāfaqāt*, 2:21.
[203] Al-Shāṭibī, *al-Muwāfaqāt*, 2:21.

factual good with normative content to render it an authoritative basis for legal analysis.

Furthermore, if pursuing such a good leads to the manifestation of some harm and hardship as a consequence, the latter are not to be viewed as intended, advocated, or rendered normative, even though the pursuit of the good is considered normative.[204] Any harm that arises from pursuing the good in such cases is certainly a negative consequence; but it carries no normative implications for the rule of law requiring pursuit of the identified good. Likewise, in the case of harm or corrupt acts, if the harm is dominant as a matter of fact, then removing the harm is intended *as a matter of law* (*al-maqṣūd sharʿan*).[205] If by prohibiting the act, some good results, that good carries no normative weight and has no normative implications for the content, nature, or authority of the prohibition. The purpose is to remove the harm and evil. Any good byproducts are consequential, but not intended *as a matter of law*.[206]

Indeed, for al-Shāṭibī, a context-sensitive inquiry allows one to understand the good and harm of an act, and the telos to which it contributes. He held that all benefits are not legally permissible and all harms are not legally prohibited.[207] Any inquiry into the good and the bad must be undertaken with due attention to the historical moment. He said:

> Where the goods and harms are included within the purview of the divine legislator, we know from His perspective that He looks to the circumstances, the people and the time such that a specific benefit may be permitted at one time or circumstance, or for one person, but not permitted in another case.[208]

Certainly, a single act will contain both good and harm. But for the purpose of law and legal ordering, we look to the predominant value that an act contains. Al-Shāṭibī wrote that when the good is deemed to be the predominant aspect of an act (as a matter of fact), it is pursued as a matter of law in no uncertain terms (*fa hiyya*

[204] Al-Shāṭibī, *al-Muwāfaqāt*, 2:21. [205] Al-Shāṭibī, *al-Muwāfaqāt*, 2:21.
[206] Al-Shāṭibī, *al-Muwāfaqāt*, 2:21.
[207] Al-Shāṭibī, *al-Muwāfaqāt*, 2:31. For the discussion by al-Rāzī, see al-Rāzī, *al-Maḥṣūl*, 6:97–108. [208] Al-Shāṭibī, *al-Muwāfaqāt*, 2:31–32.

al-maqṣūda sharʿ).[209] When something is a predominant good as a matter of fact, it becomes a goal and aim that is required of individuals *as a matter of law.*[210]

For al-Shāṭibī, the context of any act illustrates that to determine the good and the bad of a situation is a complex matter and cannot be reduced to a principle of general application alone. To presume in blanket fashion that the law upholds the good and repudiates harm could very easily be confused as a full scale endorsement of human desires in the law. Citing the Qurʾān, al-Shāṭibī wrote: 'If truth followed [human] whimsy, the heavens and earth and all that is in them would be harmed'.[211] For al-Shāṭibī, that could not be the purpose of the law. Rather, he wrote:

> The presumption of goods is not that they are absolutely permitted (*al-ibāḥa bi iṭlāq*), and the presumption of harms is not that they are absolutely prohibited (*al-manʿ bi iṭlāq*). Rather the issue concerns those things by which the worldly life is undertaken for the sake of the afterlife, even when along the way harm occurs or benefits are avoided.[212]

Al-Shāṭibī asserted that the divine legislator (*al-shāriʿ*) intends to uphold worldly and otherworldly goods (*iqāma al-maṣāliḥ al-akhrawiyya wa al-dunyawiyya*). But he did so in a manner that respects both voluntarist theology and the purpose of the Sharīʿa of guiding us to salvation in the hereafter.[213] For al-Shāṭibī, 'the goods sought after as a matter of law and the harms repelled [as a matter of law] are considered in light of living the worldly life for the sake of the eternal life, and not in light of [human] desires (*ahwāʿ al-nufūs*) for commonplace benefits or to repel commonplace harms.'[214] The goods sought after and the harms repelled as a matter of law form and shape the worldly self into something that will earn us eternal salvation. The satisfaction of worldly desires is not the goal or end that the law seeks to satisfy; rather the telos is eternal salvation. Consequently, when the law upholds the good as a matter of law, it does so in a way that ensures something other than personal delight. In fact, as al-Shāṭibī remarked, the 'Sharīʿa came in order to move

[209] Al-Shāṭibī, *al-Muwāfaqāt*, 2:21.
[210] Al-Shāṭibī, *al-Muwāfaqāt*, 2:21.
[211] Al-Shāṭibī, *al-Muwāfaqāt*, 2:30, quoting Qurʾān, 23:71.
[212] Al-Shāṭibī, *al-Muwāfaqāt*, 2:32.
[213] Al-Shāṭibī, *al-Muwāfaqāt*, 2:28.
[214] Al-Shāṭibī, *al-Muwāfaqāt*, 2:29.

individuals beyond the claims of their desires so that they can be servants of God' (*li tukhrija al-mukallafīn ʿan dawāʿī ahwāʿihim ḥattā yakūna ʿibād li Allāh*).[215]

For al-Shāṭibī, there is no doubt that *maṣlaḥa* must be considered in the law. Indeed, he recognized that most jurists, regardless of their naturalist persuasion, incorporated *maṣlaḥa* within the normative framework of their respective jurisprudence. He said: 'there is no difference between [the Hard Naturalists] and the Ashʿarite [Soft Naturalists] in the conclusion of this matter [about the role of *maṣlaḥa*]. Rather they differed over how to understand it. But their disagreement does not undermine the nature of goods (*maṣāliḥ*) as recognized under the law.'[216] Yet for al-Shāṭibī, for the *maṣlaḥa* to be part of the general jurisprudence of Sharīʿa, it must be sufficiently determinate so as to avoid allowing human whimsy an entrance into legal analysis. Consequently for al-Shāṭibī, *maṣlaḥa* must be conceptually regarded as a legally authoritative determinate good that impels someone to salvation in the afterlife. The telos of salvation contributes to al-Shāṭibī's normative foundation for resort to *maṣlaḥa*, and the obligations that arise from a *maṣlaḥa*-based analysis.

Humanity, Nature, and Obligations

The telos of salvation requires us to abide by obligations and prohibitions that contribute to our eschatological fulfillment. But the Sharīʿa, with its telos and rules, will mean little if it is so divorced from human nature as to impose impossible burdens, or to be entirely unresponsive to the human condition. To take account of human nature is not equivalent to rendering the Sharīʿa vulnerable to human contingency, if not whimsy. Al-Shāṭibī developed a jurisprudence of obligation that recognizes the necessity of accounting for human nature as inherent to the telos of salvation.

Before any obligation can take effect, people must have the capacity to fulfill its demands. Without capacity, one cannot fulfill any obligation: 'whatever the individual has no capacity to perform cannot be a legal obligation' (*fa mā lā qudra li al-mukallaf ʿalayhi lā*

[215] Al-Shāṭibī, *al-Muwāfaqāt*, 2:29. [216] Al-Shāṭibī, *al-Muwāfaqāt*, 2:35.

yaṣiḥḥu al-taklīf bihi sharʿan).[217] Human beings have certain desires (*al-shahwa*) that cannot be denied or ignored, such as those for eating and drinking. To demand that such desires be ignored would be to create obligations for which there is no capacity to satisfy (*taklīf mā lā yuṭāq*).[218] Al-Shāṭibī recognized that some human dispositions are so inherent to human nature that to deny them would be to harm human beings irreparably. Not all are inherent, and not all can or should be a basis for naturalistic reasoning in the law. But the dispositions that contribute to the good (*maṣlaḥa*) are often so linked to human nature that they must be satisfied in order for obligation to be possible in the first place. Consequently, the divine lawgiver does not want either to satisfy human desires or to prohibit them. Rather, God wants people to discipline their inclinations (*qahr al-nafs*) in order to do what is good and avoid what is prohibited. God's law ultimately respects those human dispositions that cannot be denied, while demanding of us a disciplined pursuit of the good as framed by the telos of salvation.[219]

Of course nothing prevents obligations from being difficult or hard to satisfy, especially if through such challenges we can find our way to salvation. Just because God does not impose impossible obligations does not mean that He would not impose difficult or challenging ones (*al-taklīf bi al-mashāqq*).[220] While straining against one's desires can be difficult, nonetheless one's desires alone are not necessarily pathways to salvation. Citing the Qurʾān, al-Shāṭibī said: 'Do you not see the one who takes his desires as a god. God knowingly leads him astray.'[221] The purpose of Sharīʿa, argued al-Shāṭibī, is to help people escape their whims and find salvation in the hereafter. 'The divine lawgiver imposed the Sharīʿa in order to divert the individual from following his whims so that he can be a servant of God. Thus countering whims is not among the hardships that are anticipated by legal obligations although [doing so] may involve a hardship according to customary standards.'[222] Human desires do not, and cannot, form the sole foundation of the law. Those that are inherent to human nature may certainly form a

[217] Al-Shāṭibī, *al-Muwāfaqāt*, 2:82.
[218] Al-Shāṭibī, *al-Muwāfaqāt*, 2:83.
[219] Al-Shāṭibī, *al-Muwāfaqāt*, 2:83.
[220] Al-Shāṭibī, *al-Muwāfaqāt*, 2:91.
[221] Al-Shāṭibī, *al-Muwāfaqāt*, 2:116, quoting Qurʾān, 45:23.
[222] Al-Shāṭibī, *al-Muwāfaqāt*, 2:116. See also 2:128.

part of the Sharīʿa's foundation, but not its entirety. The law must usher people along the path of salvation, which at times acknowledges certain human dispositional traits, and at other times requires us to manage our desires.

In a moment of critique, al-Shāṭibī suggested that not only the Hard Naturalists, but also even the Soft Naturalists, went too far in the way they fused fact and value in nature, and thereby in human dispositions. Certainly Hard and Soft Naturalists generally agreed (albeit on different grounds) that the Sharīʿa is intended to benefit human beings. Their fusion of fact and value suggested to al-Shāṭibī that the law should uphold human aims and aspirations (*aghrāḍ*) 'because every rational person seeks the good for himself, and what corresponds with his desires in this world and the next'.[223] Such a view, according to al-Shāṭibī, seems to invest human desires with too much animating spirit for Sharīʿa obligations. He both recognized and agreed that the Sharīʿa provides for people's affluence (*ḥuẓūẓ*) as a 'grace from God' (*tafaḍḍul min Allāh*), according to 'those adhering to the correct position' (*al-muḥaqqiqūn*). He did not agree with the Hard Naturalist approach that obligates God to benefit humanity.[224]

Nonetheless, while he shared the Soft Naturalist's theological argument, al-Shāṭibī distinguished himself by emphasizing his telos of salvation as a limit on the animating force of human dispositions in his Soft Naturalism. He argued that if the law is created for the benefit of humanity, that benefit must accord with the commands of the divine lawgiver in a way He defines, and not according to the demands of whimsy and desires (*ahwāʾ, shahwāt*).[225] For this reason, obligations may be a burden on humanity; but they are still good.[226] They require us to avoid our whims, although they also recognize our very real needs as humans. Obligations improve our lot in this life and the next; they may force us to counter our desires or may authorize our dispositions as bases for naturalistic reasoning.

[223] Al-Shāṭibī, *al-Muwāfaqāt,* 2:131. [224] Al-Shāṭibī, *al-Muwāfaqāt,* 2:131.
[225] Al-Shāṭibī, *al-Muwāfaqāt,* 2:131.
[226] Notably, other Soft Naturalists would agree with al-Shāṭibī on this point. The difference between them seems to be more a matter of degree than of kind. Arguably, al-Shāṭibī's distinctiveness may have more to do with his resort to conventionalism (discussed below), and its implication of the authority of history in his legal philosophy.

For al-Shāṭibī, to infuse human dispositions with normative content as a matter of law is not tantamount to exceeding the bounds of the law (*ḥudūd al-sharʿ*).[227] The challenge is to know which ones are authoritative and which are not. For al-Shāṭibī, we must consider the bounds set for us by God. He said: 'Commands and prohibitions lead [the individual] away from his natural dispositions and the indulgence of his aims, except where he adopts them *under the auspices of the law*.'[228] Consequently, we can follow our dispositions to the good, but only to the extent source-texts legitimate such aims (*min haythu athbatahu al-sharʿ*).[229] For al-Shāṭibī, the fusion of fact and value in nature takes into account the natural order of things, but within certain bounds defined by both the indices of God's will and the telos of salvation.

For al-Shāṭibī, the limits on the authority of our natural dispositions are based on various factors that reflect the necessities of human nature and the indices of God's will. One factor takes into account prevailing conventions in society, which will be discussed in the next section. The other factor concerns inspiration and considered reflection on an issue of legal interest. Specifically, he wrote about the role of inspiration (*ilhām*) on unprecedented matters (*khāriqa*). Al-Shāṭibī remarked that the Prophet guided people by decisions on unique issues (*muqtaḍā al-khawāriq*) on the basis of his conscientious perspicacity (*al-firāsa al-ṣādiqa*), true inspiration (*al-ilhām al-ṣaḥīḥ*), clear insights (*al-kashf al-wāḍiḥ*), and good vision (*al-ruʾyā al-ṣāliḥa*). 'One who acts in that way, among those who have these qualities, is on a correct path, and acts according to what is not outside the legally legitimate.'[230] He remarked that Muḥammad guided us in this fashion and never reserved the capacity to engage in this type of analysis only to himself.[231] In fact, al-Shaṭibī cited examples in which the Companions of Muḥammad relied on their perspicacity, insight, and inspiration to decide matters that arose amongst themselves.

This capacity for individuals to engage in reasoned deliberation is valid, though, only to the extent that the results do not violate a

[227] Al-Shāṭibī, *al-Muwāfaqāt*, 2:132.
[228] Al-Shāṭibī, *al-Muwāfaqāt*, 2:131 (emphasis added).
[229] Al-Shāṭibī, *al-Muwāfaqāt*, 2:132. [230] Al-Shāṭibī, *al-Muwāfaqāt*, 2:200.
[231] Al-Shāṭibī, *al-Muwāfaqāt*, 2:201.

fundamental principle that has some provenance with Muḥammad. He said that any unprecedented matter that arises among the scholars will concern particular legal issues (*juzʾiyyāt*) that fall within the ambit of general universal truths (*kulliyyāt*), which have a provenance from Muḥammad.[232] No one can reach an estimation of the good without respecting the mediating role of the Prophet (*fa lā yaẓannu ẓānn annahu ḥaṣala ʿalā khayr bi dūn wisāṭa nabawiyya*).[233] If an unprecedented issue (*khāriqa*) can be resolved in light of a prophetic universal principle, the new rule is valid; otherwise it is not, even if it seems obviously noble and high-minded.[234] Anything that contravenes a universal prophetic principle is invalid, and is considered the product of one's delusive imagination or is from the devil, according to al-Shāṭibī.[235]

An example of such false analysis involves a hypothetical case about a judge who has before him two witnesses who are well known for their just character. The judge has a dream in which the Prophet says to him: 'Do not judge based on this testimony, for it is void.' This sort of inspiration is not suitable for guiding the judge's determination because it violates an established principle of the Sharīʿa concerning respect for the testimony of just witnesses.[236] Another example might involve one's feeling that a certain quantity of water is unlawfully usurped or impure, or that a particular witness is a liar. No one can rely on this intuition unless there is a clear cause for such suspicion. Consequently, the person with these suspicions is not allowed to forgo ritual purification with the water in question. Nor can he ignore the testimony of the witness.[237] The obvious and clear rulings (*al-ẓawāhir*) on these matters are provided already by the Sharīʿa, and one cannot abandon them by relying purely upon intuition.[238] 'Every unprecedented inspiration that has occurred or will occur until the final day is not rejected or accepted until after subjecting it to the Sharīʿa. If it is permitted there, it is legitimate and accepted.'[239] Subjecting novel issues to this process of Sharīʿa analysis, though, means that the unprecedented rulings

[232] Al-Shāṭibī, *al-Muwāfaqāt*, 2:198.
[233] Al-Shāṭibī, *al-Muwāfaqāt*, 2:197.
[234] Al-Shāṭibī, *al-Muwāfaqāt*, 2:199–200.
[235] Al-Shāṭibī, *al-Muwāfaqāt*, 2:202–3.
[236] Al-Shāṭibī, *al-Muwāfaqāt*, 2:203.
[237] Al-Shāṭibī, *al-Muwāfaqāt*, 2:203.
[238] Al-Shāṭibī, *al-Muwāfaqāt*, 2:203.
[239] Al-Shāṭibī, *al-Muwāfaqāt*, 2:212.

must coincide with the general principles of Sharīʿa and the traditions that arise therefrom.[240]

Conventions, Soft Natural Law, and Practical Reasoning

Al-Shāṭibī's naturalism is built in part on a totalistic vision of Sharīʿa, which incorporates the conventions that reflect the demands of the human condition. He wrote that legally relevant conventions must be known with certitude and must involve general principles (*kulliyyāt*) as opposed to particular, fact-specific rules (*al-juzʾiyyāt*).[241] This sort of convention is not equivalent to human whimsy because it does not change, and generally is a constant in the universe. For instance, al-Shāṭibī said that scriptural provisions about the heavens, the earth, and the bounties of both attest to the fact that human existence is beset with structures and conventions that are eternal in nature and will not change until the Day of Resurrection. As al-Shāṭibī said: 'The style of God (*sunnat Allāh*) suffers no change. There is no change to God's creation, as illustrated by the requirements of the law pursuant to [creation's] measure of things.'[242] In other words, God puts nature into existence as a deep structure that is not susceptible to human whimsy. These natural structures are a product of God's will; they reflect the style of God and His desires for humanity. As such, they can be relied upon as authoritative standards for the purpose of legal analysis.[243]

But conventions are a complex thing. Not all of them can be relied upon as an authoritative foundation of legal analysis. The only conventions that are authoritative as a matter of law are those that pose a nexus to the totality of Sharīʿa. Al-Shāṭibī thereby broke conventions down into two types in light of their nexus to source-texts. First, there are conventions to which source-texts (*al-dalīl al-sharʿī*) clearly attest, whether approvingly or disapprovingly. The significance of these conventions is that source-texts acknowledge

240 Al-Shāṭibī, *al-Muwāfaqāt*, 2:212.

241 Al-Shāṭibī, *al-Muwāfaqāt*, 2:213.

242 Al-Shāṭibī, *al-Muwāfaqāt*, 2:213.

243 Al-Shāṭibī, *al-Muwāfaqāt*, 2:213. Al-Shāṭibī's reliance on nature's structures as a function of God's will parallels earlier theories that rely on nature's goodness as a function of God's grace (*tafaḍḍul*).

them either by commanding or recommending pursuit of them, prohibiting or cautioning against them, or simply indicating they are inconsequential. This type of convention is reflected in rules that ban slaves from testifying in court, require the removal of impurities, and demand the covering of one's genitals (*sitr al-ʿawrāt*).[244] Such conventions are generally 'matters that fall under the rule of the law, and do not change even though individuals may have different opinions about them.'[245]

The second type of convention consists of those for which no source-text exists to approve or disapprove.[246] These silent conventions may be general and static, or they may change. The consistent ones include human dispositions concerning hunger and thirst, speech, and courage—all of which offer a normative basis for practical reasoning. The divine legislator is presumed to take them into account for Sharīʿa purposes, given His deliberate creation of them. Hence, new rules that coincide with them are valid.

Silent conventions that change may be linked to the divine will once they are deconstructed to determine if there is an enduring element underlying them. One example might involve whether or not manliness and honor require men to cover their heads. Al-Shāṭibī wrote that in the East covering one's head is not looked upon with favor whereas that is not the case in the West. Here, the particular customary rule about male head-dress changes in different contexts. But both rules nonetheless reflect a more fundamental issue that does not change—namely the importance of identifying who is of just character, which has various implications in different areas of law (such as testimony). The fundamental element of identifying who is just remains constant across regions, despite the fact that how one determines if someone is just may differ from place to place and time to time.

> If the world were made to be eternal without end, and obligation likewise, there would be no need for the law to have any additions. The meaning of [legal] differences (*ikhtilāf*) is that conventions, where they differ... are reviewed in light of a fundamental legal principle by which one judges the convention, as in the case of [determining the age of] maturity.

244 Al-Shāṭibī, *al-Muwāfaqāt*, 2:215.
245 Al-Shāṭibī, *al-Muwāfaqāt*, 2:216.
246 Al-Shāṭibī, *al-Muwāfaqāt*, 2:215.

> [Requirements of] obligation are lifted from the youth prior to reaching maturity. When he reaches [maturity] obligation falls upon him. The lifting of obligations prior to maturity and their establishment after maturity are not due to differences in the divine message of obligations. Rather the difference arises in the conventions.[247]

Conventions may change due to the underlying context and circumstances. As a matter of law, obligations fall upon people once they reach the age of maturity. But for al-Shāṭibī, rules that specify *when* maturity occurs are subject to conventions that may change across societies. The validity of rules based on these changing conventions is dependent upon whether the rules can be founded upon more general conventions that the Sharīʿa upholds. Just because the specific conventions about when maturity occurs happen to change, that does not mean that rules delineating the age of majority are not valid Sharīʿa rules. 'Prevailing customs must be considered as a matter of law,' said al-Shāṭibī, whether or not they are recognized and fortified by specific source-texts.[248] Those not recognized by specific source-texts, but which nonetheless relate to a fundamental Sharīʿa value, must be given authority; otherwise, obligations that ignore such conventions will make impossible demands upon people.

Conventions that are enduring have the ontological authority to be the foundation for new rules of law because of the presumption that the divine style of God's creation is reflected in these conventions. In this case, the convention is both consistently in existence, and considered normative as a matter of law (*kānat al-ʿāda wujūdiyya aw sharʿiyya*).[249] In other words, these conventions constitute the site where fact and value are fused. The conventions that change over time and space, though, have no normative force until corroborated by the totality of Sharīʿa indicators, or until related to a more general, constant convention. If Sharīʿa source-texts attest to the value of the changing convention, the normative authority of the changing convention is derivative of the ontological authority of the source-texts. If the changing conventions are founded upon more general conventions, the normative authority of the changing

[247] Al-Shāṭibī, *al-Muwāfaqāt*, 2:217.
[248] Al-Shāṭibī, *al-Muwāfaqāt*, 2:218.
[249] Al-Shāṭibī, *al-Muwāfaqāt*, 2:227.

conventions is derivative of the ontological authority of the more general convention, as a matter of Sharīʿa. In this latter case, natural reasoning acquires sufficient ontological authority to reach conclusions about rules of Sharīʿa in light of the general and changing conventions.[250]

Maṣlaḥa Mursala and Practical Reasoning

Al-Shāṭibī's response to the four questions illustrate how he upheld his voluntarist theology, and granted ontological authority to reasoned deliberation in Sharīʿa. He was mindful of ensuring that any grant of authority to reason does not violate the central importance of God's will in the Sharīʿa. Once he separated the legal from the theological dimension of his natural law theory, he developed a model of natural reasoning that accounts for the indeterminacy that can arise from the epistemic frailty and complexity of the human condition. Certainly we are in no position to have full awareness of how a certain rule will influence and affect the social wellbeing of individuals and the polity. But legal analysis is different from an empirical analysis, in that absolute certitude is not required to justify a particular rule as authoritative. As long as that rule corresponds to a predominant good or a predominant evil in a manner that is mindful of human nature, the conventions that make social life meaningful, and ultimately the eternal salvation of each person, al-Shāṭibī held that the rule enjoys sufficient authority as a matter of Sharīʿa.

But how does one rely on reason as a source of law in light of this admittedly abstract philosophy of law? While al-Shāṭibī emphasized a general jurisprudence involving abstract principles of analysis, he specifically addressed the mechanics of practical reasoning about the good (*maṣlaḥa*) in his other jurisprudential work, *al-Iʿtiṣām*. In this work, devoted chiefly to showing how decisions based on *maṣlaḥa* are not illegitimate innovations, he wrote about the mechanism of *maṣlaḥa mursala*. Using the same vocabulary noted above in the cases of al-Ghazālī and al-Rāzī, al-Shāṭibī discussed the relationship between key technical terms like *maṣlaḥa*, *munāsaba*, *ḍarūriyyāt*,

[250] Al-Shāṭibī, *al-Muwāfaqāt*, 2:227.

and *maqāṣid*. He wrote that many people consider most rules established by *maṣlaḥa mursala* to be innovative, and attribute the practice to the first and second generation of jurists after Muḥammad's death.[251] This model of reasoning involves considering the rational nexus (*munāsab*) between a rule of law and the purpose of the law, in light of a specific good (*maṣlaḥa*).[252] In some cases, the totality of Sharīʿa may recognize the rule of law and its animating *ratio legis*, while in other cases, the rule of law may be rejected outright.[253]

Fundamentally, *maṣlaḥa mursala* is a way by which we can identify a rational nexus between a specific rule of law and the basic aims of the law (*maqāṣid al-sharʿ*). There must be no scripturally based sources that repudiate the nexus. Further, the rational nexus must conform generally to the totality of the law, address matters that pose a necessary interest, and not involve issues of ritual worship (*al-taʿabbudāt*).[254] Al-Shāṭibī's *maṣlaḥa mursala*, as a model of practical reasoning, bears much in common with the methods of practical reasoning developed by al-Ghazālī. Indeed, to illustrate his model, al-Shāṭibī expressly referred to al-Ghazālī's hypothetical about the ruler who has sex during the day in Ramaḍān. Some jurists might tell the ruler that he must fast for two consecutive months as sufficient expiation of his sin, as the other option of freeing a slave may be so easy for the ruler that it does not serve a deterrent function at all. But according to others, this selectivity violates the express terms of the Qur'ānic verse, which prioritizes freeing a slave.[255] Consequently, while the above ruling may coincide with reasonable beliefs about deterrence, it nonetheless violates the body of law already established.

In other cases, however, *maṣlaḥa*-based reasoning may affirmatively contribute to the law. Al-Shāṭibī remarked:

> When the significance [of the *munāsab*] is apparent and we understand, by [investigating the totality of] the law that it is acceptable for construing a rule, then we accept it. Intended by '*maṣlaḥa*' in our opinion is what is upheld for creation in terms of attaining benefit and repelling harm, but

[251] Al-Shāṭibī, *al-Iʿtiṣām*, 2:607.
[252] Al-Shāṭibī, *al-Iʿtiṣām*, 2:607.
[253] Al-Shāṭibī, *al-Iʿtiṣām*, 2:609.
[254] Al-Shāṭibī, *al-Iʿtiṣām*, 2:627–8, 632.
[255] Al-Shāṭibī, *al-Iʿtiṣām*, 2:610.

[only] in a way where reason does not act independently in determining the situation.[256]

If the rationale justifying a ruling on the matter coincides with the totality of Sharīʿa values and indicators (*an yulāʾima taṣarrufāt al-sharʿ*), then it bears sufficient authority to legitimate a rule of law.[257] The totality of the law may not address the rationale with any specific indicator (*bi ghayr dalīl muʿayyan*), but rather endorses it in a more general way.[258]

The discussion here on al-Shāṭibī's theory of practical reasoning is limited, in large part, because of its similarity to the theories of al-Ghazālī and al-Rāzī, which have already been discussed in detail. This is not meant to suggest he offers nothing new. Rather, for the purpose of this study, noting the general parallel between al-Shāṭibī's method of practical reasoning and those adopted by al-Ghazālī and al-Rāzī is sufficient at this stage. Al-Shāṭibī was clearly aware of the theorists who came before him. He was also keen to develop a theory of natural reasoning that incorporated more contextual content, all the while upholding (like other Soft Naturalists discussed earlier) his voluntarist theology of God's omnipotence. In his *al-Muwāfaqāt* al-Shāṭibī provided a naturalist jurisprudence that relied on a complex understanding of human nature, legal reasoning, and conventions that embodies the spirit of the law. But when writing about *maṣlaḥa*-based reasoning in *al-Iʿtiṣām*, he adopted *maṣlaḥa mursala* in a fashion akin to the methods provided by al-Ghazālī and al-Rāzī. Where he differs from the above authors is in the way he described his Soft Naturalistic account in terms of conventions, and the relationship between those conventions and the will of God.

Conclusion

Soft Naturalists recognized that at times they would need to utilize reason to create Sharīʿa rules of obligation that invoke divine reward and sanction. Jurists like al-Juwaynī held that any issue can be

[256] Al-Shāṭibī, *al-Iʿtiṣām*, 2:609–10. [257] Al-Shāṭibī, *al-Iʿtiṣām*, 2:612.
[258] Al-Shāṭibī, *al-Iʿtiṣām*, 2:612.

subjected to a Sharīʿa analysis, suggesting that while there may not be a specific source-text governing the issue, one could nevertheless derive a rule for a novel situation in a way that is consistent and coherent with the tradition of Sharīʿa. However, the challenge that remained for these jurists was how to justify this resort to reasoned deliberation while preserving both their theological commitment to an omnipotent God, and a view of legal authority that requires a sufficient degree of determinacy in the law. Jurists such as al-Ghazālī, al-Rāzī, al-Ṭūfī, and al-Shāṭibī developed Soft Natural Law theories, whereby they granted ontological authority to natural reason by fusing fact and value in nature. They developed a jurisprudence that allows us to reason about God's will through the medium of nature. Like Hard Naturalist jurists, these Voluntarist Soft Naturalists fused fact and value in nature with their use of the term *maṣlaḥa*. Their natural law theories were teleological in that they sought to guide (and thereby limit) reasoned deliberation toward the fulfillment of intuitively determined aims of the legal tradition (*maqāṣid*). The fundamental irony is that despite their theological differences, both Hard and Soft Naturalists utilized nature to provide objectivity and normativity to their reasoned conclusions about Sharīʿa norms.

What distinguishes the Hard Naturalists from the Soft Naturalists is the theological implication of their respective theories of natural law on God's omnipotence. For the Hard Naturalists, nature's beneficial quality is a constant that reflects the unchanging style of God. God only does the good, and consequently the nature that He creates only presents a good for human beings. But an implication of this theory of nature is that God is bound and obligated to do the good. He cannot act badly or will something other than the good. According to the Soft Naturalists, this implication undercuts the omnipotence of God. Soft Naturalists argued that God acts out of grace to benefit humanity. Nature's goodness does not bind God to do only the good, since He can change His will and grace. Consequently, Soft Naturalists preserved a theology of divine omnipotence while adopting a naturalistic jurisprudence that grants ontological authority to reasoned deliberation in the law. Nature is both an enduring structure that we can reliably investigate, and is subject to a change in divine will. Soft Naturalism is softer in that while it acknowledges the constancy of nature for the purposes of legal analysis, the constancy of its goodness is undermined, for theological purposes, in a way that Hard Natural Law theories avoid. For Soft Naturalists, nature's goodness must be subjected to the possibility of a divine change of mind. Possibility, however, is not the same as probability. Perhaps for that reason, they could proffer their Soft Natural Law theory without fundamentally rendering it immediately vulnerable to the specter of sudden shifts in the nature of creation.

Soft Natural Law theory both avoids theological implications that violate voluntarist commitments, and grants ontological authority to reasoned deliberation in and about Sharīʿa values. Soft Natural Law jurists recognized that not all issues of everyday life are addressed by source-texts. They knew they could not preclude reason as a source of law, lest they admit that the finitude of source-texts implies that Sharīʿa cannot speak to *de novo* issues of law. Indeed al-Juwaynī and al-Samʿānī were committed to the view that all issues in life could be captured by the Sharīʿa. But they did not suggest that authoritative source-texts address all issues that arise from lived experience. Rather they, and the other jurists surveyed above, understood that Sharīʿa modes of inquiry had to incorporate a mode of practical reasoning that did not at the same time render the Sharīʿa vulnerable to unchecked indeterminacy. For them, Sharīʿa must be able to regulate all aspects of life; consequently the epistemology of practical reasoning about fundamental values, the necessities of life, and the silence of authoritative source-texts contributed to a philosophy of law that permits extending the Sharīʿa to regulate human behavior in accordance with what God may want.

While developing a model of reasoning for *de novo* issues, Soft Naturalist jurists were also eager to ensure that their epistemology of legal reasoning would limit the scope of reasoned deliberation in the law. Jurists such as al-Ghazālī, Fakhr al-Dīn al-Rāzī, al-Qarāfī, and al-Shāṭibī developed a method of practical reasoning in Sharīʿa that centered around key concepts such as *maqāṣid* and *maṣlaḥa*. The *maqāṣid* reflect the fundamental purposes of a legal system, and which guide all legal reasoning. *Maṣlaḥa*, in this epistemic context, refers to more context-specific norms resulting from the act of practical reasoning about what the law should be for an issue not addressed by authoritative source-texts. Not all *maṣlaḥa* norms can become authoritative rules of Sharīʿa, though. Most jurists surveyed above agreed that only the *maṣlaḥa* norms that uphold the *maqāṣid*, are of general application, and contribute to the necessities of life can offer a foundation for Sharīʿa rules of obligation and prohibition. Consequently while these jurists granted ontological authority to reason in the law, they developed methods of practical reasoning that actually limited reason's scope of application and authority in the development of new rules of law.

The irony of granting ontological authority to reason while limiting its epistemic scope is most apparent when viewed in light of contemporary reformist theories that look to the *maqāṣid-maṣlaḥa* model of practical reasoning to reconsider the Sharīʿa and its substantive doctrines. Throughout the 20th century and thereafter, Muslim reformists have invoked the *maṣlaḥa-maqāṣid* model of practical reasoning to justify abandoning prior doctrine in the name of furthering the general aims of the Sharīʿa. Reformists invoke the *maqāṣid* or basic aims to override and invalidate any particular rule of law (*fiqh*) that may seem out of touch with the demands of the modern world, despite the rule's provenance in historical sources of precedent. In the pre-modern world, claiming superiority for these basic aims found expression in the writings of Ibn Qayyim al-Jawziyya (d. 751/1350) who wrote:

> The Sharīʿa is founded and built upon wisdom and the interests of people in this life and the life to come. It is justice, mercy, goodness, and wisdom. Any issue that forsakes justice for injustice, mercy for its opposite, the good for the corrupt, and wisdom for stupidity, is not part of the Sharīʿa, even if it is included in [the Sharīʿa] on the basis of an interpretation.[259]

A passage such as this fuels reformist attempts to rethink the Sharīʿa, in part, by marginalizing the pre-modern rules of law (*fiqh*) as human estimations of the Sharīʿa, which are by definition fallible, contextual, and thereby of limited authority. For instance, Khaled Abou El Fadl, who is attracted by the words of Ibn Qayyim

[259] Shams al-Dīn Abū ʿAbd Allāh Muḥammad Ibn Qayyim al-Jawziyya, *Miftāḥ Dār al-Saʿāda wa Manshūrāt Wilāyat al-ʿIlm wa al-Irāda*, Bashīr Muḥammad ʿUyūn (ed) (Damascus: Maktabat Dār al-Bayān, 1998) 3:5.

above,[260] elides the Sharīʿa with the *maqāṣid al-sharīʿa* in order to marginalize the authority of *fiqh*, which he characterizes as instrumental. He writes:

> The *Sharīʿah* is God's Will in an ideal and abstract fashion, but the *fiqh* is the product of the human attempt to understand God's Will. In this sense, the *Sharīʿah* is always fair, just, and equitable, but the *fiqh* is only an attempt at reaching the ideals and purposes of the *Sharīʿah* (*maqāṣid al-Sharīʿah*).[261]

Contextualizing the rules of *fiqh* is itself an important endeavor and one that can offer important insights into the history and evolution of the law. But to rely on the *maqāṣid-maṣlaḥa* model of practical reasoning to justify emancipation from the past tradition is not what pre-modern jurists had in mind when they developed the epistemic model to regulate the scope of reason. As suggested in the conclusion to this book, the reformists who vest hope for change in the *maqāṣid-maṣlaḥa* model give it an authority and effect that pre-modern jurists did not intend for it. While modern reformists may select from the pre-modern tradition whatever supports an agenda of reform, the pre-modern intent behind the *maqāṣid-maṣlaḥa* model is not so easily separable from the model itself. Adopting the *maqāṣid-maṣlaḥa* model without understanding its original purpose may result, ironically, in (re)inscribing pre-modern assumptions about the world and knowledge on the very present that the reformists wish to emancipate from the past.

[260] Abou El Fadl provides a translation of selections of the same passage in Ibn Qayyim's treatise. Khaled Abou El Fadl, *Speaking in God's Name: Islamic Law, Authority and Women* (Oxford: Oneworld Publications, 2001) 14.

[261] Abou El Fadl, *Speaking in God's Name*, 32.

V

Conclusion

This study has explored how pre-modern Muslim jurists theorized and justified the ontological authority of reason in Sharīʿa. As this study has shown, jurists of varying theological and legal school affiliations adopted a similar approach: the fusion of fact and value in the natural world, which is a product of God's creative will. While their philosophical emphasis was on explaining and justifying the fusion in light of certain theological pre-commitments, the fact that they located the fusion in the natural world offers the basis for meaningfully framing this study by reference to natural law philosophy. 'Natural law' as a philosophy of law offers an important lens through which to view and understand the pre-modern debates on the relationship between reason, the good and the bad (*ḥusn, qubḥ*), and obligation.

In this study, the concept of 'natural law' has been narrowly tailored to focus our investigation on the very particular question of the ontological authority of reason as a source of Sharīʿa norms. This is not to suggest that natural law theories framed in Roman, Christian, or Islamic terms of reference necessarily map onto each other concept for concept, or point for point. Rather the shared concern about reason, amidst the various differences, suggests that the frame of legal philosophy offers a window both for understanding the salience of particular legal debates, and for seeing beyond the particularities, across boundaries of time, space, and jurisdiction.[1]

[1] The literature on law and legal reasoning in the pre-modern and modern period is voluminous. Even a cursory review of different scholarly monographs shows that issues pertaining to reason and authority are shared across legal systems and approaches to legal philosophy. In the Anglo-American tradition, see Ronald Dworkin, *Law's Empire* (Cambridge: Harvard University Press, 1986), whose interpretive theory of law offers an important philosophical contribution to the debates on interpretation, objectivity and authority; Owen Fiss, 'Foreword: The Forms of Justice' (1979) 93 *Harvard Law Review* 1, who writes about the role of the judiciary in pressing for structural change; Brian Z

The frame of natural law has allowed us to capture the differences between pre-modern Muslim jurists while also transcending categories that have historically characterized Islamic intellectual historiography. The theoretical differences between the jurists discussed above are not easily captured simply by reference to their respective affiliations to one theological camp or another. Indeed, to suggest that the single dichotomy between Muʿtazilites and Ashʿarites, or Ethical Rationalists and Voluntarists, captures the relevant differences between the jurists would gloss over the rich nuances in their debates. Also it would overlook how the distinctiveness of law as a discipline challenges jurists to consider similar questions of authority, reason, and change, regardless of their historical period, religious or theological affiliations, or jurisdictional focus.

The subtle and not so subtle differences between the jurists addressed above suggest that framing our inquiry in terms of natural law can offer important insights both into theoretical trends employed by jurists across centuries, as well as how and why particular jurists might depart in slight or significant fashions from those trends. In the move from ʿAbd al-Jabbār to al-Baṣrī, we find two Hard Natural Law advocates with distinct approaches, one more concerned with philosophically justifying the ontological authority of reason and the other more attentive to the epistemology of Hard Natural Law analysis. As we witnessed in the cases of al-Jaṣṣāṣ and Ibn ʿAqīl, given the complex histories surrounding their theological affiliations, let alone their intense intellectual engagements, categorizing either of them in an exclusivist fashion does not necessarily capture their philosophy of law or the concerns that animated their legal philosophies. While a jurist such as al-Rāzī may have considered himself a Soft Naturalist, al-Qarāfī found al-Rāzī's justification of natural reason disturbingly similar to Hard Natural Law theory. And yet other Soft Naturalists such as al-Ṭūfī and al-Shāṭibī seemed to offer something significantly different from al-Ghazālī,

Tamanaha, *On the Rule of Law: History, Politics, Theory* (Cambridge: Cambridge University Press, 2004), who illustrates the relationship between substantive justice concerns and the authority of the law; John Hart Ely, *Democracy and Distrust: A Theory of Judicial Review* (Cambridge, Mass: Harvard University Press, 1980), who reflects upon the challenge judicial review can pose to prior precedent, and theorizes about that power within the framework of democratic theory.

al-Rāzī, and al-Qarāfī altogether. Al-Shāṭibī's theory of conventions in his Soft Naturalism provides a rich account of nature, which al-Shāṭibī could grant ontological authority to reason while also limiting the scope of reasoned deliberation in legal analysis. From this theoretical position, he could critique the approach of other Soft Naturalist jurists such as al-Rāzī, who adopted a conception of nature that his commentator al-Qarāfī considered to fall dangerously close to the Hard Naturalist account. Likewise, while al-Ṭūfī relied on the concept of God's grace (*tafaḍḍul*) as did other Soft Naturalist jurists, he nonetheless contended that his *maṣlaḥa*-based theory allows greater reasoned deliberation than the *maṣlaḥa mursala* of the Mālikī school, or presumably al-Ghazālī's influential model of practical reasoning. Indeed, as we have shown, al-Ghazālī's influential model considerably limits the scope of authoritative reasoned deliberation.

What we have seen throughout this study is that Muslim jurists fused fact and value in nature to grant ontological authority to reason in the law. They were concerned with how to derive and at times create Sharīʿa rules in an authoritative and determinate fashion in accordance with their conceptions of the divine will and the purposes of the law. The exigencies of daily life, coupled with the finitude of source texts suggested to them that they could not rely on prior precedent or foundational sources to address every given issue at any time in any place. For authors such as al-Juwaynī, human experience illustrates the inevitability of that truth.

Of course, jurists could have simply argued that in the lacuna of source-texts, humans can legislate as needed. Indeed, that seems to have been the conclusion of many jurists. Many would have permitted the political ruler to create rules of law pursuant to the needs of society as circumstances require.[2] So why invoke theology, God, and Sharīʿa at all? To offer a theory of law by which we can attribute the authority of certain rules to the unexpressed will of God might speak more to human hubris. But to suggest that in the absence of God's express will there is no epistemically coherent way to pursue,

[2] See, eg, Anver M Emon, '*Huquq Allah* and *Huquq al-'Ibad*: A Legal Heuristic for a Natural Rights Regime' (2006) 13 *Islamic Law and Society* 325, 386–90; Ibn Taymiyya, *al-Siyāsa al-Sharʿiyya fī Iṣlāḥ al-Rāʿī wa al-Raʿiyya* (Beirut: Dār al-Kutub al-ʿIlmiyya, 1988) esp 65.

with some degree of determinacy, what God wants, calls into question the eschatological significance of obedience in Islamic thought. In other words, if salvation depends on seeking God's pleasure, and the Sharīʿa is designed to aid our pursuit of salvation, as al-Shāṭibī suggested, then simply to remain in a state of suspended judgment about how to be in the world poses a challenge to the coherence of the Sharīʿa and contributes to eschatological anxiety. Hence, the need to render the law reflective of God's will becomes immensely important.

To concede that lacunae exist in the law is not the problem. Rather the fundamental problem is how to develop rules of law that fill the lacunae without at the same time departing from God's will. As such, we cannot develop rules of Sharīʿa without at the same time invoking God and His will. But on what basis can our reasoned deliberation reflect the will of God? Indeed, it might seem that any act of reasoned deliberation about the Sharīʿa constitutes an imposition upon God of our deliberations about the good, the just, and thereby the eschatologically redemptive. Hence we return full circle to the initial question of Islamic natural law theories—namely about the theology of God and its implications for how we can legitimately reason about Sharīʿa norms.

- On what basis can human reason ever have ontological authority to contribute to Sharīʿa rules of law?
- How do we distinguish between legitimate reasoned deliberation and mere human whimsy (*hawā*)?
- How do we account for determinacy and predictability in the law amidst the wide range of human experience and judgment?
- What bounds exist to ensure that human legislation is good and just?

These questions animated all of our jurists and contributed to the irony that, despite their theological differences, both Hard and Soft Naturalist jurists fused fact and value in nature, and recognized the ontological authority of reason in Sharīʿa. Hard Naturalists argued that God creates nature for the benefit of humanity. God acts with a purpose, namely to provide the goods that contribute to human fulfillment. Consequently, the natural order reflects not just the fact of God's creative power, but also a telos of human fulfillment whose normative import is based on a purposeful divine will. Al-Jaṣṣāṣ, Qāḍī ʿAbd al-Jabbār, and Abū al-Ḥusayn al-Baṣrī proffered the presumption of permissibility (*ibāḥa*) in order to fuse fact and value in nature. For them, the presumption of permissibility is not simply about the consequences of acting one way or another. Rather it is the conceptual device by which Hard Naturalists fused fact and value to create their natural teleology where the relevant telos was to uphold the good of humanity (*riʿāyat al-maṣāliḥ*).

Voluntarist Soft Naturalists opposed Hard Natural Law, and argued that nature is neither determinative of the good nor normative. Their opposition was based, in large part, on their theological commitment to God's unfettered omnipotence. For them, God is free to do as He pleases, with the result that any divine act is good. For them, God never commits evil because all that God does is by definition good. But they acknowledged that this theological commitment does not resolve the dilemma posed by the epistemic demands of determining the law when source-texts are silent. To uphold their theological commitment and resolve the epistemic challenge, they developed Soft Natural Law theories to account for the need for reasoned deliberation in matters unaddressed by authoritative sources. Soft Naturalists recognized as an empirical and scriptural fact that creation benefits humanity. This is not to suggest, they argued, that God is obliged to do good. Instead, relying on the *correlation* between scriptural references about the world's bounties, and the actual experience of such bounties in the world, they could reasonably posit that nature benefits humanity. Theologically this benefit is a result of God's grace (*tafaḍḍul*), and not a result of God being required to act justly and beneficently toward humanity. In this one modification of the Hard Naturalist argument, the Soft Naturalists preserved their theological commitment to divine omnipotence, and fused fact and value in nature, thereby granting ontological authority to reasoned deliberation in Sharīʿa. Al-Shāṭibī provided a similar but nonetheless modified version of Soft Natural Law. He fused fact and value in nature, but categorized nature into contingent and enduring conventions, some of which offer normative bases to justify the derivation of rules therefrom.

For both Hard and Soft Naturalists, nature is an objective basis for investigation, and a normative foundation for reasoning about Sharīʿa obligations. Consequently, while the general approaches to Hard and Soft Naturalism evince differences in theology, both versions embrace nature as embodying normative value for Sharīʿa purposes. While Soft and Hard Naturalists disagreed over the theological implications of their naturalism, they both recognized the inevitability of reasoning in the law, the need to justify the use of reason, and the way the fusion of fact and value in nature can justify the authority of reasoned deliberation in Sharīʿa.

The poignancy of this ironic congruence in natural law theories, given the fierce theological differences between both groups, is undercut by the theories of practical reasoning developed by Soft Naturalist jurists. Their theories of practical reasoning often centered around the concept of *maṣlaḥa*. Conceptually, *maṣlaḥa* operates at two levels in their theories. At a more general level, *maṣlaḥa* is the conceptual site where fact and value are fused in nature, akin to how Hard Naturalists used the presumption of permissibility (*ibāḥa*) to do the same. At the more specific epistemic level of practical reasoning, *maṣlaḥa* is a mediating concept between the purposes of the law (*maqāṣid*) and the *ratio legis* of a new rule of law (*ḥukm*). For jurists such as al-Ghazālī, al-Rāzī, and al-Shāṭibī, although reason may have ontological authority, its epistemic role is drastically circumscribed by a theory of practical reasoning that permits reasoned deliberation only on the most serious and necessary matters affecting a polity. Hence, despite the initial irony of congruence over the authority of reason, Soft Naturalist jurists—noting the possible exception of al-Ṭūfī—developed theories of practical reasoning that limited the epistemic role of reasoned deliberation in the law.

The fact that the *maqāṣid-maṣlaḥa* model of practical reasoning was designed to limit reasoned deliberation in the law, though, sets the background for a secondary irony. Modern reformers throughout the Muslim world view the *maqāṣid-maṣlaḥa* model of practical reasoning as offering an important mechanism for changing and developing the Sharīʿa in a manner that reflects the lived experience of modern Muslims. They see in the Soft Naturalist model of practical reasoning an authentically Islamic jurisprudential framework that introduces reasoned deliberation into a legal system that is often criticized as inflexible, fixed, and antiquated.[3] The irony, though, is that the pre-modern jurists who articulated the *maqāṣid-maṣlaḥa* model designed it for the purpose of limiting the kind of reasoned deliberation modern reformers often seek to legitimate by reference to the *maqāṣid-maṣlaḥa* model.

This is not to suggest that the *maqāṣid-maṣlaḥa* model cannot be refashioned, reconceived, or redeployed in light of changes in historical circumstance. Nor does this mean that reformists should abandon those parts of their tradition that contribute legitimacy and authenticity to their reform agendas. But to invoke a pre-modern model without also acknowledging the intellectual context in which the model arose may cover (and thereby perpetuate) the presumptions animating the pre-modern tradition. For instance, the modern Muslim reformer lives in a world that may be skeptical of the metaphysical presumptions underlying both Hard and Soft Natural Law theories. To cover and perpetuate those presumptions may inadvertently limit the effective use of that model in a new historical moment when such presumptions are vulnerable to critique in light of prevailing theories of knowledge, philosophies of law, and theories of government, many of which are built on presumptions different from those that animated our pre-modern jurists.

The reformer also lives in a world that is politically organized around the geo-politics of the nation-state and the international system. Modern reformers cannot underestimate the impact that the introduction of the modern nation-state has had on the nature of law and legal ordering. The state introduces a feature of legal ordering that was not part of the framework that animated the Hard and Soft Naturalists discussed. With the state come increased institutional bureaucratization; increased secularization of legal education and the legal profession; and a conception of law that is

[3] For critiques and studies on Islamic law, from the perspective of modern rule of law considerations, see Yvonne Yazbeck Haddad (ed), *Islamic Law and the Challenges of Modernity* (Lanham, Md: AltaMira Press, 2004); Abdullahi Ahmed An-Na'im, *Islam and the Secular State: Negotiating the Future of Shari'a* (Cambridge, Mass: Harvard University Press, 2008); Wael B Hallaq, 'Can the Shari'a Be Restored?' in Yvonne Haddad and Barbara Stowasser (eds), *Islamic Law and the Challenges of Modernity* (New York: Altamira Press, 2004) 21–54.

both bounded by geo-political borders and yet subjected to transnational norms arising from multilateral engagement at the international level.[4]

Additionally, as many have already noted, the institutional setting of Sharīʿa has considerably shifted. In the 19th and early 20th centuries, much of the Muslim world was under colonial rule. During this period, Sharīʿa was often marginalized by colonial powers, and viewed as a threat to the wellbeing of the colonial administration. And yet Sharīʿa remains an important feature of how Muslims constitute their identity, religiously and politically.[5] Consequently, while Sharīʿa as a rule of law system has been systematically dismantled, it continues to operate in certain fields of law to organize and manage Muslim affairs.[6] In particular, the principle subject area that is still the preserve of Sharīʿa doctrines in the Muslim world is the area of family law. Usually legislated in statutory form, Sharīʿa family law rules (such as marriage and divorce) pose serious concerns to reformers who take issue with the rules' gender-based discriminatory impact.[7]

[4] Incidentally, Islamic law is not the only tradition that has been subjected to the reconfigurations in political society—and thereby law—brought about by the modern state. Indigenous peoples across the world are aware of the impact of the state and its hegemonic enterprise on traditional modes of order and stability. See, eg, James Tully, *Strange Multiplicity: Constitutionalism in an age of diversity* (Cambridge: Cambridge University Press, 1995); John Borrows, 'Living Law on a Living Earth: Aboriginal Religion, Law, and the Constitution' in Richard Moon (ed), *Law and Religious Pluralism in Canada* (Vancouver: UBC Press, 2008) 161–91.

[5] For the relationship between religious tenets, Sharīʿa, and political identity, see Roxanne Euben, *Enemy in the Mirror* (Princeton: Princeton University Press, 1999); Emon, 'The Techniques and Limits of Rights Reasoning in *Sharīʿa* Today' (2009) 2 *UC Berkeley Journal of Middle East and Islamic Law* 1, 101–24.

[6] Wael Hallaq, on the other hand, has suggested that the modern state system has rendered Sharīʿa a poor vestige of what it once was. Hallaq, 'Can the Sharīʿa Be Restored?'.

[7] On the shift in legal frameworks in the Muslim world and the impact this has had on Sharīʿa as both legal doctrine and political symbol, see Khaled Abou El Fadl, *Speaking in God's Name: Islamic Law, Authority and Women* (Oxford: Oneworld Publications, 2001); Wael B Hallaq, *Sharīʿa: Theory, Practice, Transformations* (Cambridge: Cambridge University Press, 2009); Chibli Mallat, *Introduction to Middle Eastern Law* (Oxford: Oxford University Press, 2007); Anver M Emon,'Islamic Law and the Canadian Mosaic: Politics, Jurisprudence, and Multicultural Accommodation.' (2008) 87 Canadian Bar Review 391; Anver M Emon, 'On the Pope, Cartoons, and Apostates: Shari'a 2006' (2006/07) 22 *Journal of Law and Religion* 303. For studies on the narrow application of Sharīʿa in the realm of family law today in Muslim states, see Abdullahi

To view the *maqāṣid-maṣlaḥa* model in its intellectual context uncovers those presumptions that may, once critiqued, open the door to new research on Sharīʿa and legal philosophy for a modern period where the animating questions about ordering and the paradigms of knowledge are notably different. There are two preliminary critiques of the pre-modern tradition of Islamic natural law and the models of practical reasoning illustrated by Soft Naturalists. First, the metaphysically objective quality of nature in both Hard and Soft Natural Law as presumptively beneficial raises concerns about ongoing considerations of Sharīʿa and legal philosophy today. This is not simply to counter both theories with a version of the naturalistic fallacy, which rejects the fusion of fact and value, or of the 'is' and the 'ought'. Indeed Soft Natural Law jurists would agree that Hard Natural Law theorists engage in this fallacy, while distancing themselves from that critique on the basis of their underlying voluntarism. Rather, by suggesting that nature exists for humans to observe and understand, both naturalist camps assume a distinction between nature and how human beings construe it for legal purposes. It is as if nature stands outside and separate from the process of reasoning about nature.

The idea that nature is an objective entity separate from the individual who observes it relies on a type of scientific reduction of the world, which hides the complexity and contingency of human experience. This scientific orientation gives the natural world a type of determinacy and objectivity that allows the law to generate general norms. But in doing so, the world of law and the world of lived experience are often separated by considerable distance. The law's generality is built upon the presumption of an objective and determinate natural order, despite the often indeterminate and changing vicissitudes of human existence.[8] Indeed, even the Soft

Ahmed An-Na'im (ed), *Islamic Family Law in a Changing World: A Global Resource Book* (London: Zed Books, 2002); Judith E Tucker, *Women, Family, and Gender in Islamic Law* (Cambridge: Cambridge University Press, 2008); Jamal Nasir, *The Islamic Law of Personal Status* (3rd edn, London: Kluwer Law International, 2002).

[8] For contemporary theorists who critique the natural sciences as a model of evaluation in the human sciences, see Hans-Georg Gadamer, *Truth and Method*, Joel Weinsheimer and Donald G Marshall (trans) (2nd edn, New York: Continuum, 1989) 284; Charles Taylor, *Sources of the Self: The Making of the Modern Identity* (Cambridge, Mass: Harvard University Press 1989) 20.

Naturalist al-Ghazālī recognized that an individual who attempts to determine values like the good and the bad cannot formalistically 'find' or 'discover' them in the world. Such values are so embedded in who we are that we cannot escape our own context to find an objective position outside ourselves. Ideas of the good and the bad, according to al-Ghazālī, are ideas to which we are conditioned at a young age. One accepts something as good or bad as a result of various factors (*asbāb kathīra*) that cannot be fully determined. Yet, to assert the value as objectively true would require disassociating the truth claim from any contextuality in order to discover the essence of the thing. Such disassociation, he suggested, is impossible.

> It is possible that extensive investigation may fashion a sense of truth about [these moral values]. And perhaps they are true determinations. But [they can be known as objectively true] only through minute [analysis] (*sharṭ daqīqa*), which the mind cannot satisfy.[9]

For al-Ghazālī, the Hard Naturalists relied upon a type of rational objectivity that is impossible given that our subjective perception contributes to whether we deem something to be good or bad, with certitude.

Importantly, though, al-Ghazālī is not immune from his own critique, given his fusion of fact and value, despite qualifying it by notions of divine grace. The Soft Naturalists' adoption of God's grace to fuse fact and value in nature presumes the objectivity of the natural order, and thereby renders it separate and distinct from human reasoning and perception. Al-Ghazālī may rely on source-texts to justify his fusion of fact and value, and thereby rely on a metaphysically objective natural world to support his Soft Natural Law. But the individual nonetheless remains so embedded in his context that his ability to assert the truth or falsity of something as God's law is limited by his own situation in the world. Both Soft and Hard Naturalists philosophically presume the objective and separate existence of nature, both to ground the authority of natural reason and to limit the threat of indeterminacy in the law, given their recognition that source-texts are finite and not always

[9] Abū Ḥāmid Muḥammad b. Muḥammad al-Ghazālī, *al-Mustaṣfā min ʿIlm al-Uṣūl*, Ibrāhīm Muḥammad Ramaḍān (ed) (Beirut: Dār al-Arqam, n.d.) 1:117.

dispositive on each and every issue. Consequently, while we may be sympathetic to their philosophical aspirations, we are left asking whether nature is truly as objective as Hard and Soft Naturalists suggest. And if nature is not as objective as they suggest, what are the implications for future developments in the field of Sharīʿa and legal philosophy?

If nature is not as objective as they theorized, and yet we are aware of the need to reason in law, we must confront the ambiguity in our lives, as opposed to developing overly scientific modes of legal reasoning designed to cover the ambiguity. This leads us to the second preliminary critique, namely against the formal structuring of practical reasoning offered by Soft Naturalist jurists such as al-Ghazālī. His model of practical reasoning reflects a desire to turn reasoned deliberation into a type of scientific inquiry, despite the fact that law and legal reasoning are far from scientific. The delineation of *maṣlaḥa* into various categories—necessities, needs, and edificatory interests—presumes that the complexity of lived experience can be fitted into these three categories with a kind of exactitude that seems unbefitting for a discipline such as law. Certainly a jurist such as al-Shāṭibī might retort that his model accounts for the indeterminacy of experience by adopting a legal standard about the requisite determinacy needed to justify a rule of law. He relies on the idea of the 'dominant' good or bad as sufficiently determinate for justifying a particular legal ordering. But the resort to such a legal fiction of the good and the bad only proves the point of this critique. The complexity of lived experience is juridified into neat categories that are weighed and balanced against each other in order to offer a legal resolution that can engender authority and reliance. The fact that the law must decisively resolve disputes despite factual ambiguity is not itself the subject of this critique.[10] Rather the critique centers on the ways in which the underlying ambiguity is

[10] Indeed, the idea that the law must be general in its application to achieve justice is hardly new. Aristotle espoused the importance that law be general in order to achieve justice. Yet he was also mindful that, in some cases, equity would need to be utilized to ensure that justice prevails where the circumstances are not duly accounted for by the general rules. Aristotle, *The Nichomachean Ethics*, Harris Rackham (trans) (Hertfordshire: Wordsworth, 1996) 134. Equity offers a means (albeit a legal one) of ensuring a close relationship between experience and expectation.

erased, as if it were never there to begin with. The world of lived experience, with all its ambiguity and indeterminacy, becomes neatly categorized and organized with an efficiency that enables the law to function. Even more, the structure of practical reasoning arguably aspires to frame the way in which we see, order, and construct the world. It offers a juridical framework for our lives. As a framework, it provides an organizing template that is always and already available to us. Indeed it may be so taken for granted as an operating method of inquiry that we may even forget that it is there.

The juridification of lived experiences has come under attack in recent decades. In the field of law in the modern state system, Boaventura de Sousa Santos writes that the turn to a scientific method of legal analysis 'maximize[s] the efficiency of law as a non-scientific instrument of social control and social facilitation'.[11] The fact that law is non-scientific is another way of suggesting that it is an institution that is always and at all times beset by a degree of indeterminacy and ambiguity. The Soft Naturalists' model of practical reasoning is designed to minimize, if not hide, that indeterminacy and ambiguity by establishing categories of interest that are meant to provide exactitude and efficiency for deliberative purposes, when in fact the categories themselves are porous and indefinite.

Instead of viewing reason as a cause of indeterminacy, we must remember that the discourse on reason in the pre-modern tradition reflects the legal imperative to control and limit the indeterminacy and ambiguity that is characteristic of lived experience. The debates about natural law in Sharīʿa are contests about how we should order and live our lives in an otherwise complex and sometimes chaotic world. When we look to a tradition such as Sharīʿa—whether in the form of source-texts, doctrinal treatises, or even theoretical expositions of method—we must remember that the purpose of our practical reasoning is to understand how to be in the world *today*. As Gadamer states: 'in the human sciences, the particular research questions concerning tradition that we are interested in pursuing are

[11] Boaventura de Sousa Santos, *Toward a New Common Legal Sense* (London: Butterworths, 2002) 62.

motivated in a special way by the present and its interest.'[12] To suggest that we can make an ethical inquiry without our humanity present would make us 'deaf to what speaks to us in tradition'.[13] To assume we can absolve ourselves of our experience would create a false positive of human existence that is illusory at best and delusional at worst. As Charles Taylor argues, we cannot leap outside of our humanity and the frames of reference that situate us in the world.[14]

What we can do, though, is recognize that the law can be a force both of emancipation and of regulation, in the words of De Sousa Santos. For De Sousa Santos, who writes about modern law, regulation is 'the set of norms, institutions, and practices that guarantees the stability of expectations. They do so by establishing a politically tolerable relation between present experiences, on the one hand, and expectations about the future, on the other.'[15]

But the imperative of regulation is to maintain the status quo. It seeks to limit change in the name of stability and reliable expectation interests under the law. However, sometimes the legal status quo is too far from the experiences of lived reality. Change cannot be avoided lest the law become another artifact of history. For De Sousa Santos, the law thereby also embodies an emancipatory potential. Emancipation, for De Sousa Santos, is the 'set of oppositional aspirations and practices that aim to increase the discrepancy between experiences and expectations, by calling into question the status quo, i.e., the political institutions that constitute the extant political nexus between experiences and expectations.'[16] Emancipation will call into question the ongoing responsiveness of the law to our live experience.

Pre-modern Muslim jurists knew that lived experience presents an infinite number of questions that no finite body of source-text can be expected to answer. Consequently, they recognized the necessity to grant reason ontological authority for Sharīʿa analysis. The irony is that despite their theological differences, jurists of

[12] Gadamer, *Truth and Method*, 284. [13] Gadamer, *Truth and Method*, 270.
[14] Taylor, *Sources of the Self*, 58.
[15] De Sousa Santos, *Toward a New Common Legal Sense*, 2.
[16] De Sousa Santos, *Toward a New Common Legal Sense*, 2.

different camps employed a similar fusion of fact and value in nature, thereby providing a foundation for reason's authority. In situations where lived experience illuminates the lacuna in the law, the law responds to fill it. To let the lacuna remain is to forgo the regulatory imperative of the law. In this sense, Muslim jurists offered their respective natural law theories as regulatory instruments. Soft Natural Law theorists developed the *maqāṣid-maṣlaḥa* model of practical reasoning to respond to issues on which no source or precedent exists. In doing so, they created a legal method for ensuring regulation.

Modern Muslim reformists have often looked to the *maqāṣid-maṣlaḥa* model as an instrument of emancipation from the status quo of inherited traditions, which seem too far from the reality of lived experience. As Mohammad Hashim Kamali suggests, the *maqāṣid* model of reasoning offers contemporary Muslims a way to reform the Sharīʿa without engaging in the technical modes of legal analysis proffered in pre-modern works of Islamic legal theory (*uṣūl al-fiqh*). He writes:

'The fresh focus on *maqāṣid* is due . . . to a general awareness that the methodologies of *uṣūl al-fiqh* . . . are on the whole predicated on medieval social values, retrospective, and slow to relate effectively to the modern processes of adjudication and law making...The *maqāṣid* are inherently dynamic by comparison and capable of evolution in tandem with the changing conditions of society.'[17]

Mashood Baderin adopts the *maqāṣid-maṣlaḥa* model of legal reasoning to suggest that Islamic law offers principles of legality and legitimacy to enhance the harmony between Islamic law and international human rights. He writes:

Taking cognizance of the object and purpose of the *Sharīʿah* (*maqāṣid al-Sharīʿa*), which has been identified as promotion of human welfare and prevention of harm (*maṣlaḥa*), is an important holistic approach for realizing the proper and benevolent scope of Islamic law . . . Against the background of the nature and evolution of Islamic law...the doctrine of *maṣlaḥa* is thus

[17] Mohammad Hashim Kamali, 'Law and ethics in Islam—The role of the *maqāṣīd*' in Kari Vogt, Lena Larsen and Christian Moe (eds), *New Directions in Islamic Thought: Exploring Reform and Muslim Tradition* (London: IB Tauris, 2009) 23, 23–4.

advocated in this study as a veritable Islamic legal doctrine for the realization of international human rights within the dispensation of Islamic law.[18]

But when reformist thinkers attempt to apply the *maqāṣid* model to the challenges of modern life, they are nonetheless limited by the regulatory imperatives that underlie the legal system within which they orient themselves. For instance, reformist thinkers such as Tariq Ramadan call for a moratorium on Islamic criminal punishments (*ḥudūd*) in order to effectuate the spirit of justice that is integral to Islamic law and its aims. While Ramadan is criticized for attempting to limit the application of Islamic law, he denies the moratorium disrespects Islam and Islamic law: invoking the concept of *maqāṣid*, he writes:

> On the contrary, the legal texts must be read in light of the objectives (*maqāṣid*) that justify them, first and foremost the protection of the integrity of the person (*nafs*) and the promotion of justice (*ʿadl*). A literal and non-contextualized application of the *ḥudūd* without regard for the strictly stipulated conditions is a betrayal of the teachings of Islam, because it produces injustice.[19]

By invoking the concept of *maqāṣid*, reformists do not seek to subvert the Sharīʿa, but rather to work within the framework of Sharīʿā to effectuate increased emancipation of Muslims from the yoke of a legal tradition deemed too distant from the world of lived experience. Yet at the same time, reformists such as Ramadan are unable to go beyond a moratorium and simply deny the validity of the *ḥudūd* punishments in the modern day, while at the same time remaining firmly within the Sharīʿa tradition as he understands it. For instance, he expressly states that his call for a moratorium does not advocate setting aside the Qurʾānic texts or Sharīʿa doctrines that address these punishments. 'I have said very clearly that the texts concerning these punishments exist, that some of them are definitive as to their authenticity and their meaning . . . and that they are determined to be an essential part of the religion.'[20] Likewise, despite arguing for a

[18] Mashood Baderin, *International Human Rights and Islamic Law* (Oxford: Oxford University Press, 2003) 40, 43.

[19] Tariq Ramadan, 'A call for a moratorium on corporal punishment—The debate in review' in Vogt, Larsen and Moe (eds), *New Directions in Islamic Thought*, 163, 166.

[20] Ramadan, 'A call', 170.

harmony between international human rights and Islamic law, Baderin recognizes that to proscribe the *ḥudūd* entirely would be contrary to the Sharīʿa: 'Questioning the *hudūd* punishments is considered as questioning the divine wisdom underlying them and impugning the divinity of the Qurʾan and the theocentric nature of Islamic law.'[21] Consequently a reformist such as Abdullahi Ahmed An-Na'im has strong reasons to deny that internal, Sharīʿa-inspired reinterpretation of the *ḥudūd* can or will lead to the total abolishment of the Qurʾānic criminal penalties.[22] That does not mean there is no way to challenge the *ḥudūd*. One approach may be to adopt a legal reading of the Qurʾān that permits isolating the offending verses while introducing human rights standards in their place.[23] Such an approach may allow us to go farther than Ramadan and Baderin in condemning the *ḥudūd*, but only at the very real cost of altering the authority structure of the Sharīʿa in a manner that may provoke considerable criticism from segments of the Muslim world.[24]

The irony is that while pre-modern jurists developed the *maqāṣid-maṣlaḥa* model to limit the scope of reasoned deliberation in the name of preserving the status quo, modern Muslim reformers use it to emancipate themselves from the status quo of inherited legal norms. And yet, to invoke the *maqāṣid-maṣlaḥa* model to justify new, emancipatory rules of Sharīʿa nonetheless perpetuates the assumptions that contributed to the regulatory implications of the model. Regardless of whether one increases or modifies the content of the *maqāṣid* values to reflect better the demands of the

[21] Baderin, *International Human Rights and Islamic Law*, 84.

[22] Abdullahi Ahmed An-Na'im, 'Toward a Cross-Cultural Approach to Defining International Standards of Human Rights: The Meaning of Cruel, Inhuman or Degrading Treatment or Punishment' in Abdullahi A An-Na'im (ed), *Human Rights in Cross-Cultural Perspectives* (Philadelphia, Pa: University of Pennsylvania Press, 1992) 19, 36.

[23] An-Na'im outlines an approach to the Qurʾān that marginalizes some verses as historically contingent, and focuses on others that have a more universal message. Abdullahi Ahmed An-Na'im, *Toward an Islamic Reformation: Civil Liberties, Human Rights, and International Law* (Syracuse: Syracuse University Press, 1990).

[24] An-Na'im is no stranger to this sort of criticism. Even those favorable of his work *Towards an Islamic Reformation* have indicated that his methodology, and its implications for core sources of legal authority, will not convince more conservative segments of the Muslim world. Abdulaziz Sachedina, '[Review]' (1993) 25 *International Journal of Middle East Studies* 155; Majid Khadduri, '[Review]' (1991) 33 *Journal of Church and State* 807.

contemporary world, the model itself was designed to regulate on the basis of certain assumptions about the world and God that were of central concern to Soft Natural Law jurists. The model disciplines reasoned deliberation so that it does not stray too far from tradition and authority in a way that might impinge on the divinity of God, as understood along Voluntarist lines. The regulatory dynamic of the *maqāṣid-maṣlaḥa* model is not unique to Sharīʿa debates. To recall Rajagopal from the introduction to this study, the law 'needs to establish its own field of autonomy only by simplifying and excluding much of actual reality... indeed, each time law comes into contact with "reality", it struggles to reflect it, even as it maintains its distance from it to show that as "law", it is different from the "reality" and can therefore constrain it.'[25]

The two preliminary critiques of Islamic Natural Law theories call out for further research into the intersection between Islamic law and legal philosophy. It is hoped that future research will take account of how the theories of pre-modern Sharīʿa, no matter how regulatory or emancipatory, are nonetheless designed to limit the distance between experience and expectation. Such theories often look to presumed authorities and traditions to tell us what we should and should not expect, and thereby delegitimize the demands of experience upon the law to fulfill an emancipatory function. The challenge for researchers today is to recognize and understand the presumptions about what constitutes legitimate authority in the law, and how those presumptions contribute to a regulatory system that often obscures the distance between experience and expectation.[26] In other words, future research may want to address how much of the distance between expectation and experience is actually hidden from view by the legal methods designed to account for that distance in the first place.

[25] Balakrishnan Rajagopal, *International Law from Below: Development, Social Movements, and Third World Resistance* (Cambridge: Cambridge University Press, 2003) 65.

[26] In a recent review of reformist works, including the work of Ramadan, Richard Bulliet remarks that the future of Islamic thought will involve compromises between reformists and conservatives, who will organize and deliberate on the basis of some reformulation of legitimate authority. Richard Bulliet, 'Islamic Reformation or "Big Crunch"? A Review Essay' (2009) 8 *Harvard Middle Eastern and Islamic Review* 7, 18. The question of authority, therefore, will likely remain a point of ongoing deliberation as debates about the content and role of Islamic law continue.

Bibliography

n.d. = no date of publication available
n.p. = no place of publication available

Arabic Sources

ʿAbd al-Jabbār al-Asadʾābādī, Al-Qāḍī Abū al-Ḥasan. *al-Mughnī.* Ṭaha Ḥusayn (ed). 16 vols. Cairo: Wizārat al-Thaqāfa wa-al-Irshād al-Qawmī, al-Idārah al-ʿĀmma lil-Thaqāfa, n.d.

——. *Sharḥ al-Uṣūl al-Khamsa.* Beirut: Dār Iḥyāʾ al-Turāth al-ʿArabī, 2001.

ʿAbd al-Jabbār, al-Qāḍī Abū al-Ḥasan and al-Ḥasan b. Aḥmad b. Mattawayh. *Kitāb al-Majmūʿ fī al-Muḥīṭ bi al-Taklīf.* Yan Peters (ed). 3 vols. Beirut: Dār al-Mashriq, 1999.

Abū Zahra, Muḥammad. *Uṣūl al-Fiqh.* Cairo: Dār al-Fikr al-ʿArabī, 1957.

Al-ʿĀlim, Yūsuf Ḥāmid. *al-Maqāṣid al-ʿĀmma li al-Sharīʿa al-Islāmiyya.* Herndon, Virginia: International Institute of Islamic Thought, 1991.

Al-Āmidī, Sayf al-Dīn Abū al-Ḥasan ʿAlī b. Abī ʿAlī b. Muḥammad. *al-Iḥkām fī Uṣūl al-Aḥkām.* Beirut: Dār al-Fikr, 1997.

Al-Aṣfahānī, Abū ʿAbd Allāh Muḥammad b. Maḥmūd b. ʿAbbād. *al-Kāshif an al-Maḥṣūl fī ʿIlm al-Uṣūl.* ʿĀdil Aḥmad ʿAbd al-Mawjūd and ʿAlī Muḥammad Muʿawwaḍ (eds). Beirut: Dār al-Kutub al-ʿIlmiyya, 1998.

Al-Asnawī, Jamāl al-Dīn ʿAbd al-Raḥīm b. al-Ḥasan. *Nihāyat al-Sūl fī Sharḥ Minhāj al-Wuṣūl ilā ʿIlm al-Uṣūl.* Shaʿbān Muḥammad Ismaʿīl (ed). Beirut: Dār Ibn Ḥazm, 1999.

Al-Bājī, Abū al-Walīd. *Iḥkām al-Fuṣūl fī Aḥkām al-Uṣūl.* ʿAbd al-Majīd Turkī (ed). 2nd edn, Beirut: Dār al-Gharb al-Islāmī, 1995.

Al-Bāqillānī, Abū Bakr Muḥammad b. al-Ṭayyib. *al-Taqrīb wa al-Irshād al-Ṣaghīr.* ʿAbd al-Ḥamīd b. ʿAlī Abū Zunayd (ed). Beirut: Muʾassasat al-Risāla, 1998.

Al-Baṣrī, Abū al-Ḥusayn Muḥammad b. ʿAlī b. al-Ṭayyib. *al-Muʿtamad fī Uṣūl al-Fiqh.* Beirut: Dār al-Kutub al-ʿIlmiyya, n.d.

Al-Dār Quṭnī, ʿAlī b. ʿUmar. *Sunan al-Dār Quṭnī.* Majdī b. Manṣūr Sayyid al-Shūrā (ed). Beirut: Dār al-Kutub al-ʿIlmiyya, 1996.

Al-Dhahabī, Shams al-Dīn Muḥammad b. Aḥmad ʿUthmān. *Siyar Aʿlām al-Nubalāʾ.* Shuʿayb al-Arnaʿūt and Akram al-Būshi (eds). Beirut: Muʾassasat al-Risāla, 1986.

——. *al-ʿIbar fī Khabar man Ghabar*. Abū Ḥājir Muḥammad al-Saʿīd b. Basyūnī Zaghlūl (ed). Beirut: Dār al-Kutub al-ʿIlmiyya, n.d.

Al-Ghazālī, Abū Ḥāmid Muḥmmad b. Muḥammad. *al-Mustaṣfā min ʿIlm al-Uṣūl*. Ibrāhīm Muḥammad Ramaḍān (ed). Beirut: Dār al-Arqam, n.d.

——. *Shifāʾ al-Ghalīl fī Bayān al-Shabh wa al-Mukhīl wa Masālik al-Taʿlīl*. Muḥammad al-Kubaysī (ed). Baghdad: Raʿāsa Dīwān al-Awqāf, 1971.

Al-Ḥākim al-Nīsābūrī, ʿAbū ʿAbd Allāh Muḥammad b. ʿAbd Allāh. *al-Mustadrak ʿala al-Ṣaḥiḥayn*. Beirut: Dār al-Maʿrifa, 1998.

Ḥassān, Ḥusayn Ḥāmid. *Naẓariyyat al-Maṣlaḥa fī al-Fiqh al-Islāmī*. Cairo: Dār al-Nahḍa al-ʿArabiyya, 1971.

Ibn ʿAqīl, Abū al-Wafā ʿAlī b. ʿAqīl b. Muḥammad al-Ḥanbalī. *al-Wāḍiḥ fī Uṣūl al-Fiqh*. George Makdisi (ed). Beirut: Franz Steiner, 1996.

Ibn al-Farikān, Tāj al-Dīn ʿAbd al-Raḥmān b. Ibrāhīm. *Sharḥ al-Waraqāt*. Sārah Shāfī al-Hājirī (ed). Beirut: Dār al-Bashāʾir al-Islāmiyya, 2001.

Ibn Ḥazm, Abū Muḥammad ʿAlī. *al-Iḥkām fī Uṣūl al-Aḥkām*. Cairo: Dār al-Ḥadīth, 1984.

Ibn al-ʿImād, Abū al-Falāḥ ʿAbd al-Ḥayy. *Shadharāt al-Dhahab fī Akhbār man Dhahab*. Beirut: Dār al-Kutub al-ʿIlmiyya, n.d.

Ibn al-Jawzī, Abū al-Faraj ʿAbd al-Raḥmān b. ʿAlī b. Muḥammad. *al-Muntaẓam fī Taʾrīkh al-Mulūk wa al-Umam*. Muḥammad ʿAbd al-Qādir ʿAṭā and Muṣṭafā ʿAbd al-Qadr ʿAṭā (eds). Beirut: Dār al-Kutub al-ʿIlmiyya, n.d.

——. *Kitāb al-Aḥkām al-Nisāʾ*. Beirut: Manshūrāt al-Maktaba al-ʿAṣriyya, 1981.

Ibn Kathīr, Abū al-Fidāʾ Ismāʿīl. *al-Bidāya wa al-Nihāya*. ʿAbd al-Raḥmān al-Lawqī and Muḥammad Ghāzī Bayḍūn (eds). Beirut: Dār al-Maʿrifa, 1996.

Ibn Khallikān, Abū al-ʿAbbās Aḥmad b. Muḥammad b. Ibrāhīm b. Abī Bakr. *Wafayyāt al-Aʿyān wa Anbāʾ Abnāʾ al-Zamān*. Yūsuf ʿAlī Ṭawīl and Maryam Qāsim Ṭawīl (eds). Beirut: Dār al-Kutub al-ʿIlmiyya, 1998.

Ibn Mājah, Abū ʿAbd ʿAllāh Muḥammad b. Yazīd. *al-Sunan*. Muḥammad Nāṣir al-Dīn al-Albānī and ʿAlī b. Ḥasan b. ʿAlī b. ʿAbd al-Ḥamīd al-Ḥalabī al-Atharī (eds). Riyadh: Maktabat al-Maʿārif li al-Nashr wa al-Tawzīʿ, 1998.

Ibn Manẓūr, Abū al-Faḍl Jamāl al-Dīn Muḥammad b. Makram. *Lisān al-ʿArab*. 6th edn, Beirut: Dar al-Ṣadr, 1997.

Ibn Mattawayh, al-Ḥasan b. Aḥmad. *Majmūʿ fī al-Muḥīṭ bi al-Taklīf*. Beirut: al-Maṭbaʿa al-Kāthūlīkiyya, 1965 (see also al-Qāḍī ʿAbd al-Jabbār).

Ibn al-Murtaḍā, Aḥmad b. Yahyā. *Kitāb Ṭabaqāt al-Muʿtazila*. Beirut: al-Maṭbaʿa al-Kāthūlikiyya, 1961.

Ibn al-Qaṣṣār, Abū al-Ḥasan ʿAlī b. ʿUmar. *al-Muqaddima fī al-Uṣūl*. Muḥammad b. al-Ḥusayn al-Sulaymānī (ed). Beirut: Dār al-Gharb al-Islāmī, 1996.

Ibn Qayyim al-Jawziyya, Shams al-Dīn Abū ʿAbd Allāh Muḥammad. *Miftāḥ Dār al-Saʿāda wa Manshūrāt Wilāyat al-ʿIlm wa al-Irāda*. Bashīr Muḥammad ʿUyūn (ed). Damascus: Maktabat Dār al-Bayān, 1998.

——. *Iʿlām al-Muwaqqiʿīn ʿan Rabb al-ʿĀlamīn*. ʿAbd al-Raḥmān al-Wakīl (ed). Cairo: Maktabat Ibn Taymiyya, n.d.

Ibn Rushd (al-Ḥafīd), Abū al-Walīd Muḥammad. *al-Ḍarūrā fī Uṣūl al-Fiqh aw Mukhtaṣar al-Mustaṣfā*. Jamāl al-Dīn al-ʿAlawī (ed). Beirut: Dār al-Gharb al-Islāmī, 1994.

Ibn Taymiyya, Taqī al-Dīn Aḥmad. *al-Iḥtijāj bi al-Qadar*. Cairo: al-Maṭbaʿa al-Salafiyya, 1974.

——. *al-Siyāsa al-Sharʿiyya fī Iṣlāḥ al-Rāʿī wa al-Raʿiyya*. Beirut: Dār al-Kutub al-ʿIlmiyya, 1988.

Al-Jaṣṣāṣ, Abū Bakr Aḥmad b. ʿAlī. *Uṣūl al-Jaṣṣāṣ: al-Fuṣūl fī al-Uṣūl*. Muḥammad Muḥammad Tāmir (ed). Beirut: Dār al-Kutub al-ʿIlmiyya, 2000.

Al-Juwaynī, Abū al-Maʿālī ʿAbd al-Malik b. ʿAbd Allāh b. Yūsuf. *al-Burhān fī Uṣūl al-Fiqh*. Ṣalāḥ b. Muḥammad b. ʿAwīḍa (ed). Beirut: Dār al-Kutub al-ʿIlmiyya, 1997.

——. *Kitāb al-Talkhīṣ fī Uṣūl al-Fiqh*. ʿAbd Allāh Julam al-Nībālī and Shabbīr Aḥmad al-ʿAmrī (eds). Beirut: Dār al-Bashā'ir al-Islāmiyya, 1996.

——. *al-Ghiyāthī: Ghiyāth al-Umam fī Iltiyāth al-Ẓulam*. Khalīl al-Manṣūr (ed). Beirut: Dār al-Kutub al-ʿIlmiyya, 1997.

Al-Kankūhī, Muḥammad Fayḍ al-Ḥasan. *ʿUmdat al-Ḥawāshī*. In the margins of *Uṣūl al-Shāshī* by Abū ʿAlī al-Shāshī. Beirut: Dār al-Kitāb al-ʿArabī, 1982.

Al-Khaṭīb, Muḥammad ʿIjāj. *al-Mukhtaṣar al-Wajīz fī ʿUlūm al-Ḥadīth*. Beirut: Mu'assasat al-Risāla, 1991.

Al-Khaṭīb al-Baghdādī, Abū Bakr Aḥmad b. ʿAlī. *Ta'rīkh Baghdād*. Muṣṭafā ʿAbd al-Qādir ʿAṭā (ed). Beirut: Dār al-Kutub al-ʿIlmiyya, 1997.

——. *Kitāb al-Faqīh wa al-Mutafaqqih*. n.p.: Maṭbaʿat al-Imtiyāz, 1977.

Al-Lāmishī, Maḥmūd b. Zayd. *Kitāb fī Uṣūl al-Fiqh*. ʿAbd al-Majīd Turkī (ed). Beirut: Dār al-Gharb al-Islāmī, 1995.

Maḥmaṣṣānī, Ṣubḥī. *Falsafat al-Tashrīʿ fī al-Islām*. 3rd edn, Beirut: Dār al-ʿIlm li'l-Malāyīn, 1961.

Mālik b. Anas. *al-Muwaṭṭa'(as narrated by al-Laythī)*. Bashshār ʿAwād Maʿrūf (ed). Beirut: Dār al-Gharb al-Islāmī, 1997.

Al-Marghīnānī, Abū al-Ḥasan ʿAlī b. Abī Bakr al-Farghānī. *al-Hidāya: Sharḥ Bidāyat al-Mubtadiʾ*. Muḥammad Darwīsh (ed). Beirut: Dār al-Arqam, n.d.

Al-Nawawī, Muḥyī al-Dīn Yaḥyā b. Sharaf al-Dīn. *Kitāb al-Arbaʿīn al-Nawawiyya*. n.p.: Dār Ḥarāʾ li al-Kitāb, 1987.

Al-Nīsābūrī, Abū ʿAbd Allāh Muḥammad b. ʿAbd Allāh al-Ḥākim. *al-Mustadrak ʿalā al-Ṣaḥīḥayn*. Beirut: Dār al-Maʿrifa, 1998.

Al-Qaradāwī, Yūsuf *al-ʿAql wa al-ʿIlm fī al-Qurʾān al-Karīm*. Beirut: Mu'assasāt al-Risāla, 2001.

Al-Qarāfī, Shihāb al-Dīn Abū al-ʿAbbās Aḥmad b. Idrīs b. ʿAbd al-Raḥmān. *Nafāʾis al-Uṣūl fī Sharḥ al-Maḥṣūl*. Muḥammad ʿAbd al-Qādir ʿAṭā (ed). Beirut: Dār al-Kutub al-ʿIlmiyya, 2000.

——. *Sharḥ Tanqīḥ al-Fuṣūl fī Ikhtiṣār al-Maḥṣūl fī al-Uṣūl*. Ṭaha ʿAbd al-Raʾūf Saʿīd (ed). Cairo: Dār al-Fikr, 1973.

Al-Qaṣṣār, Abū al-Ḥasan ʿAlī b. ʿUmar *Al-Muqaddima fī al-Uṣūl*. Muḥammad b. al-Ḥusayn al-Sulaymānī (ed). Beirut: Dār al-Gharb al-Islāmī, 1996.

Al-Rāzī, Fakhr al-Dīn Muḥammad b. ʿUmar. *al-Maḥṣūl fī ʿIlm Uṣūl al-Fiqh*. Ṭaha Jābir Fayyāḍ al-ʿAlwāni (ed). 3rd edn, Beirut: Muʾassasat al-Risāla, 1997.

Al-Ṣafadī, Ṣalāḥ al-Dīn Khalīl b. Aybak. *Kitāb al-Wāfī bi al-Wafayāt*. Ayman Fuʾād Sayyid (ed). Stuttgart: Franz Steiner, 1991.

Al-Samʿānī, Abū al-Muẓaffar Manṣūr b. Muḥammad b. ʿAbd al-Jabbār. *Qawāṭiʿ al-Adilla fī al-Uṣūl*. Muḥammad Ḥasan Muḥammad Ḥasan Ismāʿīl al-Shāfiʿī (ed). Beirut: Dār al-Kutub al-ʿIlmiyya, 1997.

Al-Samarqandī, Abū Bakr Muḥammad b. Aḥmad. *Mīzān al-Uṣūl*. ʿAbd al-Malik ʿAbd al-Raḥmān al-Saʿdī (ed). n.p.: Maṭbaʿa al-Khulūd, 1987.

Al-Sarakhsī, Abū Bakr Muḥammad b. Aḥmad b. Abī Sahl. *al-Muḥarrar fī Uṣūl al-Fiqh*. Abū ʿAbd al-Raḥmān Ṣalāḥ b. Muḥammad b. ʿArīḍa (ed). Beirut: Dār al-Kutub al-ʿIlmiyya, 1996.

Al-Shāshī, Abū ʿAlī. *Uṣūl al-Shāshī*. Beirut: Dār al-Kitāb al-ʿArabī, 1982.

Al-Shāṭibī, Abū Isḥāq b. Ibrāhīm b. Mūsā b. Muḥammad. *al-Iʿtiṣām*. Salīm b. ʿīd al-Halālī (ed). Khobar: Dār Ibn ʿAffān, 1997.

——. *al-Muwāfaqāt fī Uṣul al-Sharīʿa*. ʿAbd Allāh Darāz et al (eds). 2 vols. Beirut: Dār al-Kutub al-ʿIlmiyya, n.d.

Al-Shīrāzī, Abū Isḥāq Ibrāhīm b. ʿAlī *al-Tabṣira fī Uṣūl al-Fiqh*. Muḥammad Ḥasan Haytū (ed). Damascus: Dār al-Fikr, 1983.

——. *Sharḥ al-Lumʿa*. ʿAbd al-Majīd Turkī (ed). Beirut: Dār al-Gharb al-Islāmī, 1988.

Al-Subkī, Alī b. ʿAbd al-Kāfī and Tāj al-Dīn ʿAbd al-Wahhāb b. ʿAlī al-Subkī. *al-Ibhāj fī Sharḥ al-Minhāj*. Beirut: Dār al-Kutub al-ʿIlmiyya, 1995.

Al-Subkī, Tāj al-Dīn Abū Naṣr ʿAbd al-Wahhāb b. ʿAlī b. ʿAbd al-Kāfī. *Ṭabaqāt al-Shāfiʿiyya al-Kubrā*. Beirut: Dār al-Kutub al-ʿIlmiyya, 1999.

Al-Ṭūfī, Najm al-Dīn. *'al-Ḥadīth al-Thānī wa al-Thalāthūn.'* In Muṣṭafā Zayd. *al-Maṣlaḥa fī al-Tashrīʿ al-Islāmī wa Najm al-Dīn al-Ṭūfī*. 2nd edn, n.p.: Dār al-Fikr al-ʿArabī, 1964.

Al-Zabīdī, Muḥibb al-Dīn Abū Fayḍ Muḥammad Murtaḍā al-Ḥusayni. *Tāj al-ʿUrūs min Jawāhir al-Qāmūs*. ʿAlī Shīrī (ed). 20 vols. Beirut: Dār al-Fikr, 1994.

Zayd, Muṣṭafā. *al-Maṣlaḥa fī al-Tashrīʿ al-Islāmī wa Najm al-Dīn al-Ṭūfī*. 2nd edn, n.p.: Dār al-Fikr al-ʿArabī, 1964.

Al-Ziriklī, Khayr al-Dīn. *al- Aʿlām*. 12th edn, Beirut: Dār al-ʿIlm li al-Malayīn, 1997.

English Sources

Abrahamov, Binyamin. "ʿAbd al-Jabbār's Theory of Divine Assistance (*Luṭf*)" (1993) 16 *Jerusalem Studies in Arabic and Islam* 41.

Abou El Fadl, Khaled. *Rebellion and Violence in Islamic Law* (Cambridge: Cambridge University Press, 2001).

——. *Speaking in God's Name: Islamic Law, Authority and Women* (Oxford: Oneworld Publications, 2001).

——. 'Islamic Law and Ambivalent Scholarship' (2002) 100 *Michigan Law Review* 1421.

——. *Islam and the Challenge of Democracy: A Boston Review Book*. Joshua Cohen and Deborah Chasman (eds) (Princeton: Princeton University Press, 2004).

Adam, Robert M. 'Introduction' to Immanuel Kant, *Religion within the Boundaries of Mere Reason and Other Writings*. Allen Wood and George di Giovanni (trans) (1998; Reprint, Cambridge: Cambridge University Press, 2006).

Ali-Karamali, Shiasta P and Fiona Dunne. 'The Ijtihad Controversy' (1994) 9 *Arab Law Quarterly* 238.

——. *Toward an Islamic Reformation: Civil Liberties, Human Rights, and International Law* (Syracuse: Syracuse University Press, 1990).

——. 'Toward a Cross-Cultural Approach to Defining International Standards of Human Rights: The Meaning of Cruel, Inhuman or Degrading Treatment or Punishment' in Abdullahi A. An-Na'im (ed),

Human Rights in Cross-Cultural Perspectives (Philadelphia, Pa: University of Pennsylvania Press, 1992) 19.

An-Na'im, Abdullahi Ahmed. *Islam and the Secular State: Negotiating the Future of Shari'a* (Cambridge: Harvard University Press, 2008).

An-Na'im, Abdullah Ahmad, (ed). *Islamic Family Law in a Changing World: A Global Resource Book* (London: Zed Books, 2002).

Aquinas, Thomas. *Treatise on Law (Summa Theologica, Questions 90–97)* (1956. Reprint, Washington, DC: Regnery Publishing Inc, 1998).

Aristotle. *The Nichomachean Ethics*. Harris Rackham (trans) (Hertfordshire: Wordsworth, 1996).

Arkoun, Mohammad. *Rethinking Islam: Common Questions, Uncommon Answers*. Robert D Lee (trans) (Boulder, Colo: Westview Press, 1994).

Auda, Jasser. *Maqasid al-Shariah as Philosophy of Islamic Law: A Systems Approach* (Herndon, Va: International Institute of Islamic Thought, 2008).

Baderin, Mashood. *International Human Rights and Islamic Law* (Oxford: Oxford University Press, 2003).

Bagby, Ihsan Abdul. 'Utility in Classical Islamic Law: The Concept of "Maslahah" in "Usul al-Fiqh".' (PhD dissertation, University of Michigan, 1986).

Bevir, Mark. *The Logic of the History of Ideas* (Cambridge: Cambridge University Press, 1999).

Borrows, John. 'Living Law on a Living Earth: Aboriginal Religion, Law, and the Constitution' in Richard Moon (ed), *Law and Religious Pluralism in Canada* (Vancouver: UBC Press, 2008) 161.

Bulliet, Richard. 'Islamic Reformation or "Big Crunch"? A Review Essay' (2009) 8 *Harvard Middle Eastern and Islamic Review* 7.

Calder, Norman. 'The Barahima: Literary Construct and Historical Reality' (1994) 57 *Bulletin of the School of Oriental and African Studies* 40.

——. 'The State and the Individual in Islamic Law' (1957) 6 *International and Comparative Law Quarterly* 49.

Coulson, NJ *A History of Islamic Law* (1964. Reprint, Edinburgh: Edinburgh University Press, 1997).

Crone, Patricia. *God's Rule: Government and Islam: Six Centuries of Medieval Islamic Political Thought* (New York: Columbia University Press, 2004).

De Sousa Santos, Boaventura. *Toward a New Common Legal Sense* (London: Butterworths, 2002).

Druart, Thérèse-Anne. 'Metaphysics' in Peter Adamson and Richard C Taylor (eds), *The Cambridge Companion to Arabic Philosophy* (Cambridge: Cambridge University Press, 2005) 327.

Dutton, Yasin. *The Origins of Islamic Law: The Qur'an, the Muwatta' and Madinan 'Amal* (Richmond, UK: Curzon Press, 1999).

Dworkin, Ronald. *Law's Empire* (Cambridge, Mass: Harvard University Press, 1986).

El-Affendi, Abdelwahab, (ed). *Rethinking Islam and Modernity* (London: The Islamic Foundation, 2001).

El Shamsy, Ahmed. 'The Social Construction of Orthodoxy' in Tim Winter (ed), *The Cambridge Companion to Classical Islamic Theology* (Cambridge: Cambridge University Press, 2008) 97.

——. 'Conceiving Islamic Law in a Pluralist Society: History, Politics and Multicultural Jurisprudence' [2006] *Singapore Journal of Legal Studies* 331.

——. *Ḥuqūq Allāh* and *Ḥuqūq al-ʿIbād*: A Legal Heuristic for a Natural Rights Regime' (2006) 13 *Islamic Law and Society* 325.

——. 'On the Pope, Cartoons, and Apostates: Shari'a 2006' (2006/07) 22 *Journal of Law and Religion* 303.

Ely, John Hart. *Democracy and Distrust: A Theory of Judicial Review* (Cambridge, Mass: Harvard University Press, 1980).

Emon, Anver M. 'Islamic Law and the Canadian Mosaic: Politics, Jurisprudence, and Multicultural Accommodation' (2008) 87 Canadian Bar Review 391.

——. 'Techniques and Limits of Rights Reasoning in *Shari'a* Today' (2009) 2 *UC Berkeley Journal of Middle East and Islamic Law* 1, 101–24.

Enayat, Hamid. *Modern Islamic Political Thought* (Austin, Tex: University of Texas Press, 1982).

Encyclopaedia of Islam, Second Edition. P. Bearman, T Bianquis, CE Bosworth, E van Donzel and WP Heinrichs (eds) (Leiden: Brill Online, 2009).

Euben, Roxanne. *Enemy in the Mirror* (Princeton: Princeton University Press, 1999).

Ezzati, A. *Islam and Natural Law* (London: ICAS Press, 2002).

Fadel, Mohammad H. 'Too Far From Tradition' in Khaled Abou El Fadl (ed), *Islam and the Challenge of Democracy* (Princeton: Princeton University Press, 2004).

——. 'The True, the Good and the Reasonable: The Theological and Ethical Roots of Public Reason in Islamic Law' (2008) 21 *Canadian Journal of Law and Jurisprudence* 5.

Finnis, John. *Natural Law and Natural Rights* (Oxford: Clarendon Press, 1980).

Fiss, Owen. 'Foreword: The Forms of Justice' (1979) 93 *Harvard Law Review* 1.

——. 'The Autonomy of the Human Agent in the Teaching of 'Abd al-Ǧabbar' (1982) 95 *Le Muséon: revue d'Études Orientales* 323.

Frank, Richard M. 'Moral Obligation in Classical Muslim Theology' (1983) 11 *Journal of Religious Ethics* 204.

——. 'Can God do what is wrong?' in Tamar Rudavsky (ed), *Divine Omniscience and Omnipotence in Medieval Philosophy: Islamic, Jewish and Christian Perspectives* (Boston, Mass: D Reidel Publishing Co, 1985) 69.

Fuller, Lon. *The Morality of Law* (rev edn, New Haven: Yale University Press, 1969).

Fyzee, Asaf AA. *Outlines of Muhammadan Law* (3rd edn, Oxford: Oxford University Press, 1964).

Gadamer, Hans-Georg. *Truth and Method.* Joel Weinsheimer and Donald G Marshall (trans) (2nd edn, New York: Continuum, 1989).

Gardet, L. 'al- D̲Jubbāʾī, Abū ʿAlī Muḥammad b. ʿAbd al-Wahhāb' in *Encyclopaedia of Islam, Second Edition.* P. Bearman, T Bianquis, CE Bosworth, E van Donzel and WP Heinrichs (eds) (Leiden: Brill Online, 2009).

George, Robert P (ed). *Natural Law: Contemporary Essays* (1992. Reprint, Oxford: Oxford University Press, 1996).

Gimaret, D. 'Abuʿl-Ḥosayn al-Baṣrī' in *Encyclopedia Iranica* (London: Routledge, 1983) 1:322.

Gleave, Robert. *Inevitable Doubt: Two Theories of Shiʿi Jurisprudence* (Leiden: Brill, 2000).

Grisez, Germain. *Christian Moral Principle.* Vol 1 of *The Way of the Lord Jesus* (Chicago: Franciscan Herald Press, 1983).

—— and Russell Shaw. *Fulfillment in Christ: A Summary of Christian Moral Principles* (Notre Dame: University of Notre Dame Press, 1991).

Haddad, Yvonne Yazbeck. *Contemporary Islam and the Challenge of History* (Albany, NY: State University of New York Press, 1982).

—— and Barbara Stowasser (eds). *Islamic Law and the Challenges of Modernity* (New York: AltaMira Press, 2004).

——. 'Was the Gate of Ijtihad Closed?' (1984) 16 *International Journal of Middle East Studies* 3.

——. *A History of Islamic Legal Theories: An Introduction to Sunnī Uṣūl al-Fiqh* (Cambridge: Cambridge University Press, 1997).

——. *Authority, Continuity and Change in Islamic Law* (Cambridge: Cambridge University Press, 2001).

——. 'Can the Shari'a Be Restored?' in Yvonne Haddad and Barbara Stowasser (eds), *Islamic Law and the Challenges of Modernity* (New York: Altamira Press, 2004) 21.

Hallaq, Wael B. *Shariʿa: Theory, Practice, Transformations* (Cambridge: Cambridge University Press, 2009).

Harris, JW. 'Can you believe in natural law? [Review of John Finnis, *Natural Law and Natural Rights*]' (1981) 44 MLR 729.

Hasan, Ahmad. *Analogical Reasoning in Islamic Jurisprudence: A Study of the Juridical Principle of Qiyas* (Islamabad: Islamic Research Institute, 1986).

Hawi, Sami S. *Islamic Naturalism and Mysticism: A Philosophical Study of Ibn Ṭufayl's Ḥayy b. Yaqẓān* (Leiden: Brill, 1974).

Heemskerk, Margaretha T. *Suffering in the Mu'tazilite Theology: 'Abd al-Jabbār's Teachings on Pain and Divine Justice* (Leiden: Brill, 2000).

Hildebrandt, Thomas. 'Between Muʿtazilism and Mysticism: How much of a Muʿtazilite is Naṣr Ḥāmid Abū Zayd?' in Camilla Adang, Sabine Schmidtke, and David Sklare (eds), *A Common Rationality: Muʿtazilism in Islam and Judaism* (Wrzburg: Ergon in Kommission, 2007) 495.

——. 'Two Theories of Value in Medieval Islam' (1960) 50 *Muslim World* 269.

Hourani, George F. 'The Rationalist Ethics of 'Abd al-Jabbār' in SM Stern et al (eds), *Islamic Philosophy and the Classical Tradition: Essays Presented by his friends and pupils to Richard Walzer on his Seventieth Birthday* (Oxford: Bruno Cassirer, 1972) 105.

Hovannisian, Richard G, (ed). *Ethics in Islam* (Malibu, Calif: Undena Publications, 1985).

Ibn Ashur, Muhammad al-Tahir. *Treatise on Maqāṣid al-Sharīʿa*. Mohamed el-Tahir el-Masawi (trans) (London: International Institute for Islamic Thought, 2006).

Jackson, Sherman. *Islamic Law and the State: The Constitutional Jurisprudence of Shihāb al-Dīn al-Qarāfī* (Leiden: EJ Brill, 1996).

——. 'The Alchemy of Domination? Some Ashʿarite Responses to Muʿtazilite Ethics' (1999) 31 *International Journal of Middle East Studies* 185.

Johansen, Baber. 'Apostasy as objective and depersonalized fact: two recent Egyptian court judgments' (2003) 70 *Social Research* 687.

Kamali, Mohammad Hashim. *Principles of Islamic Jurisprudence* (3rd edn, Cambridge: Islamic Texts Society, 2003).

——. 'Law and ethics in Islam—The role of the *maqāṣīd*' in Kari Vogt, Lena Larsen, and Christian Moe (eds), *New Directions in Islamic Thought: Exploring Reform and Muslim Tradition* (London: IB Tauris, 2009) 23.

Khadduri, Majid. '[Review]' (1991) 33 *Journal of Church and State* 807.

Kraemer, Joel L. *Humanism in the Renaissance of Islam: The Cultural Revival During the Buyid Age* (2nd edn, Leiden: Brill, 1992).

Lane, EW. *Arabic-English Lexicon* (Cambridge: Islamic Texts Society, 1984).

Leaman, Oliver and Sajjad Rizvi. 'The Developed *Kalām* Tradition' in Tim Winter (ed), *The Cambridge Companion to Classical Islamic Theology* (Cambridge: Cambridge University Press, 2008) 77.

Lisska, Anthony J. *Aquinas's Theory of Natural Law: An Analytic Reconstruction* (Oxford: Clarendon Press, 1996).

MacCormick, Neil. 'Natural Law Reconsidered [Review of John Finnis, *Natural Law and Natural Rights*]' (1981) 1 OJLS 99.

——. 'Ethics in Islamic Traditionalist Doctrine' in Richard G Hovannisian (ed), *Ethics in Islam* (Malibu, Calif; Undena Publications, 1985).

Makdisi, George. *Ibn 'Aqil: Religion and Culture in Classical Islam* (Edinburgh: Edinburgh University Press, 1997).

Mallat, Chibli. *Introduction to Middle Eastern Law* (Oxford: Oxford University Press, 2007).

Manji, Irshad. *The Trouble with Islam Today: A Muslim's Call for Reform in Her Faith* (New York: St Martin's Press, 2004).

Martin, Richard C, Mark R Woodward, and Dwi S Atmaja. *Defenders of Reason in Islam: Mu'tazilism from Medieval School to Modern Symbol* (Oxford: Oneworld Publications, 1997).

——. *Islamic Legal Philosophy: A Study of Abū Isḥāq al-Shāṭibī's Life and Thought* (Delhi: International Islamic Publishers, 1989).

Masud, Muhammad Khalid. *Shatibi's Philosophy of Islamic Law* (Islamabad: Islamic Research Institute, 1995).

——, Brinkley Messick, and David S Powers (eds), *Islamic Legal Interpretation: Muftis and Their Fatwas* (Cambridge, Mass: Harvard University Press, 1996).

Motzki, Harald. *The Origins of Islamic Jurisprudence: Meccan Fiqh Before the Classical Schools* (Leiden: Brill, 2001).

Mujiburrahman. 'Islam and Politics in Indonesia: the political thought of Abdurrahman Wahid' (1999) 10 *Islam and Christian-Muslim Relations* 339.

Mumīsa, Michael. *Islamic Law: Theory and Interpretation* (Beltsville, Md: Amana Publications, 2002).

Murphy, Mark C. *Natural Law and Practical Rationality* (Cambridge: Cambridge University Press, 2001).

Nagel, Tilman. *The History of Islamic Theology: From Muhammad to the Present* (Princeton: Markus Wiener Publishers, 2000).

Nasir, Jamal. *The Islamic Law of Personal Status* (3rd edn, London: Kluwer Law International, 2002).

Novak, David. *Natural Law in Judaism* (Cambridge: Cambridge University Press, 1998).

Olsson, Susanne. 'Apostasy in Egypt: Contemporary Cases of *Ḥisbah*' (2008) 98 *The Muslim World* 95.

Osman, Fathi. 'Islam and Human Rights: The Challenge to Muslims and the World' in Abdelwahab el-Affendi (ed), *Rethinking Islam and Modernity* (London: The Islamic Foundation, 2001) 27.

Pagden, Anthony. 'Rethinking the Linguistic Turn: Current Anxieties in Intellectual History' (1988) 49 *Journal of the History of Ideas* 519.

Peirce, Leslie. *Morality Tales: Law and Gender in the Ottoman Court of Aintab* (Berkeley, Calif: University of California Press, 2003).

Powers, David. *Law, Society and Culture in the Maghrib, 1300–1500* (Cambridge: Cambridge University Press, 2002).

Rahman, Fazlur. 'Law and Ethics in Islam' in Richard G Hovannisian (ed), *Ethics in Islam* (Malibu, Calif; Undena Publications, 1985).

Rahman, Fazlur. *Islam and Modernity: Transformation of an Intellectual Tradition* (Chicago: University of Chicago Press, 1982).

Rajagopal, Balakrishnan. *International Law from Below: Development, Social Movements, and Third World Resistance* (Cambridge: Cambridge University Press, 2003).

Ramadan, Tariq. *Western Muslims and the Future of Islam* (Oxford: Oxford University Press, 2004).

——. *Radical Reform: Islamic Ethics and Liberation* (Oxford: Oxford University Press, 2009).

——. 'A call for a moratorium on corporal punishment—The debate in review' in Kari Vogt, Lena Larsen and Christian Moe (eds), *New Directions in Islamic Thought: Exploring Reform and Muslim Tradition* (London: IB Tauris, 2009) 163.

Al-Raysuni, Ahmad. *Imam al-Shatibi's Theory of the Higher Objectives and Intents of Islamic Law*. Nancy Roberts (trans) (London: International Institute of Islamic Thought, 2005).

Reinhart, Kevin. *Before Revelation: The Boundaries of Muslim Moral Thought* (Albany, NY: SUNY Press, 1995).

Rosen, Lawrence. *The Anthropology of Justice: Law as Culture in Islamic Society* (1989. Reprint, Cambridge: Cambridge University Press, 1990).

——. *The Justice of Islam* (Oxford: Oxford University Press, 2000).

Sachedina, Abdulaziz. '[Review]' (1993) 25 *International Journal of Middle East Studies* 155.

Schwarz, Michael. 'The Qāḍī ʿAbd al- Ğabbārʿs Refutation of the Ašʿarite Doctrine of "Acquisition" (*kasb*)' (1976) 6 *Israel Oriental Studies* 229.

Shehabi, Nabil. 'The Influence of Stoic Logic on al-Jassasʿs Legal Theory' in John Emery Murdoch and Edith Dudley Sylla (eds), *The Cultural Context of Medieval Learning* (Boston, Mass: D Reidel Publishing Co, 1975).

Skinner, Quentin. 'Meaning and Understanding in the History of Ideas' in James Tully (ed), *Meaning and Context: Quentin Skinner and His Critics* (Princeton: Princeton University Press, 1989) 29–67.

Spiegel, Gabrielle. 'History, Historicism, and the Social Logic of the Text' in Gabrielle Spiegel (ed), *The Past as Text* (Baltimore, Md: Johns Hopkins University Press, 2006) 3.

Stern, SM. 'ʿAbd al-Djabbār' in HAR Gibb et al (eds), *Encyclopaedia of Islam* (rev edn, Leiden: Brill, 1960–) 1:59.

Tamanaha, Brian Z. *On the Rule of Law: History, Politics, Theory* (Cambridge: Cambridge University Press, 2004).

Taylor, Charles. *Sources of the Self: The Making of the Modern Identity* (Cambridge, Mass: Harvard University Press 1989).

Terminiello v Chicago, 337 US 1; 69 S Ct 894, 899 (1949).

Tibi, Bassam. *The Crisis of Modern Islam: A Preindustrial Culture in the Scientific-Technological Age*. Judith von Sivers (trans) (Salt Lake City: University of Utah Press, 1988).

Tucker, Judith E. *Women, Family, and Gender in Islamic Law* (Cambridge: Cambridge University Press, 2008).

Tully, James. *Strange Multiplicity: Constitutionalism in an age of diversity* (Cambridge: Cambridge University Press, 1995).

Turner, Bryan S. *Orientalism, Postmodernism and Globalism* (London: Routledge, 1994).

Vogt, Kari, Lena Larsen and Christian Moe (eds), *New Directions in Islamic Thought: Exploring Reform and Muslim Tradition* (London: IB Tauris, 2009).

Waldron, Jeremy. *God, Locke, and Equality: Christian Foundations in Locke's Political Thought* (Cambridge: Cambridge University Press, 2002).

Watt, W Montgomery. *The Formative Period of Islamic Thought* (Oxford: Oneworld Publications, 1998).

Weber, Max. *Economy and Society: An Outline of Interpretive Sociology*. Guenther Roth and Claus Wittich (eds). 2 vols (Berkeley, Calif: University of California Press, 1978).

Weiss, Bernard. *Spirit of Islamic Law* (Athens, Ga: University of Georgia Press, 1998).

Westerman, Pauline C. *The Disintegration of Natural Law Theory: Aquinas to Finnis* (Leiden: Brill, 1998).

Winter, Tim, (ed). *The Cambridge Companion to Classical Islamic Theology* (Cambridge: Cambridge University Press, 2008).

Wolfson, Harry Austryn. *The Philosophy of the Kalam* (Cambridge, Mass: Harvard University Press, 1976).

Index of Names

Index of Concepts

The manufacturer's authorised representative in the EU for product safety is Oxford University Press España S.A. of El Parque Empresarial San Fernando de Henares, Avenida de Castilla, 2 - 28830 Madrid (www.oup.es/en or product.safety@oup.com). OUP España S.A. also acts as importer into Spain of products made by the manufacturer.
Printed and bound by CPI Group (UK) Ltd, Croydon, CR0 4YY
14/09/2026
02216306-0001